Gramsci's Politics

Gramsci's Politics

Anne Showstack Sassoon

ST. MARTIN'S PRESS   NEW YORK

St. Martin's Press, Inc., 175 Fifth Avenue, New York, N.Y. 10010
Printed in Great Britain
First published in the United States in 1980

Library of Congress Cataloging in Publication Data

Sassoon, Anne Showstack.
   Gramsci's politics.

   Bibliography: p.
   Includes index.
   1. Gramsci, Antonio, 1891-1937 — Political science. I. Title.
JC265.G68S27 1980   335.43'092'4   79-57375
ISBN 0-312-34238-1

Printed and bound in Great Britain

CONTENTS

Contents

ACKNOWLEDGEMENTS

I would like to thank James Joll, Giuseppe Vacca, and Donald Sassoon for having read the manuscript and for giving me many useful suggestions and Ralph Miliband and Maurice Cranston for their encouragement at different stages in its development. I would also like to thank Lawrence and Wishart for permission to quote from Antonio Gramsci, *Selections from the Prison Notebooks* (London, 1971), translated by Quintin Hoare and Geoffrey Nowell Smith; Antonio Gramsci, *Selections from Political Writings, 1910-1921* (London, 1977), translated by John Mathews; Antonio Gramsci, *Selections from Political Writings, 1921-1926* (London, 1978), translated by Quintin Hoare.

TO DONALD

INTRODUCTION

In recent years reference in the English-speaking world to Gramsci's concept of hegemony and to his work on the intellectuals has greatly increased, accompanied by a growing literature on various aspects of his work without, however, always taking account of the difficulty of understanding the meaning of his concepts. Nor, despite the availability of a large portion of his writings in English,[1] has his work served as the object of theoretical discussion in the Anglo-Saxon world.[2] Moreover Gramsci's work has most often been approached from a historical point of view, rather than examined primarily as a possible contribution to political theory. Indeed, Gramsci's political theory and the consequences of his ideas for a theory of the State and of the political party was not studied in any depth in any language until recently.[3] Now at the centre of debate in Italy[4] the interest which exists in Gramsci's political theory is part of an attempt to develop further a Marxist theory of politics, an area of work which has remained comparatively neglected. In fact, many of the limits of the study of Gramsci in the Anglo-Saxon world, where adequate tools of analysis have only recently become available, have been in evidence in Italy as well. A certain tendency to attribute to Gramsci's work political positions which are not justified by a close reading of what he has actually written or by a consideration of the problems he posed, continues in recent debates on his ideas on the State and on the party. Very often the coherence of his problematic as a whole has been lost completely. An introductory survey based on his texts would therefore appear useful.

Gramsci's writings on the political party suggest themselves as a topic of investigation for several reasons. The question of the organisations of the working-class movement, of their relationship to one another and of their respective functions has been discussed since the birth of the movement while the specific configuration and *raison d'être* of the revolutionary party has been an important object of study, at least since Lenin's *What Is to Be Done*. On the other hand, the question of the relationship of the revolutionary party to the State after the socialist revolution has been a concrete problem only since 1917. Related to the relatively undeveloped nature of a Marxist political theory, the way in which political parties represent social forces in an era of mass participation in politics and the question of mass political parties in general, including mass revolutionary parties, are topics which still have largely to be investigated by Marxists.[5] Gramsci's own interest in the party, the 'Modern Prince', while not, we would argue, constituting the central organising concept of the *Prison Notebooks*, a role played rather by the concept of hegemony,[6] is a fundamental aspect of Gramsci's thinking in prison. As a significant contribution to Marxist writings on the political party after Lenin, this area of Gramsci's work deserves to be studied.

Moreover, consideration of the party leads to an investigation of what the party does, how it sees its task, and consequently to an examination of Gramsci's political theory. The topic inevitably becomes broadened and produces the question of whether Gramsci has a theory of the party separate from a theory of politics or whether indeed consideration of the organisations of the working-class movement can in fact be isolated from a view of political change in which a theory of the State is central. Here it must be observed that Gramsci's political theory is inevitably related to questions of philosophy and epistemology, to the links between a view of the world held in contradictory ways by masses of people and the hegemony of a class, to the question of the ideological and national-popular dimensions of political struggle, to the problem of the epistemological basis of the development of a revolutionary political strategy, to the question of a Marxist philosophy. These are all questions considered at times in great depth by Gramsci but which, for reasons of space, cannot be discussed in this work.

Any study of Gramsci's thought encounters some very particular problems. First of all, the nature of his texts is problematic. His pre-prison writings are embedded in a situation characterised by the dramatic changes of the years 1914 to 1926. Written 'in haste', not intended to 'outlive' their immediate purpose,[7] these texts have the form of political journalism and party documents. In addition, there is no definitive edition of these early writings and producing one will not be easy since many of Gramsci's articles in this period were unsigned or signed with pseudonyms.

Secondly, the *Prison Notebooks* were written under difficult physical, mental and intellectual conditions. No longer writing as a political actor but contemplating past experience and the contemporary world as best he could, Gramsci produced a series of notes which he considered unfinished fragments, elements and indications for further study.[8] His very language presents problems because he often used the same terms in different ways, and as the years passed, he increasingly used a code for possibly politically sensitive references. Recently a new, definitive edition of his notebooks has been published which gives us all versions of all his notes.[9] We are now better able to trace the development of his ideas and to place them within a temporal context.[10]

Yet the problem of tracing the development and change in Gramsci's thought remains difficult. Often considered in a rather superficial way, usually with reference to Lenin's thought and as part of a fairly immediate political debate concerning the relationship of the strategy of the post-war Italian Communist Party (PCI) to Gramsci's writing and activities, the problem of continuity and change in Gramsci's thought has only recently begun to be posed in more theoretical terms.[11]

Difficulties in reading Gramsci also arise for a number of other reasons. There is, for example, a special problem of establishing the historical *context* of his thought, a problem which is related to the theoretical question of the object of his work. Until recently Gramsci was placed almost completely within the context of post-First World War Italy and the experiences of the Italian working-class movement in those years. Even this historical background has been examined in an uneven way. For example, his debate with Bordiga has mostly been investigated from an historical point of view rather than as providing an important element in the development of Gramsci's political thought.[12] Little is known about what is generally recognised as a crucial influence in Gramsci's political life, the period spent working for the Comintern in 1923 to 1924 in Moscow and Vienna, and no thorough study of his writings between 1921 and 1926 has been published.[13] Moreover, his very real physical and at times political isolation in prison has produced an exaggerated picture of his intellectual isolation while writing the *Notebooks.*[14]

Another difficulty derives from the special weight of Italian culture in his work. By attempting to take account of writers like Machiavelli, Croce, and Sorel, Gramsci's writings have reference points which are very different from those of traditional Marxism. A specific national tradition is not present in the same way in Marx's texts, the product of the famous triad of German philosophy, English political economy, and French politics. Similarly, it can be argued that there is no equivalent presence of Russian culture *per se* in Lenin's texts (as differentiated from his object of analysing the concrete Russian situation).

Related to his conditions of work is the fact that Gramsci's notes in prison often have more than one object and are compounds of several concepts. Gramsci's literal object is not always his real object. His writings on the Risorgimento, for example, which for many years were the source of an historiographical debate,[15] can be analysed as a discussion of political strategy and as a reflection on the nature of the constitution of the dominance of the bourgeoisie in Italy. Each note uses concepts which are never systematically explained, whose meaning must be deduced from the whole of Gramsci's work. As a consequence each passage can serve as the raw material for a discussion of several different aspects of Gramsci's thought.

Given these difficulties, the large variety of readings of Gramsci is therefore not surprising.[16] Yet apart from the difficulty intrinsic to his texts, many of these interpretations, indeed, we would argue, until recently, the majority, had more or less immediate political intentions. His writings have been used in a dogmatic way to justify or attack a variety of contemporary political positions.[17] This political use of Gramsci's work was facilitated by the lack of study of Gramsci's political theory.[18] The undisputed emphasis Gramsci placed on cultural and ideological phenomena has often obscured his fundamental interest in the nature of the State and in the exercise of political dominance, the principles of political strategy in a specific historical period and the role of the revolutionary party. If these elements are coherently interconnected in Gramsci's conceptual framework, then it would be difficult to sustain, as some authors have implied, that his concept of hegemony is reducible to the notion of cultural influence.[19]

In order to attempt to overcome the limitations of much of the secondary literature available, particularly but not only in English, and notwithstanding the difficulties involved, a textual reading of Gramsci is necessary so that certain problems can be tackled. In particular it provides the basis for an investigation of whether there is a unity beneath the fragmentary nature of his work. An analysis of Gramsci in his own terms is a necessary pre-condition for considering his place in the Marxist tradition and in European intellectual history generally, as well as of the relationship of his thought to contemporary political practice.

These are tasks which would require more space than we have at our disposal. Nevertheless we would suggest that any comparison between Gramsci and Marx and Lenin which is not trapped within a dogmatic approach must go beyond superficial phrases. Certain aspects of the work of Lenin, for example, appear extremely influential in Gramsci's thought. Lenin's derivation of a political strategy from an analysis of a concrete social formation, and his notion of political initiative provide the foundation for and the links between his theory of the state and his writings on the party. Yet, this is also where we find a crucial difference between Lenin and Gramsci. For if the analysis of the social formation is common to the two thinkers, and here Gramsci's concept of the historic bloc is central, the *novelty* in Gramsci's work lies in his conclusions about the specific modes of the transition to socialism in advanced capitalist countries. Indeed, the re-organisation of capitalism on a world-wide scale particularly after the 1929-30 crisis and the consequences of the organisation of the masses in the modern period makes Gramsci's concept of politics relevant in a wide variety of circumstances not least with regard to the building of socialism in the USSR. The concrete analysis of the concrete situation, as undertaken by Gramsci, leads him *beyond* Lenin on the state and on the party.

Indeed, a textual reading leads inevitably to the problem of the relationship of the text to history. A textual reading isolated from Gramsci's experience and context has certain dangers. The very problems which he was considering were the results of concrete historical developments. His originality, we would argue, stems largely from his attempt to produce the concepts necessary for a comprehension of these novel realities. As a consequence of this both the questions posed and the answers given or attempted had to be more than a scholastic repetition of the classical texts, enshrined by tradition.

At the same time, an empirical discussion of the world which Gramsci was contemplating would not furnish an explanation of the extent of Gramsci's originality. The coherence of his concepts cannot be reduced to historical phenomena, although the context of Gramsci's work can help to explain the *origin*, in a linguistic sense, of certain concepts, and may indeed throw light on his particular development of a certain idea. For example, the word hegemony was quite frequently used in the Russian Social Democratic Labour Party early in the century to indicate the influence of the working class over other classes,[20] as well as by people like Bukharin and Stalin in the 1920s.[21] Yet Gramsci *extended* the concept to explain the modes of domination by the bourgeoisie and to establish a theoretical basis for a counter-strategy by the proletariat adequate to the new political forms of monopoly capital. Gramsci's development of the concept of hegemony cannot be explained by the existence of certain historical phenomena since history cannot explain why Gramsci developed this concept in a certain manner while others in the same period did not. A textual reading can attempt to trace the history of a concept internal to Gramsci's theoretical work, examining gaps, contradictions, coherence, advances.

A reading which, however, ignores its origins runs the danger of not taking into account all factors which can shed light on this work. For example, Gramsci was not completely isolated from developments in the outside world when he was in prison and was deeply interested in

the various modes of political and economic reconstitution of the bourgeoisie in response to the great economic crisis of 1929-30. These facts
cast new light on his criticism of economism and the development of the
concept of passive revolution. The richness of this latter concept deep-
ens when it is realised that he applied it, in a negative sense, to the mode
of constructing a socialist State in the USSR.[22] We would argue, therefore, that a reading of Gramsci's texts must be informed of his historical
context while avoiding the dangers of historical reductionism.

This context has several aspects. First of all, as many students of
Gramsci have emphasised, the debates and the experiences of the Second
International and of the working-class movement in post-First World War
Europe were fundamental for Gramsci. That is, from his earliest writings,
he sought to 'translate' Marx's theoretical indications into a concrete political practice of the working-class movement by going beyond the crisis
theory of the downfall of capitalism. In so doing he had to tackle problems
which revealed themselves fully only after the First World War. The crucial
starting-point for a proper reading of his thought is constituted by his
analysis of the changing relationship between State and society in the
period of monopoly capitalism, a relationship intensified and modified
by the First World War, and the new international reality created by the
Russian Revolution. This starting-point was not peculiar to Gramsci.[23] It
is Gramsci's investigation of the consequences of this new relationship
between State and society, both for changes in the modes of domination
of the bourgeoisie and for its effects on the possibility of political intervention by the proletariat, that marks Gramsci's originality in considering a problem which was at the centre of debate in the communist movement in the 1920s: the need for a revolutionary strategy in Western
Europe which took account of the special conditions of advanced capitalist societies. While the differences between East and West were widely
discussed in the forums of the Third International by political leaders
such as Bordiga and Trotsky among others, we would argue that Gramsci
was the only one to develop a theoretical basis for the necessity of a
different strategy rooted in the changed relationship between State and
society. The discussions of a strategy for revolution in the West were
closely connected with the problems of building socialism in the USSR.
Mainly but by no means entirely concerning economic policy, the hitherto hypothetical problem of the construction of socialism had become
concrete. Gramsci's work can be read from the point of view of this
question as well as in terms of the 'revolution in the West'.[24]

Furthermore, the fact that Gramsci was only relatively but not completely isolated in prison helps to explain the changes and development

of his thought. Of central concern in the *Prison Notebooks* is the ability of capitalism to survive repeated economic and political crises. Here the effects of the 1929-30 crash are crucial as they increase State intervention in the economy and society as a whole in a variety of countries. This leads Gramsci to consider the differences in the political *forms* used to tackle structurally similar problems. This is the basis of his indirect analysis of régimes as different as those in the US, the USSR and Nazi Germany. Recognition of the need to analyse the consequences of specific political forms, the potential of the working class to develop a strategy to modify the forms of domination in capitalist society, and the problems of constructing a socialist state with a wide social basis—all this leads Gramsci to face the theoretical obstacle represented by the survival of economism in the politics of the Third International. Implicitly the left turn of the Comintern in 1928 was criticised by Gramsci as he analysed the theoretical mistake on which it was based.

Gramsci's object cannot be fully understood, we would maintain, unless these reference points are taken into account. The fact that he was concerned to investigate aspects of the real world which were being studied and discussed widely in the working-class movement in the same period underlines the originality of his analysis. Gramsci's prime political concern was the significance of the latest developments of capitalism for a political strategy for the working class and its political party. Throughout his writings he considered capitalist development as contradictory in its effects which could not be correctly understood without recognising the historical novelty represented by the presence in politics of masses of people. His analysis of the modes of domination in bourgeois society in the period of mass political participation and the problems of building a socialist State are related to a theory of politics and a definition of the task of the revolutionary party, an organisation which is defined, as we shall see, in terms of enabling the proletariat to found a new State.

Notes

1. A. Gramsci, *Selections from the Prison Notebooks* (Lawrence and Wishart, London, 1971) (hereafter as *SPN*). *Selections from Political Writings, 1910-1920* (Lawrence and Wishart, London, 1977)) (hereafter as *PWI*). *Selections from Political Writings 1921-1926* (Lawrence and Wishart, London, 1978) (hereafter as *PWII*).

2, For examples of recent theoretical discussion which, it is hoped, will open up the debate, see Christine Buci-Glucksmann, *Gramsci and the State* (Lawrence and Wishart, London, 1980). Leonardo Paggi, 'The General Theory of Marxism in

Gramsci' in Chantal Mouffe (ed.), *Gramsci and Marxist Theory* (Routledge and Kegan Paul, London, 1979). See Chantal Mouffe and Anne Showstack Sassoon, 'Gramsci in France and Italy – A Review of the Literature' in *Economy and Society*, vol. 6, no. 1 (Feb. 1977) for a discussion of these and similar pieces of literature.

3. Even though Togliatti had suggested the study of Gramsci's political thought in 1958, there was a considerable lag before this aspect was studied in Italy. See Palmiro Togliatti, 'Gramsci and Leninism' in Palmiro Togliatti, *Togliatti on Gramsci and Other Writings* (Lawrence and Wishart, London, 1979).

4. See for example Norberto Bobbio, 'Esiste una dottrina marxista, dello Stato?' *Mondoperaio*, no. 8-9 (Aug.-Sept. 1975). 'Quale alternativa alla democrazia rappresentativa', *Mondoperaio*, no. 10 (Oct. 1975) and Massimo L. Salvadori, 'Gramsci and the PCI: Two Conceptions of Hegemony', in Mouffe, *Gramsci and Marxist Theory*. These challenged the position of the PCI on Gramsci, claiming that his concept of hegemony was indeed the same as the dictatorship of the proletariat. Among the many interventions in answer see Biagio De Giovanni, Valentino Gerratana, and Leonardo Paggi, *Egemonia Stato partito in Gramsci* (Editori Riuniti, Rome, 1977).

5. This 'silence' is all the more remarkable if one thinks of the contributions of writers such as Weber, Michels, Ostrogorsky and others outside the Marxist tradition at the end of the last and the beginning of this century.

6. We discuss this concept at some length below. See Part III.

7. *Lettere*, p. 58.

8. What Gramsci wrote about the way in which Marx's works should be treated in a note entitled 'Questions of Method' could well be applied to his own work: 'A distinction should be made . . . between those works which he has carried through to the end and published himself or those which remain unpublished because incomplete, and those which were published by a friend or disciple. . . . It is clear that the content of posthumous works has to be taken with great discretion and caution, because it cannot be considered definitive but only as material still being elaborated and still provisional.' *SPN*, p. 384.

9. Antonio Gramsci, *Quaderni del carcere*, vols 1-4 (Einaudi, Turin, 1975) (hereafter as *Q*). Use of the new edition makes it possible to see how often the second draft of a note employed much more obscure language.

10. It should be noted, however, that this can be done only within certain limits, since he often worked on several notebooks at the same time, subject to some extent to the availability of material.

11. See Mouffe and Showstack Sassoon, 'Gramsci in France and Italy'.

12. See Rosa Alcara, *La formazione e i primi anni del Partito comunista italiano nella storiografia marxista* (Jaca Book, Milan, 1970), and Franco Andreucci and Malcolm Sylvers, 'The Italian Communists Write Their History' in *Science and Society*, no. 1, vol. 40 (1976) for two different points of view in what is a huge literature on the subject. See also note 2, Part I below.

13. Leonardo Paggi's promised second volume of *Antonio Gramsci e il moderno principe* (Editori Riuniti, Rome, 1970), which stops at 1921, has not yet appeared. Paolo Spriano's history of the PCI in the period discusses Gramsci's ideas but its prime object lies elsewhere. *Storia del partito comunista italiano, Da Bordiga a Gramsci*, vol. 1 (Einaudi, Turin, 1967) (hereafter as PCI.) The section of Alistair Davidson's book, *Antonio Gramsci: Towards an Intellectual Biography* (Merlin Press, London, 1977) which deals with this period is more an account of various historical developments than an analysis of Gramsci's ideas.

14. See Quintin Hoare's introduction to *SPN* which tends to emphasise Gramsci's isolation. See p. lxvii.

15. For a summary of this debate see John M. Cammett's appendix 'Gramsci and the Risorgimento', in *Antonio Gramsci and the Origins of Italian Communism*

(Stanford University Press, Stanford, California, 1967).

16. The most comprehensive discussion of the various interpretations of Gramsci is Gian Carlo Jocteau, *Leggere Gramsci. Una guida alle interpretazione* (Feltrinelli, Milan, 1975).

17. A recent example of this is Maria-Antonietta Macciocchi, *Per Gramsci* (Il Mulino, Bologna, 1974).

18. Paggi blames Togliatti for the emphasis on the cultural rather than political aspects of his thought. See Paggi, *Il moderno principe*, pp. ix ff.

19. This is particularly so in the English literature. Although within the context of a very sophisticated argument about Gramsci, ultimately Perry Anderson's analysis of hegemony suffers from similar cultural reductionism. 'The Antinomies of Antonio Gramsci', *New Left Review*, no. 100 (Nov. 1976-Jan. 1977).

20. See Anderson, 'The Antinomies of Antonio Gramsci', pp. 15-17.

21. See Buci-Glucksmann, *Gramsci and the State*, pp. 174 and 171 ff.

22. See Giuseppe Vacca, 'The "Political Question of the Intellectuals" and the Marxist Theory of the State in Gramsci's Thought', in Anne Showstack Sassoon (ed.), *A Gramsci Reader* (Writers and Readers Publishing Co-operative, London, forthcoming).

23. The change in the State in the period of monopoly capitalism was discussed by Bukharin and Lenin as well as by non-Marxists. It can be argued however, that Bukharin on the whole limited his analysis to the economic functions of the State and that Lenin, concentrating mainly on the international dimension of imperialism, did not develop the consequences of imperialism on the nature of the national State.

24. Vacca, 'The "Political Question"'. As Stephen F. Cohen suggests, the more that these discussions are studied, the more restrictive appear the traditional division of positions into either the Stalin or Trotsky camp. *Bukharin and the Bolshevik Revolution, A Political Biography, 1888-1938* (Vintage Books, New York, 1975), pp. xvi-xvii.

Part I

THE YEARS IN TURIN

The historical background to Gramsci's political militancy in Turin in the period before, during and after the First World War, and the social and economic setting of his early years in Sardinia are well documented. His first acquaintance with the socialist movement, his work on various socialist journals, the intellectual climate of Sardinia and Turin, and the development of the most advanced working-class movement in Italy have been described in a number of works.[1] From the point of view of an examination of his political theory, the themes which are most discussed are the idealist language of his early works, and what has often been depicted as a spontaneist problematic in which the political party and the trade unions seem to be superseded as the most important organisations of the working-class movement by the factory councils.

Indeed, crucial questions of method immediately arise in considering Gramsci's ideas on the party in the period of his political militancy in Turin. If these writings are examined with reference to a *model* of a party, Leninist or otherwise, it is quite easy to arrive at the result that Gramsci lacked a clear idea of a political organisation alternative to that provided by the Italian socialist tradition and that his view of the need to confront the problem of the State and the political struggle was confused with the economic struggle of the factory councils. In fact, Gramsci's own development of a theory of politics contradicts this approach which is embedded in a problematic which in fact *reduces* the party and its tasks within the confines of the economism which dominated the Second International. This problematic separated the spheres of political and economic struggle in such a way, it can be argued, as to be unable to pose correctly the question of the nature of State power and therefore the requirements of a revolutionary struggle in the period of monopoly capitalism.[2]

If important aspects of Gramsci's work in this period are not to be missed altogether, the correct questions must be asked of his writings. Rather than search for an abstract model of a party, unrelated to a specific historical conjuncture or to a theory of the State and politics, those elements which come to constitute aspects of Gramsci's view of politics must be investigated in order to learn what they say about the role of political organisation and political struggle. Gramsci's own work

21

must be approached using indications from his criticism of Bordiga's view of the party as a model unrelated to historical time or space. Further, the question of whether Gramsci's ideas on the party are 'Leninist' or not, in this period or any other, is itself the product of a schematic view of party organisation and is therefore of little interest unless Lenin's own ideas on the party are considered as part of a theory of the State and politics, applied in a specific historical, national context, a task which cannot be undertaken within the space available. If then we ask the correct questions of Gramsci's ideas in this period, we will see how they represent the foundations for a theory of politics and the State and the role of the political party which represents a clear break with the tradition of the Italian socialist movement and by extension a break with the way the Second International in general viewed the problems of the institutions of the working-class movement.[3]

Revolution as Creation

While the major body of material to be considered in this period appeared in the *Ordine Nuovo*, founded in April 1919, a brief look at some selected earlier pieces of work demonstrates how Gramsci's view of the revolution as an act which must be creative if it is to break through the bounds of the present social formation goes back to his earliest activity. Of particular interest are the article, 'Active and Operative Neutrality' (*PWI*, pp. 6-9) written in 1914 concerning the position of the PSI (Italian Socialist Party) with regards to the war; the special issue published by the Piedmont Youth Federation, 'La città futura' (*SG*, pp. 73-89), indicative of Gramsci's conception of the transition to socialism at the beginning of 1917; 'Socialism and Culture' (*PWI*, pp. 10-13) an early indication of the relationship between politics and culture; and 'The Revolution Against "Capital"' (*PWI*, pp. 34-7) for his view of the Russian revolution and the lessons he drew from it.

Gramsci's position on the war is interesting to us because of his criticism of the reformist outlook of the PSI and his argument for revolutionary leadership in the crisis, an argument posed in terms of a *positive* intervention which went beyond the PSI's position of neither sabotaging nor aiding the war effort. The immediate object of Gramsci's article was a piece by Benito Mussolini, then leader of the so-called revolutionary wing of the party and editor of *Avanti!*, in which, in opposition to the official position of the PSI, Mussolini partially accepted the war since it was, as he put it, the 'destiny' of the bourgeoisie to fight.[4]

Two articles appeared in *Il Grido del Popolo*, the Turin socialist news-paper, in reaction to Mussolini's position. The first, by Angelo Tasca, firmly opposed Mussolini, defending the official party line and arguing that the only valid position for socialists was to remain absolutely neutral with regard to the war.[5] A second article, written by Gramsci, argued for a more active type of opposition to the war. Absolute neutral-ity, he said, had been necessary when the war broke out and the situation was confused, when an intransigent position was needed to counteract popular passions. But several months later when the situation had clar-ified, while absolute neutrality might be adequate for the reformists who would have liked the proletariat to act like impartial spectators, it no longer sufficed for revolutionaries.[6]

According to Gramsci, the task of revolutionaries was active opposition to the war, providing for the unhindered development of the class struggle. At this stage Gramsci contended that the heightened class struggle would reveal to the whole of society that the propertied class had reached the end of its historical role, that it had failed to supersede this role, and that the bourgeoisie no longer represented the national will.[7]

What is significant is Gramsci's interpretation of what he called Mus-solini's rather incoherent statements.[8] According to Gramsci, Mussolini was not calling for a general support of the war or abandoning the class struggle, in which case his position would have been anti-socialist, but he simply wanted to allow history to run its course. Nor, said Gramsci, did Mussolini exclude the possibility that the working class would assume power after the bourgeoisie had demonstrated its impotence. The proletariat, Gramsci thought, was well able to assume the new task of a more active role, and the 'convenient position of absolute neutrality' should not make socialists abandon themselves even for a moment to 'an over-ingenuous contemplation and Buddhist renunciation of our obligations' (*PWI*, p. 9).

Thus, the fact that the bourgeoisie was no longer progressive stems from its inability to represent the interests of the whole nation, and entrance into the war is considered an opportunity for the proletariat to demonstrate that at the present stage of history it has the potential to replace the bourgeoisie as a national class. What is missing is any indic-ation of the type of political intervention needed to do so, for Gramsci posed the question in terms of history running its course, implying that history, if left to itself, will consist of a class struggle automatically resulting in socialism.

Gramsci, then, wanted the PSI to move away from a purely formalist-ic and doctrinaire opposition to a more concrete one.[9] In line with

Gramsci's criticism of the evolutionary and deterministic view of Marxism so widely held in the party, there is an affirmation of the active role of the proletariat. However, in trying to overcome the mechanistic tendencies of Italian socialism, Gramsci remained within what can be considered the mirror opposite of a mechanistic problematic, idealism. Arguing against Tasca, he writes that

> revolutionaries who see history as the product of their own actions, made up of an uninterrupted series of wrenches executed upon the other active and passive forces in society, and prepare the most favourable conditions for the final *wrench* (the revolution), should not rest content with the provisional formula of 'absolute neutrality', but should transform it into the alternative formulation 'active and operative neutrality'. *PWI*, p. 7.

Gramsci's debt to Hegel via Croce as well as the influence of Sorel is evident in this article. Firstly, the concept of future history being reflected in the spirit of revolutionaries implies that the very activities of these revolutionaries can dominate both the active and passive forces of society. Hence, no objective relation can stand between man's will and man's future. Secondly, the revolution is viewed as the culmination of a series of crises, each of which necessarily leads to the next, as every given stage develops into a higher one. The revolution itself is seen as a finite crisis. Gramsci himself later admitted the Crocean influence on his early philosophy at a time when, as he wrote, he did not have the concept of the unity of theory and practice.[10] Moreover, the influence of Sorel's writings and his determination to rescue the class struggle from the viscosity of reformism, which affected the thinking of a whole generation of revolutionaries, also appears in Gramsci's approaches to the question of an active opposition to the war.[11]

In arguing his case, Gramsci not only tends to read intentions into Mussolini's position, but he does not see that Mussolini's notion of the forces of history working themselves out does not overcome the evolutionism of the reformists. The difficulty of in fact overcoming this kind of problematic is reflected in the lack of a coherent alternative to the superficial line of the PSI on the war.[12] In a still groping, imprecise way, he was trying to establish the active role of the masses against the formalism of the PSI leadership and was aware, more than Tasca, of the dangers of simply waiting for the crisis to pass in order to act in the future.[13]

In another article written in January 1916, Gramsci considered a theme which would remain central in his thinking, the relationship between culture and politics. Arguing against counterposing culture and concrete historical practice, and still very much within an idealist problematic, Gramsci tried to establish a definition of culture which would allow the proletariat to become conscious of an autonomous historical role.

> We need to free ourselves from the habit of seeing culture as encyclopaedic knowledge, and men as mere receptacles to be stuffed full of empirical data and a mass of unconnected raw facts, which have to be filed in the brain as in the columns of a dictionary, enabling their owner to respond to the various stimuli from the outside world. This form of culture is really dangerous, particularly for the proletariat.
> Culture is something quite different. It is organization, discipline of one's inner self, a coming to terms with one's own personality; it is the attainment of a higher awareness, with the aid of which one succeeds in understanding one's own historical value, one's own function in life, one's own rights and obligations. But none of this can come about through spontaneous evolution, through a series of actions and reactions which are independent of one's own will — as in the case in the animal and vegetable kingdoms where every unit is selected and specifies its own organs unconsciously, through a fatalistic natural law. *PWI*, pp. 10-11.

Within the context of an argument against positivism, which seemed to remove the possibility of an active intervention in history, Gramsci cites the example of the French Revolution:

> every revolution has been preceded by an intense labour of criticism, by the diffusion of culture and the spread of ideas . . .
> The same phenomenon is being repeated today in the case of socialism. It was through a critique of capitalist civilization that the unified consciousness of the proletariat was or is still being formed, and a critique implies culture, not simply a spontaneous and naturalistic evolution. . . To know oneself means to be oneself, to be master of oneself, . . . And we cannot be successful in this unless we also know others, their history, the successive efforts they have made to be what they are, to create the civilization they have created and which we seek to replace with our own. *PWI*, pp. 12-13.

The role of culture is not yet linked to a concrete political strategy, but

Gramsci's emphasis on the need for a detailed study of bourgeois culture would be extended to a study of the dominance of the bourgeoisie in all its manifestations as a prerequisite for an autonomous political intervention by the proletariat.[14]

In early February 1917 the Piedmontese Socialist Youth Federation published a special issue of a newspaper as part of a recruitment campaign. Called, *La città futura*, it was written mostly by Gramsci with selections from works by Salvemini and Croce, and can be considered the high point of his early development.[15] This work shows that on the eve of the February revolution in Russia, Gramsci was still very influenced by Croce whom he called the greatest European thinker of the period,[16] and a brief examination of his position at that time indicates the theoretical view point from which he would view the Russian revolution.

The articles which Gramsci wrote argued against fatalism and acclaimed the power of man's will to change society. Arguing against indifference, Gramsci wrote: 'The fatality that seems to dominate history is precisely the illusory appearance of this indifference, of this absenteeism' (*PWI*, p. 17). He was specifically calling on young socialists to commit themselves to the party and to the struggle, and within this context he was most particularly critical of the evolutionary standpoint of the reformists whose outlook was imbued with positivism and what he called pseudo-scientificity. Philosophical positivism, he wrote, was not really scientific but simply mechanical. It had infected the reformism of socialists like Claudio Treves whose fatalism was determined by a type of mysticism, by social energies abstracted from men so that they were incomprehensible and absurd. Within this framework, life seemed like an inevitable series of events where human will was powerless to intervene, and socialism seemed to be dead. Yet, Gramsci argued, the proletariat, casting off a blind faith in mythical science, had overcome the fatalism of the pseudo-scientists and had replaced it with the will of man.[17]

Expressed in idealist language, Gramsci criticises the reformist position for its abstractness, for its inability to relate the possibility of revolution to the concrete potential of a specific, historically determined, social force. The application of the principles of natural science to the realm of human history typical of the positivist reading of Marx implied that the class struggle was trapped within the confines of the rhythm of development of the present social formation, an historical development conceived of outside the class struggle itself. Gramsci's argument against this position is still at this stage based on the potential of human will to overcome the fatalism of a mechanistic concept of history.

In another article which considered the different forms of bourgeois

State, Gramsci maintained that it was easier to create a new order in Italy which was without a strong bourgeois State. In rather Sorelian terms he wrote:

> In countries where conflicts do not take place on the streets, where one neither observes the fundamental laws of the State being trod upon nor arbitrary rule, the class struggle loses its harshness, the revolutionary spirit loses its impact and breaks down. The so-called law of minimum effort, which is the law of armchairs, and often means not doing anything, becomes popular. In these countries the revolution is less probable. Where an order exists, it is less likely that the decision is taken to substitute it with a new order . . . Socialists must not substitute one order for another. They must found order itself. *SG*, pp. 23-4.

His argument ran counter to any suggestion that Italy would have to await full capitalist development before a socialist revolution was possible. Already interested in the different forms of bourgeois rule, Gramsci tried to assert the peculiarity of Italy as the basis for the creative institution of a new social order. Elements for an argument which paralleled that of Lenin with regards to Russia as the weakest link of the imperialist system can be found here. What is still to be developed is a view of the articulation between the international and the national contexts, as well as of the relationship between the building of a new order in Italy and the old one, however weak in comparison to England or Germany. Gramsci has established the starting point for such an analysis: the weakness of the Italian liberal State.[18]

Gramsci's emphasis, then, was on the potential of human will in history. It was with this perspective that he confronted the events in Russia.[19] In order to understand the development of Gramsci's ideas about the factory councils, and his criticism of the PSI in the post-war period, we must look at Gramsci's immediate reaction to the Russian situation in 1917 and 1918.

The first comment by Gramsci on the February Revolution was in the article, 'Notes on the Russian Revolution', written in April 1917, in which he explains why the February Revolution could be considered proletarian. It is proletarian, he writes, because its spiritual essence is proletarian, not because it was made by the proletariat. Arguing against a sociological definition, he asks:

> But is it enough that a revolution be carried out by proletarians for it

to be a proletarian revolution? War too is made by proletarians, but it is not, for this reason alone, a proletarian event. For it to be so, other, spiritual factors must be present. There must be more to the revolution than the question of power: there must be the question of morality, of a way of life. . . .

We, however, are convinced that the Russian revolution is more than simply a proletarian event, it is a proletarian act, which must naturally lead to a socialist régime. *PWI*, p. 28.

What is extremely interesting in the articles he wrote on the Russian Revolution in this period is Gramsci's description of what he considers the specifically proletarian mode of revolution. The most important aspect of the February Revolution, he argued, was that it had destroyed any authoritarianism. The liberation of the spirit and the establishment of a new moral conscience had been revealed. Elements for Gramsci's later development of the idea of the revolution as an intellectual and moral reform are evident here, and most importantly, the proletarian revolution is defined as one made by the masses rather than an élite which had forced its will on the majority. In another article,[20] contrasting the Russian revolution to the French revolution, he defined Jacobinism as an entirely bourgeois phenomenon.[21] A minority which was certain to become an absolute majority, if not directly the totality of citizens, could not be considered Jacobin and could not have as its programme perpetual dictatorship. This minority would temporarily exercise a dictatorship to permit the effective majority to organise itself, to become aware of its intrinsic needs and to establish its own order.[22] The expansive nature of the proletarian revolution, tending to win the support of the vast majority of the population, a revolution which in this sense was to be considered democratic and which could justify a dictatorship only as a temporary feature, would be taken up in the *Notebooks*. In a still rather undefined way, Gramsci was trying to establish the proper relationship between the minority which is the party and the masses during and after the revolution.

In another article, 'Russian Maximalists', he had discussed the maximalists or Bolsheviks as representing the continuity and the rhythm of the revolution, as incarnating the revolution itself, because, he wrote, it was the Bolsheviks who prevented the revolution from remaining unfinished.[23] Gramsci considers Lenin and his companions as revolutionaries who went beyond an evolutionary view of history because they did not wait for the revolution to occur automatically but had awakened and conquered the conscience of the people. In what is almost an aside, he considers the role of the party. The Bolsheviks have prevented the revolution from petering out before its full development had been achieved.

> the whole society advances because there is always at least one group that wants to advance and is working among the masses, tapping new sources of proletarian energy and organizing new social forces . . . [They have] created the very group that was necessary to oppose any final compromises, any settlement which could have become definitive. *PWI*, pp. 31-2.

The party is a propaganda instrument, one which shows the way, one which convinces and persuades, one which opposes compromising the uninterrupted development of the revolution, and pushes it to its historically most advanced conclusion. When Gramsci writes that the party should not impose its will on the majority and despotic minorities must not be formed, he reasserts his view of the proletarian revolution as expansive, involving the positive support of the mass of the population.[24]

Several of these themes are taken up in what is usually considered the most important article by Gramsci on the Russian Revolution, 'The Revolution Against "Capital"', written in November 1917.[25] Still in rather idealist language, Gramsci emphasises the role of human will in creating a revolution and says that the activity of the Bolsheviks proves that the evolutionary interpretation of Marx by the socialists of the Second International is mistaken. The article hails man as the maker of history, not 'brute economic fact'. Marx, Gramsci argues, could not foresee everything, and while the normal course of human events would indicate the need to go through a bourgeois stage in history before socialism could be achieved, the war gave revolutionaries the possibility to create in a backward country the conditions necessary for the complete realisation of their ideal. Marx, then, as interpreted by the Second International, was not as important as the will of man in making history.

This article implies several major comments on Marxism. The thesis is propounded that the laws of historical materialism are not rigid and that given certain circumstances there can be exceptions, such as in Russia, because of the particular impact of the war. The political intuition of the Bolsheviks allowed them to understand that Russia need not follow the 'normal' path of history. They were successful in making the revolution because of the very fact that they rejected the 'positivist and naturalist' shell of Marx but retained the living kernel of Marxist thought, the continuation of Italian and German idealism. The implication is obvious: it is not Marxist theory as interpreted by the Second International which guides the party, but its political will which has re-established an idealist reading of Marx.

In embracing the experience of the Bolsheviks, Gramsci nonetheless remains fundamentally within the terms of the Second International reading of Marx, while asserting his disagreement with it. A crucial dilemma had been the disjuncture between Marx's work as theory understood as predicting revolution, and the concrete experience of the working-class movement which had not actually made the revolution. Gramsci hails the Bolsheviks as having enabled the Russian proletariat to make the revolution but as an 'exception' to what should be considered the 'normal' course of history. Presumably his argument three years previously in 'Active and Operative Neutrality' that Italy could make the revolution because the existing order was weak was based on the same assumption that Italy would be an exception to the general rule.

News of the events in Russia at first was very scarce, and it was not until a year later that Gramsci would write an article discussing the history of the Russian revolution from 1905 and the role of the Bolshevik Party. In 'Lenin's Work'[26] he stresses that Lenin had continued Marx. Lenin was not a utopian or a dictator, as the bourgeoisie claimed, but the 'cool scholar of historical reality', (*SG*, p. 312) who sought to construct a new society on a permanent basis according to the outlines of Marxist theory.

In contrast to 'The Revolution Against "Capital"', there is no longer any dichotomy between Lenin and Marx or between the Russian revolution and Marxism. Gramsci's analysis is much more concrete, much more rooted in the specific experiences of the Bolsheviks. He no longer invokes the 'ethical and idealist' element of Marxism. On the contrary, he contrasts Lenin, the revolutionary who builds without illusions, who obeys 'reason and wisdom', with Dora Kaplan, the social revolutionary who attempted to kill Lenin, described as 'a humanitarian, a utopian, a spiritual daughter of French Jacobinism, who does not succeed in understanding the historical function of organization and the class struggle, who believes socialism means immediate peace among men, an idyllic paradise of joy and love'. (*SG*, p. 312.) Criticism of abstract theorising and a definition of revolutionary politics as positive, constructive intervention adhering to the potential of the concrete situation would become a permanent and vital element of Gramsci's thought.

While there is some development in Gramsci's ideas from early 1917 to late 1918, his first reactions to the Russian Revolution remain within an idealist problematic. As his view of the complexity of the revolution develops through an increasingly complex view of the State, elements from this period become reinterpreted and transformed. The emphasis on the force of the will of man against mechanical determinations, the lack of a Jacobin tradition, the majoritarian orientation of the revolution, and the liberation of man's spirit through the creation of a new order become integrated into a new concept of politics and of the terms of the political intervention of the proletariat. In this period Gramsci discusses the role of the Bolshevik party, but he is not concerned with its particular characteristics, with what differentiated it from other parties. He discusses the activities and the outlook of the Bolsheviks, but he does not discuss the role of a party as such. What begins to emerge, however, is a particular view of the proletarian revolution as a positive act of creation involving the masses which cannot be substituted by an organisation, in which the party has an as yet largely undefined role.

The Ordine Nuovo

Early in 1919, Gramsci and three other young friends from the Turin socialist youth section, Angelo Tasca, Palmiro Togliatti, and Umberto Terracini decided to found a newspaper. Called the *Ordine Nuovo*, it was in a sense a continuation of the single issue which had appeared in February 1917, *La città futura*.[27] The new weekly was to serve as an organ of 'proletarian culture' as its sub-title stated. Founded during the period of post-war revolutionary fever, in which the Turin working class achieved a series of victories, the newspaper expressed the acutely felt need for concrete preparation for the revolution.[28] The urgent necessity to prepare the working class for its historical task in a period in which the revolution was considered to be on the order of the day is a fundamental concern of Gramsci's and provides the foundation of his work in these years.[29]

By the beginning of the summer of 1919, the newspaper began its advocacy of the factory council movement and became the vehicle for Gramsci's political thought in this period. A significant question is why and how Gramsci turned to the factory councils as a focal point for his activity. Although there is no record of his being particularly concerned with the factory councils as late as 1918, he was extremely interested in the various working-class rank-and-file organisations in England, in Germany, and in the United States.[30] The experiences of the American IWW and the ideas of Daniel De Leon influenced his thinking about the structure of modern industry and the need to organise and unify the whole of the working-class movement.[31] While the Russian Revolution and those writings of Lenin which were available were of prime import-

ance for Gramsci,[32] his special interest in Russia and the Soviets was
very much within the context of seeking to learn from the varied international experiences of the working class and its theoreticians in order
to find an organisational form adequate for developments in Italy. It was
not a question of copying the Russian experience schematically but of
trying to learn from that experience as well as others[33] in order to provide the solution to a crucial problem: the organisation and preparation
of the working class for the historical task confronting it.

The idea of transforming the existing internal committees into
factory councils eventually appeared to adhere to the requirements of
the period: the need for concrete organisation to meet the revolutionary
crisis of post-war Italy and the inadequacy of both the traditional trade
union organisations and the PSI to provide it, most specifically the need
to absorb and unify large numbers of workers who were showing a new
interest in revolutionary politics, many of whom were not organised in
any way.

The necessity of overcoming the inability of the bourgeoisie to develop the forces of production without increasing State intervention, when
the bourgeois State itself was in crisis, was a fundamental factor in
Gramsci's discussion. Absolutely crucial to a proper understanding of
Gramsci's interest in the factory councils is an understanding of the way
in which he characterised the post-war period as revolutionary and of how
he analysed the weaknesses of the bourgeois order. The period is considered by Gramsci to be revolutionary because of the crisis produced by
the war, a war characterised as a conflict between imperialist powers.[34]

The internal correspondent to this international crisis was the increased dominance of finance capital over the economic system which was no
longer able to develop without State intervention in the economy. The
crisis of imperialism and the crisis of the liberal State, a State which had
never existed in its pure form in Italy because of a constant need to protect a weak economy, meant that the political and the economic spheres,
theoretically separate according to classical liberalism, were increasingly
in a new relationship. It was against these concrete developments that
the factory councils seemed the organisational form which would provide the working class with the ability to engage in the class struggle at
the specific historical level of its development, a level of development
seen by Gramsci in its complexity and in its contradictory novelty.[35]
Thus Gramsci argued that the factory councils were the required form
of organisation and the method by which the working class could be
educated to its new tasks in a specific historical reality.

Moreover, it must be emphasised that Gramsci sought to supplement

rather than to replace the traditional organisations of the working class
— the trade unions and the socialist party — when he and his collaborators
on the *Ordine Nuovo* undertook to transform the internal committees
into factory councils, democratically elected and representative of all
the workers in a plant, unionised or not, having an autonomous area of
activity and an organisation based on the structure of the industry itself, rather than on craft lines. Thus transformed, the internal committees were to become the revolutionary organisations needed to organise the masses, creating a new terrain for the political intervention of the
party and forcing the trade unions to break through their traditional
corporativism, a terrain on which to confront the problem of the most
recent developments in the changing relationship between the bourgeois
State and economic organisation.[36]

The concrete experience of the working-class movement was providing
this terrain. Within a period of approximately six months, the factory
council movement spread rapidly.[37] The rapid growth of the movement
cannot be considered simply the result of the work of propaganda of the
Ordine Nuovo, but the convergence of various factors in which the work
of Gramsci and the others was important. Based on an examination of the
potential of the mass movement in Italy, Gramsci's work in this period
is his first major attempt to grapple with the question of the modes of
organisation necessary for a socialist revolution, and he looks in the first
instance not at the need to build a revolutionary party as such, although
he criticises the PSI and the reformist trade-union leaders, but at the
factory council. In these years his ideas on the political intervention of
the working class are developed with a central object: the need to organise the masses who would be the protagonists of the revolution.

Rather than the expression of spontaneism or of a political theory
reduced to workers control, it can be argued that Gramsci developed the
concept of the factory council as that working-class institution in Italy
capable of unifying and educating the working class to fulfill its revolutionary role, and of serving as the model of the workers' state. This was
a response to the need to give political leadership to the spontaneous
militancy of the working class and of the peasants, which surpassed the
ability of the traditional working-class organisation to intervene.[38]

It was a response therefore to the great urgency to absorb and unify
this mass movement in a period in which the transition to socialism had
become a real, or concrete possibility, an attempt to translate the theoretical indications of Marx into historical reality in the period of imperialism.

Gramsci wrote in his first editorial in the *Ordine Nuovo* explaining the need to establish factory councils:

> These disorderly and chaotic energies must be given a permanent
> form and discipline. They must be absorbed, organized and strengthen-
> ed. The proletarian and semi-proletarian class must be transformed
> into an organized society that can educate itself, gain experience and
> acquire a responsible consciousness of the obligations that fall to
> classes achieving State power. *PWI*, p. 66.

Gramsci sought to find some type of existing workers' institution which
could be transformed and serve as the basis for the overthrow of capitalism and at the same time as the organ of workers' control both of
production and of the state after the socialist revolution. 'The Socialist
State already exists potentially in the institutions of social life characteristic of the exploited working class.' Organising these institutions means
replacing the bourgeois state 'here and now in all its essential functions
of administering and controlling the national heritage' (*PWI*, p. 65). The
revolution is presented as a process which begins with institutions created
by the working class within the arena of production of the present social
formation, but which can begin to create elements of a new society.

In an argument closely paralleling Lenin's ideas in *State and Revolution*,
Gramsci maintained that the proletarian State would not embrace the
institutions of the bourgeois State but would be a fundamentally new
creation. This argument must be placed alongside his criticism of the
limits of the classical liberal State. Increasingly outmoded in the present
period because of the need to intervene in the economy in the epoch of
imperialism and the dominance of finance capitalism, it creates a disjuncture between the formal democratic participation of men as citizens
and their existence as producers, since politics is presented as separate
from economics. Under the liberal State each individual has a formal
right to participation unrelated to his socio-economic position. In the
new situation created by the change in the relationship between State
and economy, Gramsci argues that the working class has the potential
to challenge the dominance of the bourgeoisie in the terrain of production,
by undertaking a *political* struggle utilising institutions based in production, themselves expressing a unity between politics and economics impossible under capitalism. The new State is thus not a new version of the
old one but a State which represents the possibility of a new mode of
democratic participation by the masses.[39]

Gramsci found the PSI and the trade union organisations inherently
inadequate as the sole instruments for the establishment of this new

State. In his articles on the factory councils he analysed what he considered to be the functions which the trade unions and the party fulfilled most usefully, and examined their limitations. His argument is not to replace traditional working-class institutions but to give them a new potential through a link with new organisations able to unite the whole of the mass movement.[40]

The concrete basis for the potential of the factory councils, according to Gramsci, was the relationship of the worker and production in the current stage of capitalism. Because of the development of monopoly capital, accelerated by the war, the State had increasingly intervened in the realm of production and the industrialist himself tended to be removed from the direct administration of the factory and of control of investment. As direct control by the owner decreased, and as the level of technological innovation was raised, the actual role of private property changed enabling the worker to develop an increased autonomy in the field of production, potentially going beyond his traditional subjection and becoming aware of his function as a producer and of his part in the overall system of production in industry.[41]

We emphasized that the *person* of the capitalist had become divorced from the world of production—not capital, whether financial or otherwise. We emphasized that the factory is no longer controlled by the person of the proprietor but by the bank, through an industrial bureaucracy which tends to lose its interest in production in the same way that the State functionary loses his interest in public administration. This served as starting-point for a historical analysis of the new system of hierarchical relations which have become established in the factory, and for locating the emergence of one of the most important historical preconditions of the working class's industrial autonomy, whose factory organization tends to embody in itself the power of initiative over production. *PWI*, p. 297.

Recognition of these changes and the implications they held for the political struggle had to be the foundation of the political intervention of the proletariat. Accusations of voluntarism are not born out by the explicit terms of Gramsci's discussion. In contrast to Bordiga who considered the councils as *economic* instruments and only Soviets after the seizure of power as political organisations,[42] Gramsci insists that the factory councils provide the basis for politics adhering to the potential of the post-war period, a potential expressed in terms of transformations in the world of production.

The communist revolution achieves autonomy for the producer both in the economic and in the political field. Political action of the part of the working class (with the aim of establishing the dictatorship, the workers' State) acquires real historical values only when it is a function of the development of new economic conditions, pregnant with possibilities and eager to expand and consolidate themselves once and for all. If political action is to have a successful outcome, it must coincide with economic action. *PWI*, p. 162.

Gramsci explains the way in which the factory council represents the worker as producer, and is the basis of the unification of the class in the following passage:

In a factory, the workers are producers in so far as they collaborate in the preparation of the object being manufactured; they are ordered in a way that is determined precisely by the industrial technique being used, which in turn is independent (in a certain sense) of the mode of appropriation of the values that are produced. All the workers in a motor vehicle factory, whether they are metalworkers, masons, electricians, carpenters or whatever, all take on the character and role of producers in so far as they are equally necessary and indispensable in the fabrication of a motor vehicle: in so far as they form a historically necessary and absolutely indivisible body, organized as they are on an industrial basis. *PWI*, p. 295.

This summary of what is a rather compressed description of the effects of the development of monopoly capitalism in Italy and the potential of the factory councils gives some indication of Gramsci's attempt to ascertain the novelty of these developments which are seen as *contradictory* in their effects.

A key part of Gramsci's approach is the way in which the divisions and fragmentation of the class struggle within and between plants can be unified through an awareness of the unity of the productive process and of the worker as producer. Gramsci argued that workers could realise their revolutionary potential only when they saw themselves as an intricate part of the whole chain of production and not just the possessor of an individual skill or craft, a possibility in the post-war period.[43] The worker would realise the unity of the industrial process, and he would no longer consider himself merely a wage-earner but as a producer,[44] that is, the worker could go beyond a position defined by the capitalist relations of production in which his existence in the factory is described as economic, in which economic is conceived of as a separate aspect of his existence, unrelated to his existence as a citizen. He could become aware of himself as a producer, and of the nation as a productive system, which, Gramsci argues, reveals the way in which the political and the economic aspects of society are intertwined.

> At this point he arrives at a conception of the 'State', i.e. he conceives a complex organization of society, a concrete form of society, because this is nothing but the form of the gigantic apparatus of production which reflects—through all the novel, superior links and relations and functions inherent in its very enormity—the life of the workshop: which represents, in a harmonized and hierarchical fashion, the complex of conditions needed for the survival and development of his industry, his workshop, and even his person as a producer. *PWI*, p. 111.

The State which Gramsci describes here is not presented as the simple instrument of a class but as the organisation enabling a class to assure the reproduction of the social relations of production. In Gramsci's attempts to grasp the significance of the changes in economics and politics confronting the working class in these early writings, we can already observe a view of the State which itself is complex and rooted in the reality of a complex social formation. This is a view of the State and politics which Gramsci would develop further in prison but which, as we shall argue, in this period is not without traces of economism. The role of political parties in articulating the spheres of politics and economics, and the nature of the changing relationship between the two spheres, is not developed. Here it should simply be noted that Gramsci expressed his argument about the role of the councils in terms of his concept of the State and its relationship to economics. In an article written a year and a half later his language is more subtle:

> Every form of political power can only be historically conceived and justified as the juridical apparatus of a real economic power. It can only be conceived and justified as the defensive organization and condition of development for a given order in the relations of production and distribution of wealth. This fundamental (and elementary) canon of historical materialism sums up the whole complex of theses we have sought to develop in an organic fasion around the problem of the Factory Councils. *PWI*, p. 305.

It was the complexity of society and of the State which the proletariat had to comprehend, and according to Gramsci it was through his participation in a factory council that the worker could become conscious of the intimate workings of the society in which he lived. Unlike the trade unions the council itself was an expression of part of the whole productive process, not simply a collection of individuals.[45] Only an organisation expressing the unity of the productive process rather than trade union divisions could serve as the basis of the transition to a new State.

> The proletarian dictatorship can only be embodied in a type of organization that is specific to the activity of producers, not wage-earners, the slaves of capital. The factory Council is the nucleus of this organization. For all sectors of the labour process are represented in the Council, in proportion to the contribution each craft and each labour sector makes to the manufacture of the object the factory is producing for the collectivity. The Council is a class, a social institution. . . .
> Hence the Council realizes in practice the unity of the working class; it gives the masses the same form and cohesion they adopt in the general organization of society. *PWI*, p. 100.

Gramsci maintained that the factory councils were an organic expression of the working class going beyond the capitalist relations of production. He agreed with Sorel in suggesting that the proletariat had to produce its own institutions,[46] but it is important to note the basis for the utility of the factory council as a form of organisation according to Gramsci. It is the concrete development of capitalism which enables the factory council to perform a certain role. It is thus an organisation related organically to the concrete situation, not the creation of an arbitrary scheme, or will. Thus Gramsci goes beyond the problematic of his earliest writings and also diverges from that of Sorel. The potential of the period for a revolution is given by the contradictory nature of the development of capitalism not by an element external to it, nor by an exception to an historical role. Gramsci argues that the factory council, far from representing a form of organisation 'uncontaminated with politics' in the Sorelian sense, allowed the working class to comprehend the variety of problems involved in building a new State.[47]

> The Factory Council is the model of the proletarian State. All the problems inherent in the organization of the proletarian State are

inherent in the organization of the Council. . . . The Council is the most effective organ for mutual education and for developing the new social spirit that the proletariat has successfully engendered from the rich and living experience of the community of labour. *PWI*, p. 100.

The necessity of equipping the working class for the constructive task of building a new State is based on the experience of the international working-class movement in the period. With the spectre of the failure of revolutions in Germany, Austria, Bavaria, and Hungary before him, the difficulties of building a new order once the bourgeoisie has been overthrown[48] provide the concrete historical raw material for Gramsci's concept of revolution as a process not only of destruction of the old order but of building a new one in which the two phases must of necessity be intimately linked and based on real historical conditions and institutions. We return to Gramsci's definition of a proletarian revolution:

We have . . . maintained: 1. that the revolution is not necessarily proletarian and communist simply because it proposes and achieves the overthrow of the political government of the bourgeois State; 2. nor is it proletarian and communist simply because it proposes and achieves the destruction of the representative institutions and administrative machinery through which the central government exercises the political power of the bourgeoisie; 3. it is not proletarian and communist even if the wave of popular insurrection places power in the hands of men who call themselves (and sincerely are) communists. *PWI*, p. 305.

Thus it is not the smashing of the bourgeois state machinery, nor the leadership of the revolution nor even the fact that it is made by the masses which defines the proletarian revolution. Gramsci goes on,

The revolution is proletarian and communist only to the extent that it is a liberation of the proletarian and communist forces of production that were developing within the very heart of the society dominated by the capitalist class. It is proletarian and communist in so far as it advances and promotes the expansion and systematization of proletarian and communist forces that are capable of beginning the patient and methodical work needed to build a new order in the relations of production and distribution: a new order in which a class divided society will become an impossibility and whose systematic development will therefore eventually coincide with the wither-

ing away of State power, i.e. with the systematic dissolution of the
political organization that defends the proletarian class, while the
latter itself dissolves as a class to become mankind. *PWI*, p. 305.

The new order which must be created and which defines the proletarian
nature of the revolution implies the establishment of a new type of
State based on fundamental changes in the economic system which provides the real basis for elimination of classes and ultimately for the dis-
appearance of a specialised political organisation of a class. This class,
the proletariat, itself disappears as a separate class as it promotes the
interests of the whole society, a theme which appears in Lenin's *State
and Revolution* and one which would occupy an important place in
Gramsci's thought when he developed new concepts to translate it into
concrete practice.

Here we would emphasise that Gramsci specifies that it is the historical development of capitalism itself which provides the possibility for
the transformation of society. The revolution is proletarian only if it is
able to represent the expansion of the forces of production and the
creation of a new social order in which the division between classes tends
to disappear on the basis of concrete elements of the present social formation. Revolution as an act of creation, not merely destruction, yet revolution not as an act of will but rooted in the real historical development
remains a crucial part of Gramsci's thinking. It is this concept of revolution which is the foundation of Gramsci's consideration of the various
working-class organisations developed in the course of this real historical
development.

In the *Ordine Nuovo* he emphasised that the need to equip the proletariat
for its historical task required special working-class institutions. He
thought that the trade unions had served a particular purpose in the
past and still served the useful job of protecting labour as a commodity
within a competitive framework, but he maintained that their form and
nature were determined and limited by the historical period in which
they developed, that is, by the capitalist system. They were limited to
acting within the realm of capitalism, and whatever claims they pressed
and won were absorbed by the present system while the principle of
private property was never attacked.[49] Most significant of all is the way
in which Gramsci discussed the inadequacies of the trade unions in terms
of their inability to challenge the basis of bourgeois legality.

In the struggle over the price of labour power, Gramsci wrote, they
dealt with the capitalist class in circumstances and concerning terms
which were imposed by capitalism within the logic of the reproduction

of capitalist relations of production, not by the working class in order to break through this logic. The trade unions had arisen in a specific historical period as a defensive reaction to the capitalist class, and indeed, for them to be successful in signing and maintaining labour contracts, they not only had to remain within the legality established by the ruling class, but they had to prevent the workers from moving beyond it. According to Gramsci, this is what made them acceptable representatives of the working class with whom the capitalists could negotiate, and what enabled them to carry out their fundamental tasks obtaining the highest price possible for labour power.[50]

What exactly is implied when Gramsci attributes the limits of the trade unions to their acceptance of bourgeois legality? He is not simply discussing reformist leadership. He is not arguing for them to break the law as such or, in his own terms, for them to destroy the very basis of their existence. What he is criticising is the limits of their acceptance of the definition of the worker under capitalism, as the provider of labour power which must be sold as a commodity in competition with other workers defined in a similar way. 'The trade union', he writes, 'has an essentially competitive, not communist, character ' (*PWI*, p. 99).

This definition maintains the *separation* between workers and other sections of the population. The *unity* between workers in the productive process can only be expressed by the factory councils which contain by implication the basis of a new legality which belongs to the logic of socialism, not capitalism. The very reason for the existence of the factory councils 'lies in the labour process, in industrial production, i.e. in something permanent. It does not lie in wages or class divisions, i.e. in something transitory and, moreover, the very thing we are trying to supersede.' (*PWI*, p. 100.) For the trade unions to have a role in the revolutionary process, they had to recognise the temporary nature of the legality and not to consider it a permanent feature of society as they unfortunately tended to do.

What then was the proper relationship between the councils and the trade unions?

> The relations between unions and Councils cannot be defined by any other device than the following: the majority or a substantial number of the electors to the Council should be organized in unions. Any attempt to link the two institutions in a relation of hierarchical dependence can only lead to the destruction of both.
>
> If the conception that sees the Councils merely as an instrument in the trade union struggle takes material form in a bureaucratic

discipline and a hierarchical structure in which the union has direct control over the Council, then the Council is sterilized as a force for revolutionary expansion. . . .

If, moreover, the unions were to lean directly on the Councils, not to dominate them, but to become their higher form, then they would reflect the Council's own tendency to break at all times with industrial legality and unleash the final phase of the class war. The union would lose its capacity to negotiate agreements, and would lose its role as an agent to regulate and discipline the impulsive forces of the working class. *PWI*, pp. 266-7.

The trade unions would retain an important role as long as society was based on the existence of private property, and as long as the wage-labour system was maintained, but what is important to note is that Gramsci assumes that with the creation of the factory councils, the activities of the trade unions themselves would change to reflect the challenge to the bourgeois definition of the terms of the class struggle.[51] Without specifying, Gramsci presumably hopes that the corporate structure of the trade unions along craft lines would begin to disappear.[52] Moreover, through the existence of the factory councils the trade unions would be able to intervene in a terrain where the mass of the unorganised workers were to be found.

For the factory councils were the democratic organs of all the workers in a factory, not just those organised in trade unions. As Gramsci explained, the nature of the membership of the two organisations was very different. 'In the Factory Council, the worker participates as a producer, i.e. as a consequence of his universal character and of his position and role in society . . .' (*PWI*, p. 295.) The Council is able to reflect the fact that the worker's role in the productive process is not simply a result of the voluntary act of selling his labour power or particular skill. He is part of a class which is part of the forces of production.

In the factory, the working class becomes a given 'instrument of production' in a given organic system. Each worker comes to play a part in this system 'by chance'—by chance as regards his own intentions, but not by chance as regards the job he does, since he represents a given necessity in the labour and productive process. This is the only way he is taken on, and it is the only way he can earn his bread. He is a cog in the division of labour machine, in the working class constituted as an instrument of production. . . . *PWI*, p. 262.

Thus it is the very development of capitalism which provides the objective basis for the unity of the class and the potential of overcoming a
certain definition of the worker as the seller of labour power and the
producer of surplus value. Gramsci calls the factory council a 'public'
organisation in contrast to the party and the trade unions which are
'private'[53] because of this ability to reflect the position of the worker
in a social whole rather than to represent a partial aspect of his position
in society. While there is an obvious contrast with the nature of membership of a trade union, Gramsci's view of the basis of membership of the
party eventually changes and comes in fact to express this universal
character.[54]

In this period Gramsci argues that for the councils to be able to fulfill
their tasks of unifying and educating the masses, they must be as democratic and as responsive as possible and unhindered by restrictions from
above, from either the trade union or party leaders. The grounds on
which Gramsci argues that the councils cannot simply be created bureau-
cratically reveal his view that any organisational form must be justified
both by the concrete reality of the historical process and by roots in the
real mass movement, if it is to be an element in guiding and educating
the experience of the masses. With reference to the German situation he
writes:

> German Social Democracy (understood as a totality involving trade-
> union and political activity) effected the paradox of violently forcing
> the process of the German proletarian revolution into the form of its
> own organization, believing it was thereby dominating history. It
> created *its own* Councils, by fiat, and made sure its own men would
> have a majority on them. It shackled and domesticated the revolution.
> Today it has lost all contact with historical reality. . . . and the revo-
> lutionary process pursues its own uncontrolled and still mysterious
> course, to well up again from unknown depths of violence and pain.
> *PWI*, p. 143.

Unless modes of organisation are rooted in an historical reality, if they
become abstract, the contradictory result is an uncontrolled spontaneity,
and the very purpose of organisation is defeated. This would be a key
argument against Bordiga.

While Gramsci had criticised the reformists in the PSI since his days at
the University of Turin, it was not until early 1920 that he began to
criticise the leadership of the party as a whole. His criticism in this period was restricted to delineating the functions and limitations of the PSI,

and he was primarily concerned with establishing the correct relationship between the party and the factory council movement. The example of the Bolsheviks is used as an illustration of how a party should work and agitate within the Soviets, not as a model of a party *per se*.[53] While the elements of a new politics begin to be developed, Gramsci does not immediately draw the implications of this new concept of politics for a new alternative party. Gramsci's writings on the role of the PSI do, however, reflect his general views on organisation. The party, he writes, has a negative function and a positive one. The negative one is to subtract the support of the masses from the present system.

> With its revolutionary programme, the Socialist Party pulls out from under the bourgeois State apparatus its democratic basis in the consent of the governed. Its influence sinks deeper and deeper into the mass of the people, and assures them that the hardship in which they are floundering is not something trifling, nor a sickness without end, but corresponds to an objective necessity: it is the ineluctable moment of a dialectical process which must debouch in a blood-letting, a regeneration of society. And so the Party comes to be identified with the historical consciousness of the mass of the people, and it governs their spontaneous, irresistible movement. *PWI*, p. 142.[56]

It is the job of the socialist party, therefore, to guide the spontaneous outbursts of revolt in such a way that they adhere to the potential of the real development of history. Political leadership is therefore quite different from volontarism.

Once the party has paralysed the present system, Gramsci writes, the most delicate and difficult phase begins, the phase of positive activity:

> The views propagated by the Party operate autonomously in the industrial consciousness, and they cause new social patterns to emerge in line with these views. They produce organs that function in accordance with their own inner laws, they produce an embryonic apparatus of power in which the masses exercise their own government and acquire a consciousness of their own historical responsibility and their own particular mission: to create the conditions for a regenerative communism. As a compact and militant ideological formation, the Party exerts an influence over this inner elaboration of new structures . . . But this influx is organic, it grows from the circulation of ideas . . . from the fact that millions and millions of workers know that, as they establish new systems and a new order, the historical

consciousness that moves them has its living embodiment in the Socialist Party. *PWI*, p. 144.

At all moments the party's work is undertaken with the objective of
organising the intervention of the masses. This is a constant in Gramsci.
Yet, the relationship between the positive and negative moments, which
appear here as two separate stages, the description of the positive political intervention of the party remains largely undefined in this early
article. We would suggest that in part this lack of definition is a result
of Gramsci's ability to determine the limitations of the PSI, without
being able at this stage of his development to have a clear idea of an
alternative.

Gramsci implies that the limitations of the PSI were largely historically determined, it having developed, as had the trade unions, as a
response to an historical period dominated by the bourgeoisie. Organised within the framework of liberal democracy to compete with the
bourgeoisie, Gramsci argued that the traditional working-class organisations tended to duplicate that aspect of bourgeois society which was
a prime object of Gramsci's criticism—the separation between politics,
an area of activity assigned to the party, and economics, the monopoly
of the trade unions, the typical division within the working-class movement during the Second International.

The factory council was the institution which was able to overcome
this split. The party itself had to be a vanguard and thus was incapable
of absorbing large masses of workers. For Gramsci, the ability of the
party to *lead* the mass movement was crucial. The PSI, he writes, is

exposed . . . to all the pressures of the masses. It shifts and alters
its colours as the masses shift and alter their colours. In fact the
Socialist Party, which proclaims itself to be the guide and master of
the masses, is nothing but a wretched clerk noting down the opera-
tions that the masses spontaneously carry out. *PWI*, pp. 337-8.

Gramsci expresses the very leadership function in terms of the ability
of the party to relate constantly to the mass movement and to maximise
the potential of this movement to intervene in a constructive way to
create a new social order. For it to be able to do this,

it is essential that the Party should immerse itself in the reality of the
class struggle as waged by the industrial and agricultural proletariat,
to be in a position to understand its different phases and episodes, its

various forms, drawing unity from this manifold diversity. It needs to
be in a position to give real leadership to the movement as a whole
and to impress upon the masses the conviction that there is an order
within the terrible disorder of the present, an order that, when system-
atized, will regenerate society and adapt the instruments of labour to
make them satisfy the basic needs of life and civil progress. *PWI*, pp.
191-2.

As we shall see, the ability to lead the masses is a problem of organisation
only in so far as organisation is itself conceived of as an integral part of
a theory of politics adequate to the intervention of the masses.

Gramsci argues that the party should not try to substitute itself for
the forms of organisation created by the masses themselves. What must
be established, according to Gramsci, is the correct relationship between
the various working-class organisations, a relationship which is part of a
process of revolution and which cannot be fixed arbitrarily.

The party and trade unions should not project themselves as tutors or
as ready-made superstructures for this new institution, in which the
historical process of the revolution takes a controllable historical
form. They should project themselves as the conscious agents of its
liberation from the restrictive forces concentrated in the bourgeois
State. They should set themselves the task of organizing the general
(political) external conditions that will allow the revolutionary process
to move at maximum speed, and the liberated productive forces to
find their maximum expansion. *PWI*, p. 261.

The chief political problem which the party had to address was the
unity of the working class, a problem which was posed by the very level
of development of the productive process. In a very explicit passage
Gramsci writes,

the historical process of capitalism has created the conditions in which
the masses themselves, using their own methods and direct action, can
achieve unity. Proletarian unity forged by the workers themselves represents a higher stage of the unity which *de facto* exists: it is the
stage in which the workers show that they have acquired a consciousness of their own unity and want to give it a concrete expression, a
sanction.

The working-class vanguard organized in the Socialist Party must
take responsibility for resolving this problem. It is clear that any effect-

ive solution can only come from the masses themselves and only through the Factory Councils. *PWI*, p. 177.

The centrality of this problem appeared historically because it was the masses themselves who would make the revolution. By encouraging the factory councils the party would be more intimately tied to the life of these masses.

> For the communists who hold to Marxist doctrine, the masses of workers and peasants are the only genuine and authentic expression of the historical development of capital . . . the masses indicate the precise direction of historical development, reveal changes in attitudes and forms, and proclaim the decomposition and imminent collapse of the capitalist organizations of society . . . these mass manifestations reveal . . . a capacity . . . the aspiration to create new institutions and the historical drive to renew society from the roots upwards . . . If one becomes estranged from the inner life of the working class, then one becomes estranged from the historical process that is unfolding implacably, in defiance of any individual will or traditional institution. *PWI*, pp. 173-4.

The revolution itself was identified with this mass movement. The party was not the form of the revolution but its greatest agent. 'The proletarian revolution', Gramsci asserts, 'is not the arbitrary act of an organization that declares itself revolutionary, or of a system of organizations that declare themselves revolutionary '(*PWI*, p. 260). It was made by the masses in a precise historical setting but expressing new institutions which indicate the ability of the working class to organise a new type of State[57] which is no longer merely an expression of formal political freedoms but of real control by the masses over the sphere of production and of politics. This new relationship between the masses and politics requires new institutions.

> The working class asserts in this way that industrial power and its source ought to return to the factory. It presents the factory in a new light, from the workers' point of view, as a form in which the working class constitutes itself into a specific organic body, as the cell of a new State—the workers' State—and as the basis of a new representative system—the system of Councils. The workers' State, since it arises in accordance with a given pattern of production, has within it the seeds of its own development, of its own dissolution as a State

and of its organic incorporation into a world system—the Communist International. *PWI*, p. 263.

A criticism which can be made of Gramsci's view of the factory councils has to do with the possibility of unifying the great majority of the population and equipping it to control the State when different groups and classes, in a very different position from the industrial working class, are not as easily organised in institutions similar to the factory councils, a question we shall return to with regards to Gramsci's writings on the peasantry in this period. None the less, the significant aspect of Gramsci's description of the mode of constructing a new type of State is his definition of the revolution in these terms, as a process made by the masses. In this perspective, a 'crisis' theory of the revolution has begun to disappear, and the withering away of the State is related to its unique form.

The transition to socialism is no longer signalled by a dramatic break based on economic contradictions but is a process which begins within the capitalist social formation as new modes of organisation and a new relationship between society and the State are created in response to the long-term contradictions of capitalism. These new organisations and this changed relationship between the mass of the population and the State are characteristics of a new mode of politics and the superseding of the traditional division between State and society.

This view of the revolution as a process made by the masses creating their own institutions had implications for the relationship between the party and the State after the revolution. The party, according to Gramsci, was to continue after the revolution as an inspiration and guide for the masses, as the depository of a doctrine which justified their activity, but the party would not itself provide this original form of State.

The Party remains the leading apparatus within this irresistible mass movement, and exercises the most effective of dictatorships, a dictatorship based on prestige, on the conscious and spontaneous acceptance of an authority that workers see as indispensable if their mission is to be accomplished. It would be disastrous if a sectarian conception of the Party's role in the revolution were to prompt the claim that this apparatus had actually assumed a concrete form, that the system for controlling the masses in movement had been frozen in mechanical forms of immediate power, forcing the revolutionary process into the forms of the Party. The result would be to successfully divert a number of men, to 'master' history: *but the real revolutionary process would slip from the control and influence of the party, which would unconsciously become an organ of conservatism. PWI, p. 144. [My emphasis.]*

A correct understanding of the relationship between the party and the mass movement and the party and the new State was not simply a question of a change of leadership or of political line. When Gramsci first wrote about creating a communist party from within the PSI in late 1920, he tried to delineate the features of a new type of party which was defined in terms of its task: to organise the will of the people to found a new State. Significantly in an article in which Gramsci criticises both the socialist party and the syndicalists for accepting the liberal notion that the institutional forms of liberal democracy are permanent, a criticism he would develop in prison, he writes:

the socialist State cannot be embodied in the institutions of the capitalist State ... the socialist State must be a fundamentally new creation. The institutions of the capitalist State are organized in such a way as to facilitate free competition: merely to change the personnel in these institutions is hardly going to change the direction of their activity. *PWI*, p. 76.

The necessity to lead the *masses* who would found a new *type* of State was the basis of Gramsci's criticism of the PSI. The urgency of preparing the proletariat for this task is reflected in the fact that two major articles in which Gramsci addressed the problem of the party were each written after crucial defeats: 'Towards a Renewal of the Socialist Party'[58] after the isolation of the Piedmont general strike in April 1920 in which Gramsci still hoped to transform the PSI, and 'The Communist Party'[59] after the defeat of the occupation of the factories when the need for a new party had become clear to him. To understand the way in which Gramsci related the question of organisation to a specific historical task we must return to his criticism of the PSI and of the trade unions as being the creation of and therefore limited by the terrain on which they were founded. When Gramsci writes that the PSI has remained 'merely a parliamentary party' (*PWI*, p. 192) and claims that it is unable to go beyond the bounds of liberal democracy, it is in terms of the lack of roots in the mass movement and the way in which the PSI reflects the concept of politics inherent in liberal democracy, in particular the split between economics and politics. As this concept is challenged during the crisis of the liberal State so too is the PSI in crisis.[60]

It is true that there is a danger of historical reductionism here and we find a critique of bourgeois democracy which might be taken for a generalised critique of democracy *per se* if it is not related to Gramsci's argument for new organisations of control by the masses over a new type of State. This argument does seem to imply the substitution of bourgeois representative institutions with institutions of direct democracy without specifying a new kind of representation. With these limits this discussion does, however, have vast implications for a new concept of political intervention by the masses which requires a new *type* of political party. The novelty of the party arises out of the need to relate to the masses which must control the State for the first time in history. It must relate positively to new organisations, in this context the factory councils, which are able to organise the masses in such a way as to make political participation meaningful, and its internal structure must be such as to provide for a real unity of purpose. It therefore cannot simply be a conglomeration of factions.[61] The PSI was 'merely a parliamentary party' *not* because it participated in parliament or because it overemphasised the parliamentary arena, but because it reproduced the limitations of bourgeois parliamentarism. Liberal democracy, according to Gramsci, was unable to provide a real means of control over the State by the masses because politics was presented as separate from the socioeconomic reality of the lives of the majority of the population. Political life was dominated by a competition which did not necessarily result in the positive good of the whole of society. These features of bourgeois democracy were reflected in the organisation of the PSI.

> The traditional organisational form of the Socialist Party is not different from the organizational form of every other party born on the terrain of liberal democracy. This form is the general assembly of members . . . All the principles of functionality belonging to a democratic political association are present in the organizational form of the party: the division of powers in deliberative, executive, judiciary and the internal competition of . . . parties (revolutionary and reformist tendencies which try to alternate in power . . .), and there are all the characteristics essential to every assembly in which fickleness and tumult are expressed; essential characteristics which come to be 'corrected' naturally . . . by the bureaucratic arbitrariness of the executive offices. *ON*, p. 141.

These features in fact negated any true democracy and resulted in control by an *élite*.

The root of Gramsci's criticism of bourgeois democracy lies in the separation between economics and politics inherent in bourgeois society. This criticism is based on the view that while the State can be seen to provide the conditions for the reproduction of the relations of production and therefore in a more or less mediated way for the economy, the political control of the State by liberal democratic institutions, based theoretically on bourgeois political thought, from Hobbes through Locke, Hegel, and Mill, did not reflect the position of men and women in the production process but rather their formal, legal equality as citizens. Gramsci's argument is that the classical separation of the State from society typical of early capitalism and of the classical liberal 'nightwatchman State' was in fact being challenged by the increasing intervention by the State in society in the period of monopoly capitalism. At the same time the division between economics and politics, already being undermined by the actual development of capitalism was explicitly reflected in the division of labour between the PSI and the CGdL (General Confederation of Labour) in which politics was recognised as the monopoly of the party and economics as the monopoly of the trade unions, a division of labour typical of the Second International.[62] Gramsci objected to this on the grounds that it did not allow for a political intervention of the working class, which took account of the very developments of capitalism itself, in which this relation between economics and politics was questioned constantly by the development of monopoly capital and its consequences for the State. It was this concrete development *under capitalism* which presented the working class with the opportunity of developing a new type of State and for this the class needed a new type of party.

What were the characteristics of this new type of party?

the assembly of members, atomic individuals, responsible only before their conscience disturbed and numbed by the din, by demagogic improvisation, and by the fear of not being at the level of the political assizes of the proletariat, will be substituted by assemblies of delegates with imperative mandates, who will want to substitute discussions on concrete problems that really interest the work-people of a factory for generic and rusty discussions. Constrained by the necessity of propaganda and struggle in the factory, they will want the party assemblies finally to become preparation for the real conquest of political and economic power by the proletarian masses. It becomes possible to foresee the transformation of the Socialist Party from an association born and developed on the terrain of liberal democracy

in a new type of organization which belongs only to proletarian culture. *ON*, p. 142.

Yet Gramsci was quite aware that this concrete reality inside the factory
was part of a complex set of class relations. In order to understand these
relations and the contradictory nature of historical development in general, theoretical tools were needed. In a passage whose implications for
the need for a new understanding of Marxism would only be developed
in prison, Gramsci wrote that the PSI 'has none of the theoretical and
practical discipline that would enable it to keep in close contact with
national and international proletarian conditions in order to master
them, to control events and not be overwhelmed and crushed by them'.
(*PWI*, p. 156) Far from suggesting a volontarist or spontaneist problematic, Gramsci argues that the proper theoretical and practical preparation
of the working class was necessary to provide for a political intervention
which adhered to the possibilities of the concrete situation.

A crucial element of the Italian social formation which had to be
understood was the peasantry and the particular relationship between
the north and the south. A central theme of Gramsci's political writings
from his earliest years in Turin was the importance of the working class
to understand and ally with the peasantry.[63] While it has been suggested
that a limit to Gramsci's work in this period is a lack of understanding
that the struggle of the peasants was qualitatively different from that of
the proletariat which implied the need for different institutions to organise them and a differentiated strategy by the party,[64] what does appear
clearly is an argument for the need for the party's strategy to be based
firmly in an examination of a specific concrete reality.

> how can the Italian working class be organized into a dominant class
> if its political party, the party which should give rise to the new govern-
> ment apparatus, does not know the real concrete terms of the prob-
> lems of the working population as a whole . . . For a party which must
> become the government party of the proletarian State, it is not only
> a matter of affirming: 'we'll build communism', it is a matter of exact
> and concrete knowledge. *ON*, pp. 432-3.

What is relevant to a discussion of Gramsci's ideas on the party is the
way the limits of his analysis of the Italian concrete situation reveals a
limit to a more general aspect of this problematic. In the *Notebooks* the
problem of alliances would be encompassed within the concept of hegemony, a concept which Gramsci develops later in part from a reflection

on the inadequacy of the political intervention of the working-class movement in this period, but which, it can be argued, is potentially present already in this period. In a passage which would be reproduced in very similar terms in prison, Gramsci expresses the hegemonic vocation of the party:

> The Communist Party is the instrument and historical form of the process of inner liberation through which the worker is transformed from *executor* to *initiator*, from *mass* to *leader* and *guide*, from brawn to brain and purpose. As the Communist Party is formed, a seed of liberty is planted that will sprout and grow to its full height only after the workers' State has organized the requisite material conditions. *PWI*, p. 333.

Here is a clear expression of Gramsci's concept of the revolution as a creative process.[65]

Gramsci also addressed the problem of the way in which the different classes making up the Italian social formation were represented politically—the problem of political parties in general. Here, too, it has been suggested that Gramsci underestimated the effects of the differences between the various non-working-class parties.[66] We would suggest that this lack of differentiation between the various political parties representing different social forces, the lack of comprehension of the qualitative differences between the situation of the peasants and the working class, and the lack of a fully developed concept of hegemony are all related. Gramsci is in this period able to observe the *crisis* of the Italian liberal State, but he is not able to understand fully the process of re-organisation of the State. In a period of social crisis in which fascism had barely appeared on the historical stage, it is not surprising that Gramsci is able to observe the *negative* features of the crisis of the traditional parties in post-war Italy, but he is not able to explain the reconstitution of what he would later call the historical bloc. Here we are not concerned with his historical analysis as such but with determining the extent to which his theory of politics had developed certain elements but not others.

The problem of the way in which political parties represent social forces is considered when Gramsci writes:

> Political parties are the reflection and nomenclature of social classes. They arise, develop, decline and renew themselves as the various strata of the social classes locked in struggle undergo shifts in their

real historical significance, find their conditions of existence and development rapidly altered, and acquire a greater and more lucid awareness of themselves and their own vital interests. What has become characteristic of the present historical period, as a consequence of the imperialist war which has profoundly altered the structure of the national and international apparatus of production and exchange, is the rapidity with which the traditional political parties that emerged on the terrain of parliamentary democracy have faded away and been replaced by new political organizations. This general process is subject to an inner, implacable logic of its own, which manifests itself in the peeling away of the old classes and groupings and in vertiginous transitions from one state to another on the part of whole strata of the population, throughout the territory of the State and frequently throughout the territory of capitalist dominion. *PWI*, p. 334.

Yet, it is very important to note that by calling political parties the *reflection* and the *nomenclature* of social classes, the possibility of there being *various* modes of representing a particular class or function of a class and of organising social forces becomes less apparent and most importantly, the specificity and relative autonomy of these various modes of political representation is not indicated.

The war had, according to Gramsci, fundamentally changed the lives of whole sections of the population and stimulated for the first time in Italy the peasantry to seek a specific political representation.

In Italy we have seen a powerful party of the rural class, the Popular Party, arise virtually from nothing within the space of two years. At its inception, it claimed to represent the economic interests and political aspirations of all the rural social strata, from the *latifundist* baron to the medium-sized landholder, from the small landholder to the tenant farmer, from the sharecropper to the poor peasant. *PWI*, p. 335.

The contradictions between the various elements represented in the Popular Party, Gramsci thought, had already resulted in a tendency towards decomposition. This general crisis of the bourgeois State and the specific appearance of the peasantry as an organised political force which, however, was in crisis appears to Gramsci as an opportunity for the working class to replace the bourgeoisie whose historical role has been exhausted.[67] He describes this in a passage which clearly shows elements for his later development of the concept of hegemony.

This profound stirring of the rural classes is shaking the framework of the democratic parliamentary State to its very foundations. As a political force, capitalism has been reduced to corporate associations of factory owners. It no longer possesses a political party whose ideology also embraces the petty-bourgeois strata in the cities and countryside, and so ensures the continued survival of a broadly-based legal State. . . .

Since the bourgeoisie is exhausted and worn out as a ruling class, capitalism is exhausted as a mode of production and exchange, and there exists no unified political force within the peasantry capable of creating a State, the working class is ineluctably summoned by history to take upon itself the responsibilities of a ruling class. *PWI*, p. 336.

Gramsci correctly notes that the direct political representation of sections of capitalism had been reduced as the crisis of the political parties had progressed, and these parties were no longer able to organise the support of the petty bourgeoisie for the present social order. But what was the alternative? Gramsci was not unusual in pointing to a military or Bonapartist solution.

Hence the political power of capitalism is tending to be identified increasingly with the upper ranks of the military . . .Thus the political power of capitalism can only be expressed today in a military *coup d'état* and the attempt to impose an iron national dictatorship which will drive the brutalized Italian masses to revive the economy by sacking neighbouring countries sword in hand. *PWI*, p. 336.

Written in September-October 1920, this is not without interest for an examination of Gramsci's analysis of fascism which he developed in the following years when the potential of fascism to reorganise the State had become concrete.

What is of particular relevance is how this relates to Gramsci's view of political parties as the reflection and nomenclature of social forces, a view which reappears in the *Notebooks*. We would suggest that there is a contradiction here which can partially be explained by the historical limits of Gramsci's experience.

What Gramsci cannot fully explain if he retains this position is the fact that in representing the attempt by different classes and factions of classes to organise the State and therefore the capitalist social formation along different and often contradictory lines, political parties increasingly represent the organisation of *masses*. A consequence is that they are never the mirror reflection of a single class or faction of class. The way in which they organise masses in relation to the present social formation and the existing State had special consequences for the political intervention of the working class in its own attempt to lead the masses to organise a different State. Thus it can be argued that the *specificity* of the political level and the competition between the political parties has an autonomous importance. The activities of the complexity of social forces represented are organised in a variety of ways one of the most important being precisely through political parties.

We would suggest that the way in which parties represent masses is only partially developed in the *Notebooks*. Without anticipating our discussion, we would merely note that as Gramsci arrives at a greater understanding of the nature of the bourgeois State and its dependence on a mass base, whatever its particular mode of constitution (i.e. including fascism), he develops elements of analysis which can be used to confront the problem of the political representation of social forces. Yet, as we will show when we consider the *Notebooks*, he does not completely resolve it. Perhaps the limitations of Gramsci's own historical experience can provide an explanation. The only mass party in Italy (and in Europe in general) had been the Socialist Party. The Popular Party had failed, and fascism as a party appeared to Gramsci primarily in its contradictions as an organisation of the petty bourgeoisie in fact promoting the interests of finance capital once constituted as a State. Gramsci quite correctly points to the novelty and the contradictory nature of fascism, but his historical experience did not provide him with an example of a mass party providing mass support for a bourgeois State on the terrain of liberal democracy. In the *Notebooks* as he focuses on the State, Gramsci only indirectly discusses the way in which fascism as a party and as a state provided a mode of organisation of the masses in Italy.[68] In his concern to show that politics and the full meaning of the State implies a new look at a variety of political and cultural institutions, he only begins to see that the development of the State under monopoly capitalism requires a new type of bourgeois party as well as a new type of proletarian party.[69]

What remains fairly obscure in Gramsci's work in this period is the nature of the new relation which he suggests between economics and politics. To some extent he provides the answer by saying that it is only the concrete experience of the mass movement which can provide the modes of a new kind of politics which is no longer separated from the socio-economic reality which itself changes as the class struggle progresses.

In addition, it is not until he begins to write his *Notebooks* in prison that he has a full idea of the need for a new understanding of Marxism which can provide the tools for understanding theoretically this new relationship between politics and economics. What is already implicit in this period, however, is a challenge to the structure-superstructure model as Gramsci attempts to grasp the consequences for the political tasks of the proletariat of a changed relationship between the State and society in the period of the organisation of the masses. What is lacking are clear indications about the content of a political strategy which will enable the working class to relate to other classes, the alliance between the proletariat and other classes and strata remaining to a large extent limited to other groups which identify the dictatorship of the proletariat with the resolution of the problems of their existence.

The way in which the present State rested on the concrete relations between these groups and the specificity of their modes of existence and modes of struggle is not yet understood by Gramsci. Tools for determining this strategy and for understanding the qualitative differences between these different social strata and the proletariat would be provided by Gramsci in prison as he studied the complex way in which a social formation is reproduced and in which a social class can maintain its dominance. What he has begun to develop in the years preceding the foundation of the PCd'I (Communist Party of Italy) in January 1921 is a view of political organisation rooted in a theory of politics, of the State, and of the revolution as a process made by the masses with concrete historical forms. This would be the basis of the battle he eventually undertook against Bordiga to transform the PCd'I.

Notes

1. See, for example, Giuseppe Fiori, *Antonio Gramsci* (New Left Books, London, 1970). For a discussion of the intellectual influences on Gramsci in these years see Paggi, *Il moderno principe*, and Alistair Davidson, *Antonio Gramsci: Towards an Intellectual Biography*.

2. This is implicit in Bordiga's criticism and also in the approach of various articles which appeared in the 1960s in the *Rivista storica del socialismo*. See for example Luigi Cortesi, 'Alcuni problemi della storia del PCI', vol. 8, no. 24 (Jan.-April 1965) and Andreina DeClementi, 'La politica del PCI nel 1921-22 e il rapporto Bordiga-Gramsci', *Rivista storica del socialismo*, vol. 9, no. 28 (May-Aug.) and no. 29 (Sept.-Dec. 1966). For a summary of the debate about this period in the history of the PCI, much of which concerns Gramsci's ideas and activities see Alcara, *La formazione e i primi anni*. Her approach is similar to that of Cortesi and De Clementi. There is a certain logical coherence in the criticism made of Gramsci's view of the party in these studies which are based on an abstract and

formal concept of organisation which, we would argue, makes it quite impossible to understand important aspects of Gramsci's discussion.

3. It can be argued that Gramsci's ideas in this period only in part share points in common with other exponents of the European 'ultra-left', e.g. Pannekoek, Korsch, Lukacs, Gorter, Luxemburg, and that crucially he is able to go beyond an economistic problematic. For a comparison of Gramsci and Korsch see Paggi, *Il moderno principe*, pp. 245-53. With regards to Pannekoek, Franco De Felice, *Serrati, Bordiga, Gramsci e il problema della rivoluzione in Italia 1919-1920* (De Donato, Bari, 1971), pp. 285ff and Paggi, *Il moderno principe*, pp. 239-40. With regards to Luxemburg, see Paggi, pp. 255-6.

Revolution as Creation

4. Some of the points which Mussolini made were that there were differing opinions regarding the war within the PSI, that there were differences between the two sides which were significant for the working class, that irredentism or the claim for additional territory for Italy was an important issue that should be considered by the socialists, and that the socialists should face the possibility that Italian entry at some point might help to end the war more quickly. It was one of a series of articles in which he finally came out in full support of the war.

5. See Paolo Spriano, *Torino operaia nella grande guerra* (Einaudi, Turin, 1960), p. 85 for a quote from this article.

6. *PWI*, p. 7.

7. Ibid.

8. Ibid., p. 9.

9. Ibid., p. 8.

10. *Q*, p. 1233.

11. For a discussion of the influence of Sorel's ideas in Italy early in the century see Enzo Santarelli, *La revisione del marxismo in Italia* (Feltrinelli, Milan, 1964), ch. 2, 'L'esperienza soreliana'. For the way in which Sorel influenced Gramsci and how this differed from the general syndicalist use of Sorel, see Paggi, *Il moderno principe*, pp. 124-36.

12. See Spriano, *Torino operaia*, p. 87 and Angelo Tasca, *I primi dieci anni del PCI* (Laterza, Bari, 1971), pp. 92-3.

13. See Spriano, *Torino operaia*, p. 88.

14. Paggi writes: 'Culture was considered in the first place as the instrument and the necessary form of the *political* emancipation of a class. The first position to be clearly rejected was that of Bordiga which perceived the strong point of socialism in 'the feeling of class solidarity . . . When culture is understood as the criticism of the preceding civilization, every revolution is also a great cultural event.' *Il moderno principe*, p. 106.

15. Fiori, *Antonio Gramsci*, p. 106.

16. Ibid.

17. *SG*, p. 85.

18. De Felice discusses how Gramsci is later able to relate the national and the international dimensions in his work on the *Ordine Nuovo*. De Felice writes that Gramsci particularly wanted to overturn the traditional socialist position which argued that the very backwardness of Italian society made revolutionary socialist policies impossible. *Serrati, Bordiga, Gramsci*, p. 270 and p. 271. This of course paralleled the Menshevik position in Russia.

19. With regard to Gramsci's view of socialism in these articles see Gianni Scalia, 'Il Giovane Gramsci', *Passato e presente*, no. 9 (1959), pp. 1146-7.

20. 'Constituent and Soviet', *SG*, pp. 160-1.

21. Scalia says that Gramsci's anti-Jacobinism is very much aimed at the tradition in Italy represented by Gaetano Salvemini, particularly its Messianic and

utopian qualities, 'Il giovane Gramsci', p. 1153. Gramsci's concern to show that Lenin and the Bolsheviks were not utopians is related to the claim that the Russian Revolution was fundamentally different from a bourgeois revolution. *PWI*, pp. 28-9. Gramsci's definition of Jacobinism and therefore his opinion of it changes in the *Notebooks*. See our discussion below and our criticism of the article by Hughes Portelli, 'Jacobinisme et anti-Jacobinisme de Gramsci', *Dialectiques*, no. 4/5 (March 1974).

22. *SG*, p. 161.

23. *PWI*, pp. 31-3.

24. See also an article published shortly thereafter, 'Kerensky-Cernov', *Il Grido del Popolo* (29 September 1917) in Antonio Gramsci, *Scritti 1915-1921, Nuovi Contributi*, pp. 35-6. In this article Gramsci stressed once more that the work done by the Bolsheviks prevented the revolution from stopping at a compromise and out of chaos created a collective consciousness, an idea which is transformed into the making of a collective will in the *Notebooks*.

25. *PWI*, pp. 34-7, Aurelio Lepre considers 'Lenin's Work' which is discussed further on, to be more important. See his article, 'Bordiga e Gramsci di fronte alla guerra e alla Rivoluzione d'ottobre', *Critica marxista*, vol. 5 (July-Oct. 1967), p. 132.

26. *SG*, pp. 307-12.

The Ordine Nuovo

27. Piero Gobetti, *La rivoluzione liberale* (Einaudi, Turin, 1948), p. 107.

28. See Spriano, *Gramsci e l'Ordine Nuovo*, pp. 10-12, and *PWI*, p. 291.

29. See Paggi, *Il moderno principe*, p. 109.

30. See Franco Ferri, 'Consigli di fabbrica e partito nel pensiero di Antonio Gramsci', *Rinascita*, vol. 14, no. 9. Ferri tends to exaggerate somewhat the presence of a clear concept of an alternative party in Gramsci's ideas in these years.

31. Daniel De Leon's concept of organising workers according to industry seems to have influenced Gramsci. See De Leon's *Socialist Reconstruction of Society*, 1905. Gramsci mentions De Leon in 'On the *L'Ordine Nuovo* Programme', *PWI*, pp. 291-8. Emilio Soave discusses the international and, in particular the Anglo-Saxon influences on Gramsci in 'Appunti sulle origini teoriche e pratiche dei Consigli di fabbrica a Torino', *Rivista storica del socialismo*, vol. 8 (Jan.-April 1964), pp. 2-3. See Spriano, *Gramsci e l'Ordine Nuovo*, p. 72. See also Paggi, *Il moderno principe*, pp. 240-5 for a discussion of Anglo-Saxon influences on Gramsci.

32. Spriano, *Gramsci e l'Ordine Nuovo*, p. 45, p. 65. Of course the specific weight of Lenin's thought in Gramsci's work is the subject of much controversy. Spriano, for example, argues in another article that while this influence was very important, there were crucial differences with Gramsci giving much more emphasis to the push from the masses. Paolo Spriano, 'Gramsci dirigente politico', *Studi Storici* (1967). Concentrating on the organisational question in the rather restricted framework discussed above (see note 2), Carlo Cicerchia maintains that the influence of Lenin had to do with the factory councils rather than the party. 'Rapporto col leninismo e il problema della rivoluzione italiana', in Alberto Caracciolo and Gianni Scalia (eds.), *La città futura. Saggi sulla figure e il pensiero di Antonio Gramsci* (Feltrinelli, Milan, 1959). See also Alistair Davidson, 'Gramsci and Lenin, 1917-1922'. There is some confusion as to which of Lenin's writings Gramsci was familiar with and when. The discussion of the relationship between Gramsci and Lenin does not in fact depend on this kind of direct influence in any case since it is quite possible to ascertain similarities and differences from a comparison of the two systems of thought without a discussion of Gramsci's intellectual history.

33. Alberto Caracciolo suggests that Gramsci read a good deal into the Russian experience of the Soviets, particularly in attributing a greater extent of workers'

control to them than they had, and in considering them as the nucleus of a new State. 'A proposito di Gramsci, la Russia, e il movimento bolscevico', in Eugenio Garin, *et al., Studi gramsciani* (Editori Riuniti, Rome, 1958), pp. 99-100.

34. See De Felice, p. 270.

35. This is an argument put forward by both De Felice and Paggi. See for example, De Felice, *Serrati, Bordiga, Gramsci*, pp. 291ff and Paggi, *Il moderno principe*, pp. 257ff.

36, De Felice considers the councilar experience from this point of view. In particular see his chapter 'Gli istituti della rivoluzione', in *Serrati, Bordiga, Gramsci*, pp. 346-91. According to De Felice, Gramsci thought that the factory councils, by relating economics and politics continuously, would provide the basis for a transformation of both the party and the trade unions and the relationship between them, ibid., p. 347. See also Paggi, *Il moderno principe*, pp. 253-64. Paggi says that it is in Gramsci's position on the factory councils that his break with the Italian socialist tradition is most complete, especially his insistence that the revolutionary process could not be identified simply with the traditional organisations, ibid., p. 260.

37. For the historical dimension see John M. Cammett, *Antonio Gramsci and the Origins of Italian Communism* (Stanford University Press, Stanford, California, 1967); Martin Clark, *Antonio Gramsci and the Revolution that Failed* (Yale University Press, New Haven and London, 1977); Gwyn A. Williams, *Proletarian Order* (Pluto Press, London, 1975).

38. See *PWI*, pp. 66-7 and p. 77. Paggi maintains that Gramsci was concerned with the relative lack of organisational forms created by the Italian working-class movement in the course of often very militant 'spontaneous' struggles such as the 'red week' of 1915. *Il moderno principe*, pp. 253-5.

39. See De Felice, *Serrati, Bordiga, Gramsci*, pp. 275ff for a discussion along these lines. A fundamental aspect of Gramsci's position, this is completely ignored in Perry Anderson's analysis of Gramsci's view of the State. Anderson, 'The Antinomies of Antonio Gramsci'.

40. The councils had a double role according to De Felice, 'of re-organization of the entire Italian trade union structure to be capable of organizing permanently the totality of the working class, of responding to the strong demand for democracy and workers' control that developed after the war, and at the same time . . . of creating an organism which made a revolutionary policy possible for the party', *Serrati, Bordiga, Gramsci*, p. 187.

41. *PWI*, p. 164.

42. See De Felice, *Serrati, Bordiga, Gramsci*, pp. 189-92.

43. See *PWI*, pp. 110-11.

44. The worker as producer (and the relationship between the ideas of Sorel and Gramsci) is considered in depth by Nicola Badaloni in *Il marxismo di Gramsci* (Einaudi, Turin, 1975).

45. See *PWI*, p. 100. Gramsci argues that: 'Trade unionism stands revealed as nothing other than a form of capitalist society, not a potential successor to that society. It organizes workers not as producers, but as wage-earners, i.e. as creatures of the capitalist, private property regime, selling the commodity labour . . . in other words, trade unionism combines workers on the basis of the form that the capitalist regime, the regime of economic individualism, impresses on them.' *PWI*, p. 110.

46. *ON*, pp. 460-1.

47. The question of the relationship between Sorel and Gramsci has only recently begun to be considered in any depth, particularly by Nicola Badaloni, *Il marxismo di Gramsci*, and in 'Gramsci and the Problem of Revolution', in Mouffe, *Gramsci and Marxist Theory*.

48. *PWI*, pp. 306-7.

ll
CT

PARTIAL SHIPMENT

in stock
/or

49. *PWI*, pp. 104-5.

50. *PWI*, pp. 265-8.

51. See De Felice, *Serrati, Bordiga, Gramsci*, p. 347.

52. Gramsci was critical of the corporativism of trade unions organised along craft lines, and considered this kind of organisation inadequate for the kind of struggles taking place in a number of countries. See 'The Strikes of Canada', *ON*, p. 251.

53. See *PWI*, p. 295.

54. This is when the party's policy is what Gramsci calls truly political, 'posing all the questions around which the struggle rages not on a corporate but on a "universal" plane', *SPN*, pp. 181-2. See our discussion below of Gramsci's definition of politics in the *Notebooks* as the ability of a class to go beyond corporativism.

55. See, for example, *PWI*, p. 68.

56. See also *PWI*, p. 191.

57. The socialist State is a new type of State according to De Felice because it expresses, 'the *tendential* overcoming of the bourgeois distinction between economics and politics. Precisely those elements which according to Gramsci made the revolution actual had to characterize the state which was to be built, that is the relation between revolution and production', *Serrati, Bordiga, Gramsci*, p. 277.

58. *PWI*, pp. 190-6.

59. *PWI*, pp. 330-9.

60. The differentiation of tasks between the PSI and the CGdL, giving 'politics' to the first and 'economics' to the second, was the most obvious example of the reflection of a liberal notion of politics.

61. The result of the existence of factions was that the party was unable to carry out its revolutionary task. See *PWI*, p. 337.

62. In a passage which is also interesting for its reflections on the Labour Party, Gramsci writes: 'In fact, in terms of its traditions; in terms of the historical origins of the various currents that formed it; in terms of its pact of alliance, whether tacit or explicit, with the General Confederation of Labour (a pact which has the effect of giving an unwarranted power and influence to trade-union bureaucrats at every congress, Council or authoritative assembly); in terms of the unlimited autonomy conceded to the parliamentary group (which gives deputies too a power and influence in congresses, Councils and high-ranking discussions that is similar to that enjoyed by union bureaucrats and just as unwarranted) — in terms of all these things, the Italian Socialist Party is no different from the English Labour Party.' *PWI*, p. 337.

63. For a discussion of various early influences on Gramsci's position on the south see Paggi, *Il moderno principe*, ch. 2, 'Il liberismo, lo Stato e la storia d'Italia'.

64. See De Felice, *Serrati, Bordiga, Gramsci*, p. 321, pp. 328-37.

65. This passage indicates what Christine Buci-Glucksmann calls the 'practical state' of the concept of hegemony in the experience of the *Ordine Nuovo* which, she says, begins to take theoretical shape for Gramsci from 1924 (the period of Gramsci's debate with Bordiga and his work to transform the politics of the PCI). *Gramsci and the State*, pp. 6-7.

66. See De Felice, *Serrati, Bordiga, Gramsci*, pp. 342-3.

67. *PWI*, p. 335. See Massimo L. Salvadori, 'Gramsci e la quistione meridionale', in *Gramsci e il problema storico della democrazia* (Einaudi, Turin, 1970), pp. 77-8, for a discussion of the Popular Party and a criticism of Gramsci's interpretation.

68. The most important discussion is in the context of the passive revolution. See below. Togliatti later discussed fascism in these terms. See his *Lectures on Fascism* (Lawrence and Wishart, London, 1976).

69. Thus it can be argued that there are no 'pure' bourgeois parties in an advanced stage of capitalism. The British Conservative Party, for example,

cannot simply be defined by its policies, nor by its membership, nor by its voting support but by the articulation of all of these *and* its relationship to a specific field of conflicting social forces organised in other parties and organisations.

Part II

THE STRUGGLE FOR A NEW TYPE OF PARTY

The new party which was founded as a minority split from the PSI at Leghorn in January 1921 did not reflect the ideas of Gramsci on politics and organisation. From the founding of the party until the spring of 1922 Gramsci was the editor of the new daily *Ordine Nuovo* the contents of which resembled only to a limited extent the weekly of 1919-20. As one of the daily newspapers of the PCd'I, it reflected the Bordighist line of the party in the way it engaged in polemic with the PSI and the daily political debate.

Gramsci's own articles are written in a harsh, strident language very unlike his previous style.[1] This period can be considered a hiatus in a certain sense in his own political development. Subsumed under the Bordighist leadership, isolated from his colleagues of 1919-20,[2] Gramsci's most original contribution of the years before going to Moscow was his analysis of fascism which departed considerably from Bordiga's own understanding of the phenomenon. There continue to be traces of Gramsci's earlier ideas in various articles,[3] but a further development of his political thought awaited a crucial experience—the year and a half spent working for the Comintern in Moscow and Vienna in 1922 and 1923.[4]

While abroad Gramsci wrote little, in part because he was confined to a sanatorium for six months. It was none the less a period of intense study and political experiences. The debates about the building of socialism in the Soviet Union, the differences between the situation in Russia and Western Europe, and the problems of implementing the line of the United Front provided the background for Gramsci's application of the ideas of 1919-20 to what he came to realise was a crucial problem—the creation of a political party able to relate to the mass movement whatever the circumstances. The struggle to transform the PCd'I into a new type of party still had to be undertaken.

Beginning with letters from Moscow and Vienna and continuing in the newly founded national daily, *L'Unità*, after his return to Italy in the spring of 1924, Gramsci's work focused on the relationship between a particular concept of politics and the problem of political organisation. In the letters in which he put forward his ideas to his former colleagues of 1919-20, Gramsci outlined the differences between himself and

Bordiga on politics and the party. In the newspaper articles, addressing a wider audience and intervening in a period of severe fascist oppression, we find a very direct discussion of the party which was part of the struggle to change the ideas of the rank and file away from the Bordighist conception to a new mode of political intervention.[5] Given the difficulty of the party surviving in any form in these years, it is significant that Gramsci insists on the need for a full discussion to improve the political preparation for the rank and file to allow the party to intervene effectively, an argument for internal democracy on political-functional grounds which he would develop further in a still more difficult period in prison.

Organisation as a Political Problem

In terms of specific policies one of the most contentious issues was the application of the United Front strategy in Italy. Without entering into a very complex historical debate[6] and noting that on this issue Gramsci did not at first oppose Bordiga, the important aspect for us to consider is the way Gramsci relates their differences to a different concept of the revolution. Bordiga's opposition to the line of the International, Gramsci wrote, derived from his belief that it

> was born on the terrain of a backward and primitive capitalist civilization. For him, this tactic is extremely voluntaristic and theatrical, because only with an extreme effort of will was it possible to obtain from the Russian masses a revolutionary activity which was *not determined by the historical situation*. He thinks that for the more developed countries of central and western Europe, this tactic is inadequate or even useless. In these countries, *the historical mechanism functions according to all the approved schemes of Marxism. There exists the historical determinism which was lacking in Russia*, and therefore the over-riding task must be the organization of the party as an end in itself. *PWII*, p. 199. [My emphasis.]

What is significant is Bordiga's view that the revolution in Russia was the *exception* to an historical rule, a rule established by a Marxist orthodoxy which applied in Western Europe, a view with certain points in common with Gramsci's earliest position on the Russian Revolution. Bordiga's insistence on the need for organisation *per se* in the West when it might seem more appropriate to what he considered the voluntarist task of the Bolsheviks is explained by Bordiga's concept of the revolution as determined by an historical process which was separate from the political intervention of the party. The party therefore had to be prepared for the moment of revolutionary crisis, a moment which the party could do little if anything to create. In the meantime, the efforts of the party were to be directed to its own organisation so that it would be prepared when the crisis took place.

In a passage which contains several of the themes which he developed in the *Notebooks*, Gramsci argued that just the opposite to Bordiga's view of the differences between East and West was true.

> Firstly, because the political conception of the Russian communists was formed on an international and not on a national terrain. Secondly, because in central and western Europe the development of capitalism has not only determined the formation of the broad proletarian strata, but also—and as a consequence—has created the higher stratum, the labour aristocracy, with its appendages in the trade-union bureaucracy and the social-democratic groups. The determination, which in Russia was direct and drove the masses onto the streets for a revolutionary uprising, in central and western Europe is complicated by *all these political super-structures*, created by the greater development of capitalism. This makes the action of the masses slower and more prudent, and therefore requires of the revolutionary party a strategy and tactics altogether more complex and long-term than those which were necessary for the Bolsheviks in the period between March and November 1917. *PWII*, pp. 199-200. [My emphasis.]

The justification of trying to translate the lessons of the political experiences of the Bolsheviks and the theories developed by Lenin into the Italian situation was the international context, imperialism. But the development of capitalism in the West had created a much more complex situation which required a much more complicated strategy, a strategy which was *not* based on an analysis of a specific defeat or series of defeats of the working-class movement but which was made necessary by the very complexity of the political superstructures. What is extremely interesting is the way in which Gramsci implies that organisations which are normally considered part of *civil* society are in fact part of the *political* superstructure. The intimate relationship between political and civil society would be a central theme in the *Notebooks*.

A strong element in Gramsci's letters was the need to adhere to the line of the International because of the party's experience in Italy although Bordiga's position might seem the more independent one.

Gramsci's chief concern was to improve the ability of the party to intervene in a specific national context.[7] Bordiga's polemic with the International seemed to be derived from the point of view of a minority faction within the International. 'We', Gramsci writes, 'must approach things from the viewpoint of a national majority '(*PWII*, p. 200). The need to relate to the *majority* which would make the revolution was one of the arguments used to justify the United Front policy and had been central in Gramsci's work from his earliest writings.

Gramsci thought that the most important question was whether each party, in its own particular conditions, had understood how to apply the United Front policy. The answer, he concluded, was 'no'. One reason for this was the way in which the so-called centralism of the Comintern was applied.

> so far it has not been successful in creating parties which know how to undertake a *creative autonomous policy* which is automatically centralized, in as much as it corresponds to the general plans of action drawn up in the congresses. I believe therefore that it would be difficult to change the present situation by establishing obligatory tactics, because in reality this has been fruitless. *La form*, p. 261.

A number of assumptions about the role of the International and of the national parties is contained in this passage. In a letter to Terracini from Vienna in March 1924, Gramsci accepts the establishment of broad strategic indications by the International which must, however, be applied in the national context by 'autonomous, creative politics'. The establishment of obligatory tactics is fruitless.[8] Without entering a discussion about the ability of an international organisation to establish even strategic guidelines, an assumption which was practically unquestioned in the communist movement in the 1920s, and without insisting on a detailed comparison, we would simply point out that Gramsci portrays the relationship of a party centre to its rank and file cadres in a similar way, stressing that the rank and file must be prepared to intervene creatively in a concrete political reality.

It was this ability to relate to a concrete reality which had been the chief merit of the *Ordine Nuovo* group, the most important aspect of which was to build and organise a strong mass movement which gave the party the only real base that it had had. Rather than identify the changes he sought in the party with a very specific group of people, however, Gramsci argued that what should be emulated was a method of work which sought to unite theory and practice.

We must try to reconstruct an environment for ourselves like that of '19-'20 . . . then no initiative was taken if it had not been tested against reality, if first we had not sounded out the opinions of the workers with various means. Therefore our initiatives almost always had an immediate and widespread success and they appeared as the interpretation of a widely felt need, never as the cold application of an intellectual schema. *La form*, p. 257.

In a passage which would almost be duplicated in the *Notebooks*,[9] Gramsci was in fact criticising an abstract, 'rationalistic' approach to politics which was unable to relate specific questions of organisation and tactics to the real experiences of the mass movement. He suggests that the success of the *Ordine Nuovo* derived from this ability to undertake activities which corresponded to the needs of the working class. It was this method which had to be adopted by the PCd'I in very different circumstances. Thus Gramsci is not arguing for a resuscitation of the factory councils *per se* but of the need to derive the politics and the organisation of the party from an examination of concrete reality.

In these letters Gramsci insisted that the debate with Bordiga concerned not just organisational questions but political ones. These were the terms in which Gramsci presented his ideas of centralism, the relationship of the class to the party and of the members of the party to the leadership, the need for discussion and debate, and the role of illegal work.

As early as July 1923, with regard to discussions in Moscow about unification between the socialist and communists within the framework of the United Front, he wrote to Togliatti, 'I am absolutely convinced that today any discussion on our part that is limited to the organisational and juridical aspects of the Italian question can have no useful result ' (*PWII*, p. 159.) The discussion in Moscow was concerned with far broader and more significant issues than the question of unification. It was

whether the PCI has understood the overall Italian situation, and whether it is capable of giving a lead to the proletariat; whether the PCI is capable of developing a vast political campaign, i.e. whether it is ideologically and organizationally equipped for a specific activity; whether the leading group of the PCI has assimilated the political doctrine of the Communist International which is Marxism as it developed into Leninism, i.e. into an organic and systematic body of organizational principles and tactical viewpoints. *PWII*, p. 159.

Thus organisational questions, Marxist theory and the ability to intervene effectively were intricately related for Gramsci.

While in the above passage Gramsci seems to accept a certain theory of organisation, he insisted in succeeding letters that organisation itself derived from a theory of politics. In another letter six months later, Gramsci reiterated that the problems in the party could not be reduced to organisational questions but that the general situation of the party, which was reflected in its organisation, itself was the reflection of a general political view of the revolution and of the workers State.

> Today, it is a problem of relations on the one hand between the party leaders and the mass of members, on the other between the party and the proletariat. Tomorrow, it will be a vaster problem, which will influence the organization and solidity of the workers' State. Not to pose the question to its full extent today would mean going back to the Socialist tradition, and waiting to differentiate oneself until the revolution is at the door, or even until it is already in course. *PWII*, p. 187.

The originality of the communist tradition, the way in which it was differentiated from the socialist heritage, a topic which was very much in the centre of the debate within the PCd'I, was found, according to Gramsci, in a conception of the revolution as a *process*. This conception implied that the activities of the party and its view of its role in the present social formation were crucial to the new type of State and society which would develop. The question of the relationship between the leadership of the party and its members on the one hand and the party and the class on the other had implications for the very foundation of the socialist State. Significantly Gramsci portrays the difference between the socialists and the communists in terms of the way in which the view of the party was related to its task of founding a new State. Thus, the problem of the relationship between leaders and led could not be left to be resolved spontaneously at the time of the revolution. Implicitly he is arguing that Bordiga, who separated the question of the party from the new type of State, had been unable to go beyond the socialist tradition despite his rhetoric.[10]

Central to Gramsci's argument against Bordiga was a different view of the revolution, which implied a different relation between the party and the masses. Referring to opposition from the Bordiga leadership to the formation of factory cells,[11] Gramsci wrote:

> Any participation of the masses in the activity and internal life of the

party, other than on big occasions and following a formal decree from the centre, has been seen as a danger to unity and centralism. The party has not been seen as the result of a dialectical process, in which the spontaneous movement of the revolutionary masses and the organizing and directing will of the centre converge. It has been seen merely as something suspended in the air: something with its own autonomous and self-generated development; something which the masses will join when the situation is right and the crest of the revolutionary wave is at its highest point, or when the party centre decides to initiate an offensive and stoops to the level of the masses in order to arouse them and lead them into action. *PWII*, p. 198.

Gramsci is indicating the way in which Bordiga's problematic was at one and the same time voluntarist and mechanistic. The activities of the masses were feared if they were not the result of the intervention of the party. Rather than depend on a dialectic between the activities of the mass movement and the conscious leadership of the party the revolution appeared as a spontaneous development of history. Thus posed, the potential of the party for political intervention to change the balance of forces and the potential of the mass movement to make the revolution are mutually diminished.

There was a correspondence between Bordiga's views of the revolution, of the role of the party and the masses, and of the *internal* organisation of the party. Gramsci argued that the conception of the role of individual members was seriously mistaken as it was expressed in the second thesis on tactics approved at the Rome Congress, which he said, stressed that the consciousness and will of the individual members of the party were not important because they had no meaning except as the member was integrated in a unitary collective organism.[12] Gramsci claimed that, in fact, it reproduced the position of Serrati the leader of the PSI.[13] as well as that of the Mensheviks. At the same time Gramsci thought that the emphasis on the collective organism was correct if applied to the working class as a whole because the class could only act politically through a political party, that is, the consciousness and will of a class could only be translated into constructive political intervention through a party. In prison Gramsci would develop the idea that one of the tasks of the party was to create a collective will. Here, recalling the discussion which led to the split between the Bolsheviks and the Mensheviks, he maintained that in a revolutionary party every member had to be an active and prepared element in order for the organisation to be effective.

Bordiga's view that the individual party member was significant only in so far as he was part of the collectivity had had several consequences for the party. On the one hand the lack of discussion inside the party, which indicated that the party leadership was not giving due consideration to the development of single militants, provided the conditions for what Gramsci called 'the opportunist danger', that is, the right-wing minority led by Tasca, to gain strength. Thus, far from protecting the party from being infected by petty bourgeois ideas, as Bordiga intended by maintaining a doctrinal purity in the central party organs which established a political line to be carried out by militants who did not fully understand it and who lacked theoretical and political preparation, Bordiga's rigid concept of the party actually created the basis for factions to arise. It also led to 'the withering of all individual activity; the passivity of the mass of members; the stupid confidence that there is always somebody else who is thinking of everything and taking care of everything'. (*PWII*, p. 197.)

This mistaken conception of the role of the individual members, in leading to their relative passivity, had very specific effects on detailed organisational questions.

> The party has lacked the possibility of choosing, with rational criteria, the trustworthy elements to whom particular tasks could be assigned. The choice has been made empirically, according to the personal knowledge of individual leaders, and has most often fallen on elements who did not enjoy the confidence of the local organizations and therefore saw their work sabotaged. And it should be added that the work carried out has only been controlled to the most minimal extent, and that in the party there has therefore been produced a real separation between the membership and the leadership. . . . The error of the party has been to have accorded priority in an abstract fashion to the problem of party organization, which in practice has simply meant creating an apparatus of functionaries who could be depended on for their orthodoxy towards the official view. It was believed, and it is still believed, that the revolution depends only on the existence of such an apparatus; and it is sometimes even believed that its existence can bring about the revolution. *PWII*, pp. 197-8.

Gramsci is arguing that unless the rank and file fully understand the party line, it will not in fact be applied in the daily practice of the party militants. Thus the application of a particular line of politics is not a question of an iron discipline, but, in the absence of the political preparation of the individual member, quite the opposite happens. The centre is unable to control the activities of the base. The split which is created between the party leadership and the mass of party members reproduces the kind of division between leaders and led inherent in the politics of capitalist society. Thus, abstractly posing the question of organisation had the contradictory result that the organisation was unable to go beyond the historical limits of the socialist party. In a passage full of implications for the experience of the communist movement, Gramsci suggests that the mere creation of an apparatus which adheres to an official orthodoxy, itself derived from this abstract approach to organisational questions, does not represent a break with the socialist tradition and indeed implies a mistaken concept of the revolution which, according to Gramsci, is made by the masses and is not determined by the mere existence of a rigidly organised party.

Questions of discipline and centralism were an important element in the attempt, both within Italy and internationally, to differentiate a communist party from the socialist parties of the Second International. It is worthwhile to consider further the way in which Gramsci argued that, despite the exaggerated concern for unity manifested by Bordiga, the PCd'I was in fact seriously deficient in the most basic, day to day, organisation. This was particularly evident because of the difficult conditions of semi-legality under which the party had to work. He was convinced, he wrote in January 1924,

> that the so-highly praised and lauded centralism of the Italian party comes down in reality to a very ordinary lack of any division of labour, or precise allocation of responsibilities and spheres of authority. . . . Everyone takes initiatives without warning the centre responsible, which has often already initiated work along the same lines which it has to discontinue. All continuity of initiatives ends by disappearing. Too many people end up knowing the most highly confidential matters; every possibility of control or checking vanishes. People are introduced into the movement whose seriousness and responsibility have not been checked out in advance in any way. *PWII*, p. 184.

The need for the party to be organised differently would not be addressed, according to Gramsci, merely by outlining a new organisational framework. First of all, Gramsci suggested that it was through political education of all party militants, not an abstract discipline, which would insure that they could react in a unified way to any political situation, and secondly, he wanted closer contact with party members through establishing an intermediate stratum between the rank and file and the leadership.[14]

Gramsci would return to the topic of centralism and hierarchy in the party in terms of a division of labour in the *Notebooks*. Here it should be noted that Gramsci is particularly concerned with the effectiveness of the party in a state of semi-clandestinity, a situation which called for a creative rather than a mechanical application of the party line. Thus not even in the most difficult circumstances was rigid organisation derived from abstract schema.

This does not mean, however, that Gramsci was not concerned with party unity. Centralisation, he wrote, 'means that when a decision has to be taken it cannot be modified by anybody . . . and that no one can create *faits accomplis*' (*PWII*, p. 185). It was the way in which the rank and file kept the leadership informed of developments in the mass movement and then took part in applying decisions taken by the centre in day-to-day activities which determined the ability of the party to intervene effectively. Yet Gramsci was not suggesting that there would necessarily be a uniformity of opinions. Gramsci foresaw the possibility of the co-existence of quite different ideas in the party. By stressing the need to make use of the talents of Bordiga and Tasca, he applied this not just to himself when he felt in a weak position but to his opposition, when he later was confident of being able to form a new leadership. The collaboration of individual leaders with different ideas was not the same, however, as allowing for the existence of different factions.

In a letter referring to a conversation with Tasca, Gramsci outlined what he considered the particular nature of a communist party:

The internal life of a communist party cannot be conceived as the arena for a parliamentary type of struggle, in which the various factions fulfil a function which is determined, like that of the different parliamentary parties, by their origins, which in turn depend on the different classes in society. In the party, one single class is represented and the different positions which from time to time become currents and factions are determined by divergent assessments of the events which are taking place; they therefore cannot become solidified into a permanent structure. *PWII*, p. 178.

With echoes from his earlier writings, Gramsci stresses that the party of a new type must not reflect the principles of a bourgeois democracy but must achieve a greater positive unity. When he discussed the formation of his own group in the struggle for the leadership, it was a question of winning over the whole of the party to a new line, not of the coexistence of different factions within the party over a period of time. A faction, he

said, 'exists even when only two or three comrades come to an agreement
in advance to draw up a common platform which concerns the entire activity of the P. (party)'. (*La Form*, p. 252.)

Several problems arise here with regards to the internal democracy
of the party. First, the labelling of various opinions as representing class
interests divergent from those of the proletariat could hardly encourage
the kind of internal discussion which Gramsci sought. Nor do we find
an argument for any formal structures guaranteeing that this discussion
takes place. The first aspect will be considered albeit only indirectly in
prison while the second poses questions of organisational structures in
the very abstract way Gramsci attacks. We shall return to this when we
discuss the *Notebooks*.

The belief that there was some kind of model of organisation, which
was considered a fixed goal without relation to the development of the
class struggle had influenced the PCd'I's opposition to the Comintern's
directives to unite with the PSI.

> The question that was always put to the Comintern was the following:
> 'Do you think that our party is still at the nebular stage, or that its
> formation has been completed?' The truth is that historically a party
> is never definitive and never will be. For it will become definitive only
> when it has become the whole population, in other words when it has
> disappeared. Until it disappears because it has achieved the ultimate
> aims of communism, it will pass through a whole series of transitory
> phases. *PWII*, p. 198.

In terms which he would repeat almost exactly in prison,[15] Gramsci
argues that until the class struggle itself is surpassed and communism is
established the party must continually evolve and develop. Until its task
is complete the party will constantly change. Since the transition to socialism is a process with different phases, rather than the result of a single
dramatic event, it should be assumed that the party will grow and change,
absorbing new members either as individuals or groups as its influence
spreads and the concrete situation changes. Thus there is no abstract
moment when the party is complete and 'ready' to accept new members.

On approaching the question of the United Front and the need to
win over the mass of the PSI, Gramsci thought that the problem could be
tackled only if the subtle ramifications of the development of social
democracy in Italy were understood, and he stressed that a patient, comprehensive programme of political activity was needed, and that mere
ideological debate was not sufficient. Written in a very different tone

from the polemical articles which he wrote for the daily *Ordine Nuovo*, Gramsci argues that the mass movement could only be won over to the politics of the Communist Party if the activity of the party went beyond mere propaganda and represented an articulate political initiative.[16] It was this patient, constructive intervention which was the concrete basis for a change in the political orientation of masses of people at present influenced by the Socialist Party. A similar argument would be developed in prison with regards to changing the balance of forces and winning sections of the population away from support of the present social system.

Gramsci argued that the PCd'I had to approach unity with the PSI on the basis of the political strength of the party. Without considering the historical discussion of the correctness of the Comintern line, what should be noted is a more general point. Gramsci assumes that various movements can develop outside the party which express an advanced revolutionary position. The party must recognise this and welcome new members. Its own revolutionary nature will be guaranteed not by the personnel at the top but by the correctness of its politics.[17]

In approaching the question of relations with the PSI, Gramsci analysed the particular role which the socialist movement had had in Italian history. Rather than succeeding in unifying the working class and placing it at the head of all the oppressed classes in Italy, Gramsci suggested that in the previous thirty years the working-class movement had in fact served as a method of selecting new leading elements for the bourgeois State.[18] The ability of the working class to establish an autonomous political role is defined by Gramsci in terms of the unity of the working class and contemporaneously its leadership of other classes. Thus even its own unity implies achieving a level of political development which goes beyond corporativism.[19] The need to unify the masses who would make the revolution was the background for considering areas where he thought the party's activities had been particularly weak.

With regards to the detailed type of work which the party should undertake, Gramsci insisted that the specific policies of the party had to be determined on the basis of a central question: what was the relationship between this work and the mass movement? He was worried, for example, that the launching of a new fortnightly series called the *Ordine Nuovo* was not connected to a specific movement as had been the case with the earlier weekly, even though he still thought that the specific programme of the new journal should be factory organisation. He sought criticism of this idea from the party members with whom he was corresponding because he felt, 'suspended in mid-air: I am always afraid of being detached from actual reality and of building sand castles.' (*La form,*

p. 256.) It was only if the party succeeded in creating an atmosphere similar to the one which existed in 1919-20 when workers were consulted in various ways before any activity was undertaken that the appropriateness of any specific initiative could be determined.[20]

Gramsci was especially concerned with the party's attitude toward the south. He had already discussed the need for an alliance between the northern working class and the southern peasantry when he was writing for the weekly *Ordine Nuovo*,[21] and now he insisted that the PCI should give due attention to the problem. He connected an improved policy towards the south with the struggle against reformism which he identified with the traditional neglect with which the PSI leadership had treated the southern question. One of the many problems facing the party, he wrote,

> is that of the South, which we have misunderstood just as the socialists did, considering that it could be solved within the normal framework of our general political activity. I have always been convinced that the South would become the grave of fascism, but I also think that it will be the greatest reservoir and the marshalling-ground for national and international reaction if, before the revolution, we do not adequately study its problems and are not prepared for everything. *PWII*, p. 203.[22]

Again, with regard to the problem of the south, the party had been unable to go beyond the limits of the PSI. The complex social reality of the south had to be studied to enable the party to intervene effectively in what Gramsci presents as a contradictory reality which had the potential either to serve as the base for reaction or to undermine fascism. This view of the peasants and of rural areas as potentially allying with either the proletariat or with the bourgeoisie is not particularly original, but Gramsci came to consider the complex situation in the south as the key to the political unity of the Italian social formation.

Another of the areas of party work which concerned Gramsci in these letters had to do with the trade unions. Gramsci wanted the party to pursue a policy of intensifying the campaign for workers to return to the trade unions whose organising ability had been severely limited by the fascist régime, and at the same time to work to organise factory cells in the factory along the lines of the factory councils or the internal commissions.[23] He stressed that it was not a matter of trying to create a separate trade union organisation, as some members of the party feared would be the outcome, but of making the party's political presence felt in a practical way inside the factory. Once more emphasising the need to maintain roots in the mass movement, Gramsci was arguing that the factory represented a contradictory reality. In an article which he wrote while abroad, Gramsci explained how the development of capitalism required a certain organisation of the working class. Noting that while the trade unions had lost ground, the internal commissions had expanded their organisation, he asked:

> Why have the capitalists and fascists allowed, and why do they continue to allow, such a situation to arise and persist? For capitalism and fascism, it is necessary that the working class should be deprived of its historical function as leader of the other oppressed classes of the population (peasants, especially in the South and the Islands; urban and rural petty bourgeois). It is necessary, in other words, to destroy organizations that are external to the factory and territorially centralized (unions and parties), since they exercise a revolutionary influence on all the oppressed and remove from the government the democratic basis of its power. *But the capitalists, for industrial reasons, cannot want all forms of organization to be destroyed. In the factory, discipline and the smooth flow of production is only possible if there exists at least a minimum degree of constitutionality, a minimum degree of consent on the part of the workers. PWII*, p. 167. [My emphasis.]

This organisation of the working class, which if isolated was limited in its political potential, was the reality in which the party had to intervene. For this intervention to be as effective as possible, the development of capitalism had to be understood as producing contradictory effects which could be in the political interests of *either* the bourgeoisie *or* the proletariat. In the *Notebooks*, Gramsci will analyse further this potential of the organisation of the masses as he investigates the changed reality of the dominance of the bourgeoisie. The modes of this dominance change to include what Gramsci calls hegemony as a response to changes in the organisation of the economy and society as a whole. In this sense the roots of hegemony lie in the factory, in the type of consensus created there.

One of the criticisms which has been made concerns Gramsci's underestimation of the ability of the bourgeoisie to re-organise the State, and his insistence that the period was revolutionary.[24] We would suggest that it is a reconsideration and a redefinition of the revolutionary potential of the period of advanced capitalism rather than the abandonment of this perspective which forms the basis of his work in prison. It is therefore interesting to consider the terms in which he described the revolutionary nature of the situation, leaving aside the *historical* discussion of the accurateness of his analysis which would require a detailed historical investigation.

He writes, for example:

> That the situation is actively revolutionary, I do not doubt; and that therefore within a given space of time *our party will have the majority with it.* But if this period will perhaps not be long chronologically, it will undoubtedly be packed with supplementary phases, which we will have to foresee with some accuracy *in order to be able to manoeuvre and avoid making mistakes* which would prolong the trials of the proletariat. *PWI*, p. 202. [My emphasis.]

In another letter written 24 March 1924 shortly before he returned to Italy, Gramsci posed the question in the following way:

> In short: the present situation must have a political resolution; what is the most likely form for this resolution to take? Is it possible to believe that we will pass directly from fascism to the dictatorship of the proletariat? What intermediate phases are possible and likely? We must carry out this task of political study, both for our own sake and for the mass of party members and for the masses in general. I think that in the crisis which the country will undergo, that party will gain the upper hand which has best understood *this necessary transition process*, and thus impressed its seriousness on the broad masses. From this point of view, we are very weak, undoubtedly weaker than the socialists—who, well or badly, do carry out some agitational work, and what is more have a whole popular tradition to sustain them. *PWII*, p. 221. [My emphasis.]

Gramsci foresees a result which is not very different from Bordiga's view that the party would soon be able to influence the *majority*, but what is significant is the party's role in achieving this outcome. The fact that the situation was extremely complex, much more complex than Bordiga imagined,[25] both made necessary an adequate analysis by the party and provided the possibility for the party to intervene to shorten the process in which the majority could be influenced by the party. Thus the development of the situation is posed in terms of the party's own ability to intervene rather than as something unrelated to this intervention. The masses, according to Gramsci, would not automatically reach the position of a party which maintained its orthodoxy but which undertook little more than propaganda activity. Rather, that party which was best able to understand the situation and to relate to the masses would be able to achieve a political leadership, a leadership which did not automatically ensue from an abstractly 'correct' theory schematically conceived.

The reality of the roots of the social democratic tradition in the masses was an historical problem which was too complex to be resolved by simple manoeuvres between the leaders of the parties concerned or by some kind of elimination of these leaders.[26] The problem of the political organisation of the mass movement depended on the party's ability to understand all the implications of the historically given conditions of the masses and its ability to intervene in this concrete reality 'from now'. The possibility of creating a revolutionary organisation rooted in the mass movement, the winning of millions of people to a revolutionary position depended on the activities of the party, not on some external force.

By posing the question of the revolutionary nature of the period in these terms, Gramsci places a great responsibility on the party and by the same token gives it great creative potential. The detailed aspects of building a party adequate to this task would be considered by Gramsci upon his return to Italy.

Gramsci's New Emphasis on the Party

The articles which Gramsci wrote in the period between returning from his stay abroad and his imprisonment are in marked contrast in many respects with his works in the preceding years. After returning to Italy, there was a clear change in style, a new emphasis and clarity in his work which concentrated on the question of the organisation and the role of the revolutionary party as it had never done before. What is most significant is the way in which Gramsci's discussion of the party continues and develops a certain view of the revolution and of the relationship between organisation and politics.

There were three interrelated factors which together gave Gramsci reason to emphasise the discussion of the revolutionary party. After the Matteotti crisis of 1924, fascism had become firmly entrenched in Italy without any successful opposition from the working-class movement. This represented a defeat for the working class and its organisations which made Gramsci more than ever concerned with the role of the communist party in leading the working class and other potential anti-fascist allies.

Secondly, the polemic with Bordiga continued in increasingly acute tones. The relative isolation of the PCd'I and its sectarian policies limited its ability to lead the working class in the political struggles of the period while Bordiga's refusal to participate in the party leadership and his dissident activities in such a difficult time increased the bitterness of the dispute.[27] As Gramsci carried on the struggle to change the ideas of the rank and file of the party, he re-articulated the argument which he had put forward in his letters to Togliatti and others. The problem was not simply to change the leadership of the party, but to transform its politics. Thus the discussion of the proper relationship between the party and the working class, the need for increasing the ties between the party and the masses, and the relationship which Gramsci thought should exist between the leadership and its rank and file involved the very nature of the party.

The third factor which influenced Gramsci was his increased knowledge of the Russian Revolution and the experiences of the Bolshevik Party. The debates within the Comintern about the problems of building socialism took on a new meaning for him after his visit to Russia and his work for the International. The need to translate the lessons of the Russian experience into Italian terms seemed more complex and yet all the more necessary.[28]

Gramsci's discussion of the form and role of the revolutionary party in this period also had a very specific international dimension. The debate with Bordiga in particular took place within a larger discussion which was going on in the International about the need to 'bolshevise' the communist parties in the West. This played an important role in the very complicated debates within the leadership of the CPSU. None the less, while there were echoes of the Russian debate within the Italian party, the influence on the PCd'I of the growing split in the USSR must not be overemphasised. Gramsci's increasing stress on the need for centralisation and discipline arose very much out of the internal situation in the PCd'I during a period of intensified fascist repression in Italy and is an example of the coincidence of interests between the leadership of the PCd'I and the CPSU majority.[29]

Leaving aside a complex historical discussion about the relationship between the Italian party and the Comintern, Gramsci's interpretation of this policy is of central interest here. Gramsci defined the bolshevisation of the party as the way in which the PCd'I might become 'a unity capable of leading the proletariat into struggle; capable of winning and winning permanently.' (*PWII*, p. 305.) In forging this type of weapon the questions of internal organisation and ideological development were primary. The aim was to change what Gramsci termed the extreme sectarianism of the Italian party which prevented it from applying two political principles which had characterised Bolshevism: the alliance between the workers and peasants and the hegemony of the proletariat in the anti-capitalist revolutionary movement.[30]

There were four fundamental aspects connected with the campaign to build a Bolshevik party: first, the ideology of the party; second, the form and compactness of its organisation; third, its ability to function in contact with the masses; and finally, its strategic and tactical strength.[31] The first two points had to do with the ideological development of the individual members of the party, the relationship between the centre and the rank and file, and the type of unity and discipline existing in the party. The third and fourth points were connected with an understanding of the relationship between the party and the working class and its allies. 'Each of these points', Gramsci wrote, 'is closely linked with the others, and cannot logically be separated from them ' (*PWII*, p. 351). Thus ideological and organisational questions could not be separated from the ability of the party to maintain roots in the mass movement, or from its potential for effective political intervention.

The Need to Forge a Revolutionary Party Adequate to Its Task

The defeat of the working-class movement in Italy was now connected in Gramsci's mind even more clearly with the problems of the political organisation of the proletariat.

> The defeat of the revolutionary proletariat in this decisive period was due to political, organizational, tactical and strategic deficiencies of the workers' party. As a consequence of these deficiencies, the proletariat did not succeed in placing itself at the head of the insurrection of the great majority of the population, and channelling it towards the creation of a workers' State. Instead, it was itself influenced by other social classes, which paralysed its activity. The victory of fascism in 1922 must be seen, therefore, not as a victory won over the revolution, but as a consequence of the defeat suffered by the revolutionary forces through their own intrinsic weakness. *PWII*, p. 349.[32]

This description of the inability of the communist party to lead the mass movement constituted not just a criticism of Bordiga but also a self-criticism in so far as Gramsci had shared in the leadership of the party and had failed to establish an independent line until the winter of 1923-4.

The need for a revolutionary party, which would lead the masses who would make the revolution, was emphasised by Gramsci over and over again.[33] This was expressed in a military image which would appear often in the *Prison Notebooks* in which he compared the working class to a great army employed in the class struggle in need of a high command.[34] Of the various organisations of the working-class movement such as the trade unions, co-operatives, and cultural and youth organisations, Gramsci stressed that the revolutionary party had a special role as the organised vanguard of the proletariat. It had to be the personification of discipline and organisation, and it had to unify the various activities of the very different organisations of the working class. In a passage echoing some of the themes of the *Ordine Nuovo* period, he writes:

> First of all, it contains within it the best part of the working class, a vanguard tied directly to non-party proletarian organizations, which the communists frequently lead. Secondly, because of its experience and authority, the party is the only organization able to centralize the struggle of the proletariat and thus to transform the political organizations of the working class into its own coordinating organs. The party is the highest form of class organization of the proletariat. *CPC*, p. 206.

What had become much clearer to Gramsci is the precise role of the party *vis-à-vis* the other organisations of the working class. Whereas in the earlier period he was mainly concerned to establish a new relationship between the various working-class organisations in order to adhere to the changes brought about by the development of monopoly capitalism, in this period in a very difficult situation under the consolidation of the fascist régime, he attempts to determine more precisely the specificity of the political struggle.

In terms which were very different in their tone and in their mode of expression from his earlier work, and which echo the language of Marx, Engels and Lenin, Gramsci maintained that the struggle of the working class was fought on three fronts, the economic, the political and the ideological. The trade union struggle, he emphasised, was in the first instance spontaneous and hence not by itself revolutionary. It had to be accompanied by a political struggle in order to lead to revolution, in which the ideological element was crucial.

The element of 'spontaneity' is not sufficient for revolutionary struggle; it never leads the working class beyond the limits of the existing bourgeois democracy. The element of consciousness is needed, the 'ideological' element: in other words, an understanding of the conditions of the struggle, the social relations in which the worker lives, the fundamental tendencies at work in the system of those relations, and the process of development which society undergoes as a result of the existence within it of insoluble antagonisms, etc. *PWII*, p. 288.

This ideological function and the vanguard nature of the party, then, were derived from the different ideological levels present in the working class at any one time because of the situation of the proletariat under capitalism.

One certainly cannot ask every worker from the masses to be completely aware of the whole complex function which his class is destined to perform in the process of development of humanity. But this must be asked of members of the party. One cannot aim, before the conquest of the State, to change completely the consciousness of the entire working class. To do so would be utopian, because class consciousness as such is only changed when the way of living of the class itself has been changed; in other words, when the proletariat has become a ruling class and has at its disposal the apparatus of production and exchange and the power of the State. But the party can and must, as a whole, represent this higher consciousness. Otherwise, it will not lead them but be dragged along by them. Hence, the party must assimilate Marxism, and assimilate it in its present form, as Leninism. *PWII*, p. 288.

The mere emphasis on the vanguard role of the party, while articulated for the first time in such a precise manner by Gramsci does not in itself mark his originality.[35] Indeed Bordiga had attempted to create just such a vanguard. What is original is Gramsci's approach to this crucial political problem. In arguing that Bordiga had in fact failed to produce a new *type* of party, Gramsci implicitly or explicitly maintained a certain view of the revolution as a process and of Marxist theory. The first is very much rooted in the experiences of the *Ordine Nuovo* period while his attempt in prison to develop Marxist theory to provide tools adequate to the needs of the struggle in advanced capitalist countries and for building socialism in the Soviet Union is related to his struggle against Bordiga's politics which he came to realise was rooted in a dogmatic conception of Marxism as a closed system.

The task of creating a party qualitatively different from the PSI entailed a new assertion of the importance of the theoretical struggle. Gramsci's argument about the inadequacies of the theoretical preparation of the PSI had roots in his criticism in Turin of the positivist influence on Italian socialism. The leadership of the PSI had discounted the importance of Marxist theory.

> Theoretical activity, in other words struggle on the ideological front, has always been neglected in the Italian workers' movement. In Italy, Marxism (apart from Antonio Labriola) has been studied more by bourgeois intellectuals, in order to denature it and turn it to the purposes of bourgeois policy, than by revolutionaries. . . . The party leaders never imagined that in order to struggle against bourgeois ideology, i.e. in order to free the masses from the influence of capitalism, it was first necessary to disseminate Marxist doctrine in the party itself and defend it against all false substitutes. *PWII*, pp. 288-9.

Yet, and this is central to Gramsci's argument against him, Bordiga had not succeeded in breaking with this tradition. He was so afraid that the party would be contaminated with incorrect ideas that he concentrated above all on preserving the purity of a set doctrine. He thought of Marxism as a completed system which Lenin had interpreted but not developed.[36] This conception of Marxist theory had consequences for both the organisation and the politics of the party. The party, by refusing to take part in a whole range of struggles, had remained an isolated sect, detached from the masses. Bordiga's emphasis on the theoretical purity of the leadership above all else prevented him from being concerned with the problem of raising the theoretical level of the ordinary members of the party.[37]

Theoretical preparation of the members of the party but also a new relationship between the party and the mass movement differentiated Gramsci's view of the party from Bordiga's. Related to this is Gramsci's particular approach to the question of the intellectuals. Rooted in his long-standing interest in culture, he later developed this discussion at great length in the *Prison Notebooks*. In this period, he attributed a role to the intellectuals in the socialist movement very similar to that articulated by Lenin in 'What Is to Be Done' but with a crucial development. Gramsci writes that the working class is able to become aware of its historical role, only because the representatives of science and of technology on the basis of bourgeois science construct a proletarian science. They are able to do this because of their specific class position. (The intellectuals are a class which serves the bourgeoisie and are not the same thing as the bourgeoisie.) They arrive at the conclusion that a further development is impossible if the proletariat does not seize power, does not constitute itself as a dominant class, imprinting on the whole of society its specific class characteristics. *CPC*, p. 250.

What is interesting is Gramsci's broadening of the social group of the intellectuals to include those who study technology who become aware that a further development of the forces of production is not possible in the present social system. This widening of the definition of intellectuals is made much more explicit and goes much further in the *Notebooks.*

At the same time, Gramsci was at great pains to emphasise that the intellectual skills and theoretical knowledge could be acquired and developed further by workers themselves.[38] He argued that Bordiga had overemphasised the difficulties a worker faced in overcoming the limitations of his position in capitalist society and in developing a revolutionary consciousness. In answer to Bordiga who was particularly concerned about the divisions in the working class according to skills and trades, Gramsci explained the specific role of the party in uniting the class. He argued that it was in the trade union that a worker entered as a worker and remained identified as such while in a revolutionary party he became a political man, a theoretician of socialism. It is the party which allows the worker to go beyond an economic corporative definition of his position, as a wage labourer divided from his fellow workers because of his skill, a definition remaining within the logic of capitalist relations of production. It is the party which allows him to become a political leader, a builder of a new order, socialism, rather than simply rebelling in a negative way against the existing one. In a passage which would be echoed in the *Notebooks*, Gramsci defines the achievement of a political consciousness as the ability to become the theoretician of a new social formation, of socialism. The positive constructive role of the party and of every member who must constantly develop and the creative potential of the mass movement are always implicit in Gramsci's discussion of party organisation. The acquisition of knowledge by the new protagonists of social change as the basis of an expanded democracy related to an intellectual and moral reform is a theme Gramsci would develop in prison.

The Organisation of the Party

This later discussion is rooted in Gramsci's writings on party organisation. In order for the party to be able to intervene creatively in even the most difficult reality, the *whole* of the party had to be prepared theoretically and politically. Gramsci writes, 'Our party is not a democratic party, at least in the vulgar sense commonly given to this word.' (*PWII*, p. 290) Yet, as he defines what he considers the proper type of centralism, he bases his argument on the need for the individual members to be able to undertake political initiatives even when the centre of the party was unable to function. Gramsci in fact attempts to establish a new concept of internal democracy which depends on the active participation of the members of the party rather than on a formal 'right'.

> Internal democracy is also relative to the degree of political capacity possessed by the local bodies, and by the individual comrades working in the localities. The activity which the centre carries on to increase this capacity makes possible an extension of 'democratic' methods, and a growing reduction of the system of 'cooptation' and of interventions from above to sort out local organisational questions. *PWII*, p. 364.

Through a constant process of theoretical preparation and political education, members of the rank and file could develop their political capacities and eventually become leaders. In this way the necessary division between leader and lead was no longer arbitrary and formal, but merely functional. Gramsci's very definition of the proper type of centralism, a centralism which was not simply reduced to rigidly applying the line laid down by the central leadership but which depended on full discussion of crucial issues and on the ideological preparation of each member of the party, was based on a crucial political objective. 'A Bolshevik party', he wrote, 'must be organized in such a way that it can function in contact with the masses whatever the conditions may be.' (*PWII*, p. 366)

Gramsci's discussion of centralism grows out of this fundamental political objective. We shall discuss the relationship between the party and the mass movement later. Here it should simply be noted that Gramsci's discussion of centralism *within* the party assumes a certain relationship between party and masses. The aim of maintaining this kind of contact with the mass movement demands a certain kind of preparation of each party cadre who represents the real link with the masses in the party's day-to-day activity.

> In order for the party to live and be in contact with the masses, it is
> necessary for every member of the party to be an active political
> element, a leader. Precisely because the party is strongly centralized,
> a vast amount of propaganda and agitation among its ranks is re-
> quired. It is necessary for the party in an organized fashion to educate
> its members and raise their ideological level. Centralization means, in
> particular, that in any situation whatsoever—even when the most
> rigorous Emergency Laws are in operation, and even if the leading
> committees are unable to function for a given period or are put in a
> situation where they cannot maintain contact with the local organ-
> izations—all members of the party, and everyone in its ambit, have
> been rendered capable of orienting themselves and knowing how to
> derive from reality the elements with which to establish a line, so that
> the working class will not be cast down but will feel that it is being
> led and can still fight. Mass ideological preparation is thus a necessity
> of revolutionary struggle, and one of the indispensable conditions for
> victory. *PWII*, p. 290.

Centralism is not an end in itself but is necessary only in so far as it
serves the political effectiveness of the party as a whole and it depends
intimately on the full preparation of every member of the party.

Gramsci's discussion of the kind of centralisation and unity which
should exist in the party is based on the argument that Bordiga's mechanical concept of centralisation was an exaggerated reaction to the tradition of the PSI which in fact did not overcome the organisational
problem of the PSI—its inability to function as an effective political
instrument and its reproduction of the bourgeois mode of politics. That
is, neither Bordiga nor the PSI had been able to go beyond the type of
division between leaders and lead which was inherent in bourgeois politics.

> As a reaction against the usual custom in the Socialist Party—in which
> much was discussed and little resolved; where unity was shattered
> into an infinity of disconnected fragments by the continuous clash
> of factions, tendencies and often personal cliques—in our party we
> had ended up by no longer discussing anything. Centralization, unity
> of approach and conception, had turned into intellectual stag-
> nation. . . . Centralization and unity were understood in too
> mechanical a fashion: the Central Committee, indeed the Executive

Committee, was the entire party, instead of representing and leading it. *PWII*, p. 290.

Bordiga's version of party organisation corresponded to his view of the revolutionary struggle. Just as he tended to substitute the party for the masses, he substituted the central organs for the full political preparation and effectiveness of the rank and file, which in fact guarantees that the party is rooted in the mass movement. The possibility of politics made by masses rather than an *élite* had implications for the very organisation of the party.

What, then, was a correct concept of democratic centralism according to Gramsci? The most explicit discussion is found in the 'Lyons Theses'.[39] Internal democracy, he said, had a very specific meaning. The kind of iron discipline which was needed was not to be confused with an autocratic system.

Both the Central Committee and the subordinate leading bodies are formed on the basis of election, and on the basis of a selection of capable elements carried out through the test of work and through the experience of the movement. This second element guarantees that the criteria for the formation of the local leading groups and of the central leading group *are not mechanical, external and 'parliamentary'*, but correspond to a real process of formation of a homogeneous proletarian vanguard *linked to the masses. PWII*, p. 364. [My emphasis.]

Gramsci's rejection of a formal, 'parliamentary' definition of internal democracy does not mean that he rejects democracy *tout court.* Quite the opposite. Even in the most difficult conditions, the authority of the leadership had to be conceived of as derived from the party as a whole.

The principle of election of the leading bodies — internal democracy — is not an absolute one, but relative to the conditions of political struggle. Even when it is restricted, the central and local organs must always consider their power not as being super-imposed, but as springing from the party's will, and must strive to accentuate their proletarian character and to multiply their links with the mass of comrades and with the working class. This last necessity is felt particularly keenly in Italy, where reaction has imposed and continues to impose a strict limitation of internal democracy. *PWII*, p. 364.

At the same time the vital need for unity is a constant theme in these years, in large part because of the pressures of the external situation but also due to the need for an effective political instrument for the working class. Gramsci's argument against the existence of factions within the PCd'I or within any communist party was based on the idea that a communist party differed profoundly from a social democratic party on this point.[40] While a social democratic party could and did allow factions because it did not insist on a unified programme as the basis of membership, first principles could not, Gramsci said, be continually challenged in a revolutionary party as they were in a social democratic party.[41] For a revolutionary party to be the weapon which the working class needs to seize state power, it had to be unified and disciplined and threats of splits had to be avoided. The question of organisation is related to the political task of the revolutionary party: the recomposition of the division within the working class and between the working class and other sectors of society under capitalism. The internal life of the party had to represent the kind of organic unity it sought to create in society at large. It was for these reasons that factions were not to be organised. Gramsci wrote that, 'posing the problem of the organization of a faction in a Communist Party, means posing the problem of a split'. (*CPC*, p. 225.)

Yet Gramsci was equally at pains to deny that this was an infringement on discussion within the party. Organisation of a faction was a danger to the party because it in fact prevented the kind of positive discussion which should take place.[42]

> No confusion is possible between those who weaken the compactness of the party and the advocates of tactical criteria opposing those of the centre. The former cannot have and will not have the right and the possibility in any case of defending and advocating . . . their activity hostile to the party; the latter . . . will and must, without any restriction, expound and support their ideas and their convictions. *CPC*, p. 220.

Thus Gramsci differentiates between free discussion of tactical questions concerning the way in which the general line was to be carried out, a discussion which derived from the day-to-day experience of the rank and file, and an organised faction which argues for an alternative line as a party within a party.

But what was the difference between a constructive type of criticism and a destructive one? It was not simply a question of the subject of the criticism but of its method and intention:

> inside the party criticism is useful and necessary when it tends to correct errors committed in the application of a particular method . . . but when criticism itself becomes a method and it is believed always necessary to be original to everyone and for everything, then one falls right in a petty bourgeois position. *CPC*, p. 261.

The fact that there was a danger of a serious split within the Communist Party was related to the very class nature of society.

> As long as there is the class struggle, as long as a society divided in classes exists (and that is, therefore, even after the revolutionary victory, since the dictatorship of the proletariat is only the supreme form of the proletarian class struggle), the party can always become the theatre of internal struggles, provoked by the influence of non-proletarian classes and especially of those who historically can become and will become allies of the workers, that is peasants and intellectuals. If the party is not consolidated, if it has not succeeded through experience in understanding how manoeuvres aiming at modifying its proletarian character can assume initially even the most innocent appearance of purely organizational questions, the party always runs the risk of deviating or breaking up; no guarantee can be given because this *cannot happen except through proletarian consciousness and mass political and ideological preparation. CPC*, pp. 260-1. [My emphasis.]

It must be made clear that Gramsci is not so much defining the revolutionary capacity of the party in terms of limiting membership of the party to workers, nor is he ignoring the need for the working class to ally with other classes. Rather he is arguing that an effective autonomous political intervention by the party must be based on a fundamentally new type of politics which historically only the proletariat can develop as a class. What is interesting is Gramsci's idea of the way in which unity can be guaranteed. The actual argument for unity is not so very different from that of Bordiga, but the method of achieving it is radically different: the theoretical and political preparation of the whole party.

Although the discussion on factions is so embedded in the heated polemic against Bordiga in the difficult situation under fascism that it is particularly hard to establish general principles in these writings, the political and ideological rather than formal, bureaucratic guarantees of both unity and democracy are fundamental. If we consider Gramsci's ideas in the 'Lyons Theses', the argument becomes somewhat clearer. Here he wrote:

The Communist Parties and International emerged after a factional struggle waged inside the Second International. Establishing themselves as the parties and world organization of the proletariat, they chose as the norm of their internal life and development, in place of factional struggle, *the organic collaboration of all tendencies* through participation in the leading bodies.

The existence of, and struggle between, factions are in fact incompatible with the essence of the proletarian party, since they break its unity and open a path for the influence of other classes. *This does not mean that tendencies may not arise in the party*, and that these tendencies may not on occasion seek to organize themselves as factions; but it does mean that a vigorous struggle must be conducted to prevent this latter eventuality, by *reducing tendency conflicts*, theoretical discussions and the selection of leaders to the form appropriate to communist parties, i.e. to a process of *real and unitary (dialectical)* evolution and not to 'parliamentary' modes of debate or struggle. *PWII*, p. 365. [My emphasis.]

Unity in the party does not mean uniformity of opinion. It is the *form* of different tendencies and the way unity of purpose is actually achieved which differentiates a communist party from the socialist tradition. In the communist party, differences are to be resolved dialectically to create an organic unity; that is, once a question had been decided the decision must be accepted by all in the party, but in such a way that the reasons for the decision, the basis of the party's strategy, are fully understood.

In a social democratic party these differences were never resolved but continued to exist in organisational form. In a revolutionary party it is not sufficient for the majority to win formally and thereafter to impose its will on an unconvinced minority so that the divisions themselves become formalised as in a bourgeois parliament. There must be a continual process of discussion and interchange between the leadership and the rank and file to explain and to convince the whole of the party of the correctness of the party line and to test the line against the experiences of the rank and file. One of the chief reasons communist parties were organised in the first place was to carry on internal discussion and debate in a different manner.[43] We find echoes here of Gramsci's earlier analysis of the crisis of the liberal State and his argument that the political organisation of the working class had to be an *autonomous* creation, superceding the limitations of bourgeois politics.

Within such a highly disciplined and centralised party, the Central

Committee had a special role in maintaining unity. The place for a debate about the party line was before and during the party congress which was the source of the authority of the Central Committee.[44] Once decisions had been taken, they had to be carried out by the whole of the party in a united political intervention. The actual form of tactics could be continually debated as they would depend on the requirements of a concrete situation which was constantly in flux, but the line itself should only be questioned at the time of the congress.

Gramsci defended the right and the duty of the Central Committee to make its opinion known and to campaign for the line which it had decided. It was inconceivable that the Central Committee would abdicate its duty in a discussion leading to a congress, for example, so that opinions could be formed 'freely'. This, Gramsci said, was only acceptable in a social democratic organisation.[45] Nor was it correct to place the activities of a small group of party members who had formed a faction on the same level as that of the Central Committee, and to demand that the faction be allowed the same debating time and facilities. According to Gramsci, the Central Committee should in any case represent a cross-section of opinion in the party.[46]

There is an implicit assumption here about the discussion of the party line. When Gramsci puts the word 'freely' between inverted commas, he indicates that the development of a political line derived from an analysis of the situation never arises spontaneously or freely. In the *Notebooks* he would explain that there is no such thing as true spontaneity because there is always an ideology implicit or explicit in any political activity.[47] An adequate analysis of the concrete situation requires the use of scientific tools. The leadership of the party is made aware of many of the complex aspects of the conjuncture from the experiences of the rank and file. The actual establishment of a strategy must be done, however, by skilled people who, through a *technical* division of labour, are in the leadership because of their experience and knowledge. According to Gramsci, they must work on the assumption that the authority they enjoy is not imposed upon the party but is derived from it. The continual discussion and verification of the line which takes place within the party has two functions: to keep the leadership in contact with the reality of the mass movement and to maintain a process of education and development of the rank and file to enable them to understand the concrete situation and the party line so that they can intervene creatively without waiting for orders from the centre. Their contribution to the party line is not a formal one but rather a practical, functional one. The implications for party democracy based on a qualitatively new relationship between leaders and led would be developed further by Gramsci in prison.

The concern for the need for unity in a communist party was one aspect of Gramsci's preoccupation about the growing strife within the Soviet Communist Party (CPSU). While he fully supported the line held by the majority of the CPSU leadership against Trotsky and the opposition, Gramsci was very critical about the manner in which the discussion was being carried on and the political differences about the building of socialism which the dispute reflected. In an exchange of letters in October 1926,[48] he expressed his worry about the effects this had on the communist parties and the masses in the West.

There are two inter-related aspects of Gramsci's intervention in the Russian debate which are of particular interest. First his letters immediately express the need for unity on *political* rather than formal grounds related to the specific necessity for the working class in the Soviet Union to be able to build socialism based on its hegemony over other classes. Secondly, he maintained that this overcoming of an economic-corporative position, entailing many sacrifices by the working class, had to be fully understood by the masses in the West in order for the reformist, syndicalist tradition to be replaced by a revolutionary influence. This, Gramsci writes, is the political essence of the 'bolshevisation' of the communist parties.

There was a *political* necessity, therefore, of a certain *mode* of debate with a constant reference point – the situation of the mass movement. The masses in the West, Gramsci writes,

> cannot understand the discussions which are taking place in the Communist Party of the USSR, especially if they are as violent as the present one and concern not some question of detail, but the political line of the party in its entirety. *PWII*, p. 428.

He goes on,

> We repeat that we are struck by the fact that the attitude of the opposition concerns the entire political line of the Central Committee, and touches the very heart of the Leninist doctrine and the political action of our Soviet party. It is the principle and practice of the proletariat's hegemony that are brought into question; the fundamental relations of alliance between workers and peasants that are disturbed and placed in danger: i.e. the pillars of the workers' State and the revolution. . . .

Yet the proletariat cannot become the dominant class if it does not overcome this contradiction through the sacrifice of its corporate interests. It cannot maintain its hegemony and its dictatorship if, even when it has become dominant, it does not sacrifice these immediate interests for the general and permanent interests of the class. *PWII*, p. 431.[49]

He explains the political reasons for opposing the opposition. 'In the ideology and practice of the Joint Opposition are born again, to the full, the whole tradition of social-democracy and syndicalism which has hitherto prevented the Western proletariat from organizing itself as a leading class.' (*PWII*, p. 432.) In the particularly acute situation of the NEP which required huge sacrifices of the working class when other classes were better off materially, unity and discipline in the party were vitally necessary, but Gramsci specifies the nature of this unity and discipline.

But the unity and discipline in this case cannot be mechanical and enforced. They must be loyal and due to conviction, and not those of an enemy unit imprisoned or besieged, whose only thought is of escape or an unexpected sortie. *PWII*, p. 432.

This is also reflected in the nature of the loyalty and discipline which the communist parties and the mass movement in the West felt towards the first socialist State.

Today, at nine years distance from October 1917, it is no longer *the fact of the seizure of power* by the Bolsheviks which can revolutionize the Western masses, because this has already been allowed for and has produced its effects. What is active today, ideologically and politically, is the conviction (if it exists) that the proletariat, once power has been taken, *can construct socialism*. The authority of the party is bound up with this conviction, which cannot be instilled in the broad masses by the methods of school pedagogy, but only by those of revolutionary pedagogy, i.e. only by the *political fact* that the Russian Party as a whole is convinced of it, and is fighting in a united fashion. *PWII*, p. 440.

The foundation of loyalty to the Soviet Union and the basis of its influences on the masses in the West was not simply the October Revolution, the seizure of state power, or the 'negative' moment of revolutionary activity, but the ability of the Russian proletariat to construct a new society based on its hegemony. Written shortly before he was imprisoned, many of the lines of reflection in the *Notebooks* are already evident.

The Relationship Between the Party and the Class

The political rather than formal basis of the leadership by the communist party over the working class was fundamental to Gramsci's argument against Bordiga and paralleled the kind of relationship which he felt should exist between the Russian party and other communist parties. It also implied a certain mode of building socialism.

> The principle that the party leads the working class must not be interpreted in a mechanical manner. It is not necessary to believe that the party can lead the working class through an external imposition of authority. This is not true, either with respect to the period which precedes the winning of power, or with respect to the period which follows it. . . . We assert that the capacity to lead the class is related, not to the fact that the party 'proclaims' itself its revolutionary organ, but to the fact that it 'really' succeeds, as a part of the working class, in linking itself with all the sections of that class and impressing upon the masses a movement in the direction desired and favoured by objective conditions. *PWII*, pp. 367-8.

In the objective conditions of the struggle in Italy in these years, a necessary aspect of the 'bolshevisation' of the party and one of the issues most contested by Bordiga, was the attempt to transform the base of the organisation into cells at the place of work. Gramsci defended this specific mode of organisation on general grounds as an essential part of the Leninist conception of the party. The vehicle for the extension of contact with the masses was to be the organisation of cells in the factories. Gramsci once more called upon the experience of the Bolshevik party before the revolution although he considered the situation of the PCI to be even more difficult, and he defended the application of what he considered Leninist ideas of organisation to Italy. He claimed that opposition to the organisation of cells signified that Bordiga and others were still tied to social democratic ideas.[50]

Gramsci stressed, however, that the question of cell organisation, as with other organisational matters, was not simply an organisational but a political question which had to do with preparing the working class for the seizure of State power.[51]

The organisation of cells within the factories was in keeping with Gramsci's earlier activities when he worked in Turin with the *Ordine Nuovo* to establish the closest possible contact between the party and the mass of the working class and to root politics in the productive sphere based on the creation of the factory councils. In this later period, the argument for cell organisation was part of the campaign to establish the party as an integral part of the class, not an organ set off and above the class. It was an aspect of the attempt to lead the party out of its previous isolation, to develop it into a mass party in a period when the establishment of factory councils was not feasible. This was the crucial difference between Gramsci and Bordiga on the revolutionary party and the key to Gramsci's interpretation of 'bolshevisation'.[52] Thus a constant in Gramsci's ideas on organisation is not only the need for strong ties between the party and the class but of unity between different sections of the class rooted in the sphere of production and based on the very potential of the development of capitalism. This is the general principle which can be extracted from Gramsci's discussion of organisational forms which appears within the context of a very specific concrete situation in 1924-6 and a principle which had its origins in his discussion of the factory councils in 1919-20.

Bordiga's stand against basing the party on cell organisation in the factories was consistent with his idea of a party set off from the class, ready to lead it in the revolutionary struggle, but not in the immediate and intermediate battles. A factory cell organisation would be intimately involved in the day-to-day struggle. Bordiga had previously criticised Gramsci and the work of the *Ordine Nuovo* in the factory council movement, accusing Gramsci of ignoring the political task of conquering the state by concentrating on what he defined as the economistic level inside the factory. In 1925-6 he still maintained that it was the *place* and the *mode* of organisation of a particular political initiative which defined its nature rather than the content of its politics.

For Gramsci no abstract form of organisation could be universally valid. 'No organisational form can be absolutely perfect: *the important thing is to establish which type of organisation corresponds best to the conditions and to the needs of the proletarian struggle.*' (*CPC*, p. 275.) [My emphasis.] Thus the exact *form* of the party at any particular time was related to the task of the party in the class struggle. Nor could an organisational form or a fixed strategy guarantee the revolutionary nature of the organisation. Gramsci maintained that the best guarantee

against any degeneration in the party was not a tactic determined by
formalistic concerns, but the nature of the politics of the party.[53]

When Gramsci argued that the party should be considered a *part* of
the working class and not an *organ* of the class as Bordiga suggested, he
stressed the need for the closest possible relationship between party
and class. The party had to be viewed as an integral part of the proletariat rather than an organisation separated from it. As with the other
important themes of the period, Gramsci summarised his ideas in the
'Lyons Theses' where he argued that the left's mistaken conception of
the revolutionary process led it to pose organisational and tactical problems in the wrong way.

> For the far left, the function of the Party is not to lead the class at
> all moments, striving to remain in contact with it through all changes
> in the objective situation, but to form and prepare cadres, who can
> lead the masses when the evolution of the situation has brought them
> to the party and made them accept the programmatic and principled
> positions it has fixed. *PWII*, p. 360.

Most importantly, the difference between the positions of Gramsci
and Bordiga on the party involved different ideas of the nature of the
revolution. Because Bordiga thought that the party simply had to wait
for the situation to develop positively, his attitude led to a high degree
of passivity and pessimism in a period of reaction, reducing the potential
of political initiative. Gramsci maintained that this was a result of the
same formalistic and mechanical conception of Marxist doctrine as held
by the maximalists, an argument which he would elaborate in his criticism of economism in the *Notebooks*. Imbued with a crisis theory of the
collapse of capitalism, both the maximalist, he wrote (and the communist
who followed Bordiga's ideas) thinks 'that it is useless to . . . struggle
day by day; he waits only for the great day. The masses—he says—cannot
not come to us, because the objective situation pushes them towards the
revolution.' (*CPC*, p. 248.)

Gramsci opposed this position with a view of the revolution as a
process with intermediate phases in which the political intervention of
the party was vital to the outcome. In a passage which closely pre-figures
his discussion of strategy in prison, he writes that Lenin,

> has taught us that in a war between armies, one cannot reach the
> strategic goal, which is the destruction of the enemy and the occupation
> of his territory, without first having arrived at a series of tactical object-

ives tending to break up the enemy before confronting him in the field. The whole revolutionary period appears as a predominantly tactical activity, addressed to acquiring new allies for the proletariat, to breaking up the offensive and defensive organisational apparatus of the enemy and to exhausting his reserves. *CPC*, p. 249.

In the context of the debate with Bordiga, Gramsci cited the Russian experience in 1907-9 as a precedent for the type of problem which the party was facing in Italy. At that time there were tendencies within the Bolshevik Party which argued that in a period of reaction the only activity the party could undertake was general propaganda. The majority, however, maintained that

> even in a period of reaction the party had to be a party of the masses, working and struggling in close contact with them, reinforcing its influence and its position in the heart of the proletariat day by day, placing itself at the head of the working class in its daily struggles and not waiting for the revolution to fall from a tree like a piece of ripe fruit. *CPC*, p. 222.

Showing a clear development from his earliest writings, the lesson which Gramsci now draws from the experience of the Bolsheviks is the need to maintain roots in the mass movement whatever the circumstances and a view of revolution which implies a creative potential for the masses if led by the party.

Gramsci discussed the party both as a vanguard and as a mass party. In what sense did he think that the party should be a mass party? Should it be large in terms of membership, or should it simply maintain as close links as possible with the masses?[54] The two aspects are closely related. In an article he wrote shortly before returning to Italy, Gramsci posed the problem in the following terms:

> We do not have the cadres, we do not have the links, we do not have the services to spread our influence over the broad mass of union members, to strengthen it and to make it once again an effective instrument of revolutionary struggle. *PWII*, p. 166.

Shortly thereafter he wrote of the need to build a large mass party:

> We are today, in relative terms, as a result of the conditions created by white terror, a little party. But we must consider our present

organization, given the conditions in which it exists and develops, as the element that is destined to provide the framework for a great mass party. *PWII*, p. 226.

Thus, the activities and organisation of the party in the difficult circumstances under fascism had to be the basis of the eventual creation of a mass party.

Criticising the development of the PCd'I in its first years, Gramsci attacked Bordiga's leadership for not trying to gain as wide an influence as possible after the split at Leghorn when the question of organisation was detached from the political task of the party which, according to Gramsci, should have aimed at winning over the mass of the population to the conquest of power.[55] This political task and the mass character of the party were intimately related to its ability to intervene in the concrete situation to modify the balance of forces. Arguing against Bordiga, Gramsci writes,

> The ideological struggle against ultra-leftism must be waged by counterposing to it the Marxist and Leninist conception of the proletarian party as a mass party. And by demonstrating the need for the latter to adapt its tactics to situations in order to be able to modify them; in order not to lose contact with the masses; and in order to acquire continually new zones of influence. *PWII*, p. 361.

But although Gramsci wrote about a party with a mass membership which had close ties with the masses, he insisted on the vanguard character of the party.[56] He was emphatic that a communist party had the duty to *lead* not to tail the masses. This brought him to consider the political will or the political consciousness of the masses, another subject which he would discuss in the *Notebooks*. He was most interested in this context to differentiate the theory of a communist party from that of a social democratic party.

In answer to an article in *Avanti!*, he denied that the PCI should 'obey' the will of the masses understood in a general, amorphous way because the masses, of necessity in the existing state of society, had not one but many wills reflecting the different ideologies which influence them. Reflecting without doubt the particularly difficult situation of 1925, Gramsci asked:

> Does there exist a will of the masses taken as a whole and can the Communist Party . . . 'obey the will of the masses in general'? No.

There are many and distinct wills in the working masses as a whole: there is a communist will, a maximalist will, a reformist will, a liberal democratic will. There also exists a fascist will, in a certain sense and within certain limits. As long as the bourgeois regime exists, with the monopoly of the press in the hands of the capitalists and therefore with the possibility for the government and for the bourgeois parties to define political questions according to their interest, presented as general interests, as long as the freedom of association of the working class is suppressed and limited, or the most impudent lies can be spread with impunity, it is inevitable that the working classes remain divided, that is, that they have many wills. *CPC*, pp. 238-9.

He would later discuss the role of the party in creating a unified, collective will in the *Prison Notebooks*. In this period Gramsci's discussion of the variety of ideologies influencing the mass movement already contains the notion that social groups are always organised by some ideology and that pure spontaneity cannot exist.

According to Gramsci, it was the condition of the working class and of other classes under capitalism which prevented the labouring masses from being able to create a unified will spontaneously. At the same time the very development of capitalism furnished a potential for unity of the working class and for a new unity in society as a whole. The duty of the communist party, therefore, was to lead the struggle from the most advanced position as the party of the working class, while at the same time representing the long-term interests and gaining the support of the working classes as a whole. Gramsci's vision would broaden considerably in prison. Here his argument is based on a certain premise. The working class, according to Marxist doctrine, is potentially the most progressive because, by the nature of its position in the capitalist mode of production, it is the one and only class able to develop a revolutionary theory and a revolutionary practice. In emancipating itself and abolishing wage labour, it is also able to emancipate the great majority of the population. In this context Gramsci described the role of the revolutionary party in the following way:

The Communist Party 'represents' the interests of all the labouring masses, but it 'puts into effect' only the will of a particular part of the masses, of the most advanced part, of that (proletarian) part that wants to overturn the existing regime with revolutionary means to found communism. *CPC*, p. 293.

This kind of differentiation is in fact open to question within Gramsci's own terms as he discusses in prison the establishment of a collective will unifying various sections of the population. Indeed, Gramsci's discussion of the vanguard nature of the party in this period has several problems. The difference between 'represent' and 'put into effect' is not very clear. There is also some confusion between the concept of the proletariat as the most progressive class in society in the abstract and the actual divisions and levels of consciousness within the proletariat.

When *Avanti!* suggested that it was necessary to follow the will of the masses in general, Gramsci claimed that this was simply an attempt to justify the socialists' opportunism and their policy of trying to collaborate with sections of the bourgeoisie by using the argument that certain segments of the working classes, which were still under the influence of the bourgeoisie, 'wished' such collaboration. In opposition to this Gramsci emphasised that 'The proletarian party cannot "tail" the masses. It must go ahead of the masses, nonetheless objectively taking account of the existence of these backward strata.' *CPC*, p. 239. By attempting to obey the will of the masses defined in a general way, a 'proletarian' party abandoned its proletarian nature and became simply another bourgeois party because it abandoned its role as the bearer of revolutionary theory. As a revolutionary party, according to Gramsci, it could not bow to other non-revolutionary ideologies which only served the bourgeoisie in preserving the existing relations of production.

> The party not only represents the working masses, but also a doctrine, the doctrine of socialism, and therefore it struggles to unify the will of the masses in the direction of socialism, while keeping itself on the real terrain of what exists, but which exists *moving and developing* itself. Our party puts into effect the will of the most advanced part of the masses which fights for socialism and it knows that it cannot have the bourgeoisie as allies in this struggle, which is precisely against the bourgeoisie. This 'will', in as much as it coincides with the general development of bourgeois society and with the vital needs of all the working masses, is progressive. It spreads, wins over ever new strata of workers, splits the other working class parties—working class in their social composition, not in their political line. *CPC*, p. 239.

In the first part of the quotation there is evidence of Gramsci's long-term concern to overcome the mechanistic interpretation of Marxism which had so long been prevalent in the socialist movement, while at the same time guarding against a voluntaristic distortion. In the second part it is clear that he does not escape from an interpretation which puts the working class directly against the bourgeoisie even in the period of fascist reaction without any possibility of temporary alliances between the working class and sections of the bourgeoisie. In the last sentence he is continuing the fight 'on two fronts' with his argument against the socialists, and the specificity of the context of Gramsci's debate against the socialists in the difficult conditions of 1925 must not be underestimated. The position still held by Gramsci that the period was potentially revolutionary in the fairly immediate sense has an echo in these writings. Yet, we can derive a general statement about Marxist theory from this passage.

For Gramsci, Marxist theory had to be able to analyse a complex, changing reality. It could not do this if it were considered a schema which had simply to be interpreted. During the course of the struggle, the party would attempt to unify theory and practice in order to influence new strata and thus to challenge non-revolutionary ideologies. But this was the result of more than propaganda. The question of who, the communists or the socialists, represented and led the masses as a whole could only be answered, said Gramsci, in the course of practical work.[57]

Two crucial areas of such work had to do with rejuvenating the trade unions and with posing concretely the problem of creating an alliance between the working class and the peasants. While Gramsci maintained that the party had to be active in all the organisations where the working class was to be found, he particularly stressed the importance of the trade unions. He argued that the trade unions as such were neither revolutionary nor counter-revolutionary. In Italy the trade unions provided a particularly important terrain for a political initiative aimed at restoring an autonomous role to the industrial and agricultural proletariat. 'Thus the party must manage to carry out activity to defend the class trade union and demand freedom for it, and at the same time it must encourage and stimulate the tendency to create representative mass organisms adapted to the system of production. (*PWII*, p. 369.)

Gramsci insisted now, as he had when he was in Turin, on the need to work for the unity of the entire working class,[58] and he invoked the experience of the factory councils to indicate the type of unitary work which was more than ever important in a period when the very ability of the working class to organise in any way was threatened. Unity and autonomous action taken by an independent class were prime goals. And in polemic with Bordiga, Gramsci asserted the duty of the party to take part in partial struggles not only with regard to intermediate objectives such as the unity of the working class, but he argued that it was through these partial struggles that the class could eventually be mobilised for a revolutionary struggle.

> The party combats the conception according to which one should abstain from supporting or taking part in partial actions, because the problems which interest the working class can be solved only by the overthrow of the capitalist order and by a general action on the part of all the anti-capitalist forces. It is aware of the impossibility for the workers' conditions to be improved in a serious or lasting way, in the period of imperialism and before the capitalist order has been overthrown. However, agitation around a programme of immediate demands and support for partial struggles is the only way of reaching the broad masses and mobilizing them against capital. Moreover, any agitation carried out or victory won by categories of workers in the field of immediate demands makes the crisis of capitalism more acute, and accelerates its fall subjectively too, insofar as it shifts the unstable economic equilibrium upon which it bases its power today. *PWII*, pp. 369-70.

While the actual link between the myriad of daily struggles and the eventual transformation of the social formation is not entirely satisfactorily explained by Gramsci,[59] the party's initiative is undertaken with a specific political goal. The decision to undertake any particular activity will depend on whether a political initiative by the party will lead 'to a shift in its favour of the balance of forces, and represents a step forward in the unification and mobilization of the class upon revolutionary terrain.' (*PWII*, p. 370.)

Thus the question of whether a particular activity was economistic or not depended on its role in a complex reality and its potential for a change in the balance of forces. It was not determined by the form or particular content of the activity in the abstract. The actual ability of the party to intervene to create a more favourable situation was at issue between Gramsci and Bordiga. At the Congress of Lyons, Gramsci argued that,

> Bordiga has said that he is favourable to the winning over of the masses in the period immediately preceding the revolution. But how do we know when we are in this period? It depends precisely on the work which we know how to develop among the masses whether this period begins or not. Only if we work and achieve some success

in the winning over of the masses will we arrive at a pre-revolutionary period. *CPC*, p. 487.

Even though Gramsci uses the term 'pre-revolutionary', he implies a view of the revolution as a process in which the outcome is determined not in a single dramatic moment but by the whole of the party's activities, each of which is aimed at changing the balance of forces. A key element in creating a strategy adequate to this task was the development of a strategy of alliances which would enable the working class, in a minority in Italy, to defeat the bourgeoisie.[60] One of the most important problems which the PCd'I had to face was the question of the relationship of the working class to the other social forces which were potentially anti-capitalist even if they might be led by parties and political groups tied to the bourgeoisie, in particular the peasantry.[61] This, of course, was not a new theme for Gramsci. His own analysis of the peasantry in this period, however, is more elaborate and attempts to take account of the specificity of the struggles in the countryside.[62] Without considering this in any detail, what is of particular relevance is the basis on which Gramsci maintained that, along with the problem of organising the revolutionary party, the worker-peasant alliance was the key problem facing the working class in Italy.

In no country is the proletariat capable of winning power and keeping it with its own forces alone. It must therefore obtain allies: in other words, it must follow a policy that will enable it to place itself at the head of the other classes who have anti-capitalist interests, and guide them in the struggle to overthrow bourgeois society. The question is of particular importance for Italy, where the proletariat is a minority of the working population and geographically distributed in such a manner, that it cannot presume to lead a victorious struggle unless it has resolved very precisely the problem of its relations with the peasant class. *PWII*, p. 316.

Thus Gramsci goes beyond a definition of the socialist revolution as a proletarian revolution. The transition from capitalism to socialism requires the proletariat to create a system of alliances. In posing the question in this way, Gramsci indicates the need to consider the relationship between democratic struggle and the general transformation of society or the relationship between democracy and socialism. While this question assumes a specific significance in Italy where the very national, territorial integrity of the country is at stake (the basis for the special national role attributed to the working class), Gramsci argues that in *no* country can the revolution be made by the proletariat alone.

In Italy the tactics which had to be followed in forming an alliance with the peasantry constituted one of the most important tactical and strategic problems that had to be solved by the party and was an area of work which had to adhere to the actual situation and not be determined on a mechanical or formalistic basis. Significantly, Gramsci links the very form of the party to its ability to pose this and other political questions properly.[63] The relationship between the organisation of the party and its task to found a new State was rooted in a concrete reality which had to be understood in all its complexity if the intervention of the party was to have a maximum effectiveness. When, shortly before his arrest, Gramsci began writing an essay on the Southern question which was not, however, published until after his imprisonment, he attempted to analyse the way in which Italian society was composed. In this essay, he introduced many of the themes which he went on to develop more fully in prison and which we discuss below—the role of the intellectuals, the historical bloc and the concept of hegemony, and the role of the proletariat and its political party.[64]

In the years 1924-6, Gramsci portrayed the party in language which appears neither in his earlier nor in his later work; yet his view of organisation as a political problem rooted in a specific view of the revolution and his concern for the effectiveness of the party's political intervention never change. In prison he elaborated the nature of the extremely complex task of the party, that of enabling the working class to found a new State. This leads him to develop his ideas on the nature of the State and consequently on the strategy of the party, an undertaking with great implications for the working-class movement and for Marxist theory.

Notes

1. See for example *PWII*, pp. 12-13, 14 and *SF*, p. 349.

2. See Tasca, *Il primi dieci anni del PCI*, p. 108; Paolo Spriano, 'Il dibattito tra il "Soviet" e "l'Ordine Nuovo"', *Rinascita*, vol. 18, no. 1 (Jan. 1961), p. 51; Franco Ferri, 'La situazione interna della sezione socialista torinese nell' estate del 1920', *Rinascita*, vol. 15, no. 4 (April 1958), pp. 259-65.

3. See for example, 'Controllo operaio', *SF*, pp. 67-9.

4. Little is known about this period. See Spriano, *PCI*, vol. 1, pp. 291ff for the most complete account.

5. It is the political theory underlying this change in the mode of political intervention which is relevant here. The specific role of the International must be considered only one of several factors influencing the change in leadership. See

Hoare, *Selections from the Prison Notebooks*, p. liii and Spriano, *PCI*, vol. 1, p. 285.

6. The attitude of the PCI and other communist parties to the united front policy and the various 'right' and 'left' interpretations of it have been widely discussed. See for example Spriano, *PCI*, vol. 1, ch. 10, 'Il dissenso con il Komintern'. What we would like to emphasise is the way in which the United Front policy was rooted in a problem which was at the heart of Gramsci's work: the need for communist parties to be able to influence the masses. As Hoare writes: 'The slogan "To the masses" which was launched at the Third World Congress in 1921 was a recognition that in most cases . . . the communist parties were not yet followed by the majority of workers, and that only when they were would revolution be attainable.' *Selections from the Prison Notebooks*, p. xlviii. Lenin had, of course, argued in 'Left-Wing Communism' among other works that not only the majority of workers but also of the potential allies of the working class had to be influenced by the communist parties.

7. See *PWII*, p. 139 and Hoare, *Selections from the Prison Notebooks*, p. liii.

8. *La form.*, p. 26.

9. See *SPN*, p. 198.

10. See Franco De Felice, *Serrati, Bordiga, Gramsci*, pp. 129-33, 143, 194, 226 with regard to Bordiga's view of politics.

11. Gramsci probably also had in mind the opposition to the *arditi del popolo*, the volunteer organisations formed on a local basis to fight the fascist squads. See Spriano, *PCI*, vol. 1, ch. 9, 'Gli arditi del popolo', pp. 139-51.

12. See *PWII*, p. 93. At the second congress of the PCI in Rome in 1922 the theses on tactics were written by Bordiga and Terracini while those on trade union matters were drafted by Gramsci and Tasca. The latter contained the only evidence of the ideas of the *Ordine Nuovo* group while the former established the Bordighist politics of the new party. Gramsci's uncritical adherence to the whole of the document has produced a good deal of historical debate. See Spriano, ibid., ch. XII, 'Le tesi di Roma e il II Congresso del PCd'I', pp. 178-91.

13. See *PWII*, p. 197. De Felice maintains that at the root of Serrati's efforts to maintain the unity of the PSI and his refusal to expel the reformists was a particular view of the revolution as developing mechanically, automatically, which simply had to be organised by the party. The effectiveness of the intervention by the party was therefore reduced to a pedagogic and organisational role while Serrati thought that the few reformists would be unable to block the revolution. *Serrati, Bordiga, Gramsci*, p. 120 and pp. 121 ff.

14. See *La form.*, p. 225 and *SPN*, p. 152.

15. See *SPN*, pp. 151-2.

16. *PWII*, p. 139.

17. *La form.*, p. 226.

18. The way in which the reformist leadership had been co-opted by the bourgeoisie in particular through the policies of Giolitti had been a point of criticism of the PSI since at least the beginning of the century exemplified by the writing of Salvemini. It was re-examined by Gramsci in the *Notebooks* in his discussion of the passive revolution. See section 13 below.

19. See *PWII*, p. 160.

20. *La form.*, p. 257.

21. See for example *PWI*, pp. 83-7 and *PWI*, pp. 147-9.

22. In a letter sent from Russia 12 September 1923, Gramsci had suggested that a new party daily be called *L'Unità* to indicate the special importance which should be given to the Southern question. Further he discussed the full range of social forces which should be employed in the fight against fascism. The letter can be considered a prelude to his writing on hegemony and the historical bloc while

in prison. See Spriano *PCI*, vol. 1, pp. 298-9. The letter is reprinted in its entirety
in *Rivista storica del socialismo*, vol. 6, no. 18 (Jan.-April 1963), pp. 115-16.
    23. *La form.*, p. 244.
    24. See Hoare, *Selections from the Prison Notebooks*, pp. lxxiii-lxxiv, and
Massimo L. Salvadori, *Gramsci e il problema storico della democrazia*, (Einaudi,
Turin, 1970), p. 77. The party under Gramsci's leadership never totally abandoned
Bordiga's view that the régime would face a crisis which would lead to a compromise between the fascists and the democratic opposition including the socialists,
the so-called 'legitimisation of the reaction'. This underestimation of the capacity
of the régime for internal development led to a paradox. The PCI under Gramsci
sought to widen its base and to work actively for the formation of a united front,
but at the same time it continued to view the other opposition parties, including
the two socialist parties, as potential allies of the fascists and therefore as enemies.
Projecting a political crisis from an analysis of the economic situation, Gramsci
and other leaders in the PCI failed to take into account the effect of the institution
of a totalitarian system with its special means of suppression and the unification
of virtually the whole of the bourgeoisie around the fascist régime.
    25. See *PWII*, pp. 201-2. While we are not able to discuss in any depth the dif-
ferent interpretations of fascism of Gramsci and Bordiga, there are several aspects
of Gramsci's approach which are particularly relevant. Firstly, he assumes the possibility of contradictions between sections of the bourgeoisie and fascism. Moreover the territorial dimension of potential opposition in the south would
provide an argument for the national role of the proletariat in its alliance with
the peasants. But the central question he was posing concerned the political leadership of the mass movement as the situation developed.
    26. See *PWII*, p. 221.

Gramsci's New Emphasis on the Party

    27. Bordiga came to lead the so-called *Comitato d'intesa*, a group of dissidents
within the party, organised in June 1925, which was the object of Gramsci's attack
on factionalism. See Spriano, *PCI*, vol. 1, pp. 453-6.
    28. See for example Gramsci's letter to the Central Committee of the CPSU,
PWII, pp. 426-32, and our discussion, pp. 109ff, below.
    29. Hoare writes: '1924-6 was a transitional phase, and it is extremely impor-
tant to stress the room for manoeuvre still remaining in this period to an individual
party such as the PCI. The coincidence between Comintern strategy and that of
the Italian party after the Fifth World Congress in June 1924 was not simply a
question of cause and effect; it was rather a question of a somewhat tactical 'left'
turn by the Comintern meshing in with the pre-existing 'leftism' of the PCI.'
Selections from the Prison Notebooks, p. lxviii.
    30. *PWII*, pp. 297-8 and pp. 299-300.
    31. *PWII*, p. 357. The theses for the Lyons Congress were in fact the product
of collaboration between Gramsci and Togliatti. Gramsci not only accepted but
argued for them and they clearly reflect his ideas.
    32. For a criticism by Gramsci of the PSI *vis-à-vis* its position on fascism in the
years 1920-2 see *CPC*, pp. 163-4.
    33. See for example, *PWII*, p. 209, pp. 214-15, p. 226.
    34. *PWII*, p. 166.
    35. The 'orthodoxy' of his terminology in these articles presumably reflects in
part his experiences working for the Comintern. These articles, we would suggest,
indicate that he took for granted a certain Marxist and Leninist tradition of thought
which would be the basis of his own development of Marxist theory in prison, including his criticism of aspects of it. We would therefore agree in a certain sense
with Anderson that Gramsci 'presumed the gains of the Comintern tradition',

Anderson, 'The Antinomies of Antonio Gramsci', p. 49. We would argue, however, that he considered this tradition, and most importantly the experience of building socialism in the USSR, from a critical perspective and that in addition to exploring areas neglected by Marxists, his own contribution revises some fundamental assumptions of Marxism such as the utopianism associated with assuming that socialism is constructed entirely *after* the seizure of power, rather than in the process of transforming power rooted in developments within the capitalist social formation.

36. For Bordiga's views in this regard see Andreina De Clementi, *Amadeo Bordiga* (Einaudi, Turin, 1971), p. 115. For a discussion of Bordiga's marxism see also Santarelli, *La revisione del marxisme*, pp. 231-92.

37. See *PWII*, p. 298.

38. See *CPC*, p. 251.

The Organisation of the Party

39. See note 31 above.

40. See *CPC*, p. 243, and *PWII*, pp. 364-6. There is no direct discussion of factions in the *Notebooks*.

41. *CPC*, pp. 240-1.

42. See *CPC*, p. 92 regarding the lack of discussion within the party after the split at Leghorn.

43. Gramsci said that while factions could not be allowed within a revolutionary party, this did not mean that factions *per se* were not useful in certain situations. It was perfectly justified, for example, to organise as a faction within a social democratic party to win over the majority of the party to revolutionary positions. It was not only justified but obligatory for communists to work as a faction within a trade union which did not have the same political function as the party. See *CPC*, pp. 243-4.

44. *CPC*, p. 97.

45. See *CPC*, p. 295.

46. *CPC*, p. 297.

47. See *SPN*, p. 196.

48. Gramsci sent a letter to the Central Committee of the CPSU via Togliatti who did not pass it on but answered Gramsci, disagreeing with him. Gramsci in turn sent a second letter to Togliatti. All are found in *PWII*, pp. 426-40.

49. In his second letter he writes,

   'the opposition represents in Russia all the old prejudices of class corporativism and syndicalism which weigh upon the tradition of the Western proletariat, and delay its ideological and political development ... the difficulty also arises for the proletarian vanguard which is not suspended in mid air but united to the masses. And it arises all the more in that reformism, with its tendencies to class corporativism – i.e. to not understanding the leading role of the vanguard: a role to be preserved even at the price of sacrifices – has far deeper roots in the West than it had in Russia.' *PWII*, p. 439.

50. *PWII*, pp. 296-7.

51. *PWII*, pp. 272-3.

52. See *PWII*, pp. 362-4.

53. *PWII*, p. 360 and *CPC*, p. 293.

54. In the original Italian Gramsci either writes 'partito di massa', which is most common, or 'partito delle più larghe masse'.

55. *CPC*, p. 90.

56. *CPC*, pp. 205-6.

57. *CPC*, p. 240.

58. *PWII*, p. 372.

59. At times he seems to imply a rather rhetorical and propagandistic link. See *PWII*, p. 370.

60. *PWII*, pp. 304-5, p. 395.

61. *PWII*, p. 388.

62. *PWII*, pp. 395-8, and 354-6. See also De Felice, *Serrati, Bordiga, Gramsci*, pp. 328-37, and Salvadori, *Gramsci e il problema storico della democrazia*, p. 75.

63. See *CPC*, p. 483.

64. This essay was published in Paris in January 1930 in *Lo Stato operaio*. The following passage shows how it links themes of the pre-prison period with concepts only later fully developed:

> The proletariat can become the leading [dirigente] and the dominant class to the extent that it succeeds in creating a system of class alliances which allows it to mobilize the majority of the working population against capitalism and the bourgeois State. In Italy, in the real class relations which exist there, this means to the extent that it succeeds in gaining the consent of the broad peasant masses. But the peasant question is historically determined in Italy; it is not the 'peasant and agrarian question in general'. In Italy the peasant question, through the specific Italian tradition, and the specific development of Italian history, has taken two typical and particular forms – the Southern question and that of the Vatican. Winning the majority of the peasant masses thus means, for the Italian proletariat, making these two questions its own from the social point of view; understanding the class demands which they represent; incorporating these demands into its revolutionary transitional programme; placing these demands among the objectives for which it struggles. *PWII*, p. 443.

Part III

GRAMSCI'S CONCEPT OF THE PARTY AND POLITICS IN THE PRISON NOTEBOOKS

1. Introduction

When Gramsci undertook to study the role of intellectuals in Italian history, in prison, he began a process of reconsidering the political experiences of his years as an active militant. The more recent developments of the consolidation of the fascist régime in Italy, the great economic crisis of 1929-30, the difficulties in the course of building socialism in the Soviet Union, and the 'left turn' of the Comintern provided the occasion for rethinking the nature of the resilience of capitalism and the problems of creating a new society. The precise nature of the relationship between Gramsci's earlier writings and his notes in prison has been the object of much discussion. We would argue that certain themes from his earlier work, among them revolution as a process, the political nature of organisational questions, the changed relationship between economics and politics, the importance of culture and the role of the intellectuals, the argument against a mechanistic interpretation of Marxism, and the novel nature of the socialist State and hence of the revolutionary party, continue to be important in the *Notebooks*. Yet Gramsci develops these themes within a problematic whose object is broadened to include the nature of the dominance of the bourgeoisie, a dominance which Gramsci comes to realise cannot be comprehended unless the very tools of analysis at the disposition of the working-class movement, of Marxist theory, are developed and the consequences of economism in theory and in political organisation and practice are criticised. Within the confines of prison, Gramsci attempts to contribute to the resurrection of the communist party as a political force by constructing a theoretical basis which would enable its political intervention to be adequate to the potential of the historical epoch.

2. The State as 'Hegemony Fortified by Coercion'

Thus, it can be argued that any discussion of Gramsci's concept of the revolutionary party must begin from a very particular point of departure – his extended, or integral, concept of the State. It is his concept of the State, in particular those manifestations of class rule which he calls hegemony,[1] which defines his concept of politics and consequently the task of the party. He is very specific about this when he writes,

> The concept of revolutionary and of internationalist, in the modern sense of the word, is correlative with the precise concept of State and of class: little understanding of the State means little class consciousness (and understanding of the State exists not only when one defends it, but also when one attacks it in order to overthrow it); hence low level of effectiveness of the parties, etc. *SPN*, p. 275.

It is only by taking the State as the starting-point, we would suggest, that the full range of concepts in the *Notebooks* can be appreciated.[2] In particular, with regard to the party, its very task and therefore its form and functioning, depends in the most immediate sense on Gramsci's view of the nature of the State and hence the nature of the political struggle. The central problems which Gramsci faced, the making of the revolution in the West, the disjuncture between economic and political crises, and the ability of the organised working-class movement to intervene in the historical process whatever the objective difficulties, are all considered from the point of view of a 'precise concept of the State'. (*SPN*, p. 275.) It should be made clear that the argument here is not that this starting-point is the only one which will lead us to the whole range of concepts in the *Notebooks*. The nature of Gramsci's work in prison, in which he compounds several notions in each fragmentary note, makes it possible to start with a number of concepts which touch on the whole range of his ideas. We would argue, however, that the key concept in terms of organising his thought is the State as 'hegemony armoured by coercion' (*SPN*, p. 263) and that beginning anywhere else diminishes the political nature of his work and restricts the discussion of the revolutionary party. Furthermore, Gramsci's view of the State and the nature of political rule encapsulates a whole notion of revolutionary change which has important implications not only for the struggle before the achievement of State power but also for the building of socialism and consequently for the role of the party in a socialist State. He presents, in fact, theoretical considerations which apply to *any form* of class rule, be it bourgeois or proletarian, whatever the precise configuration of State power.

In terms of defining his concept of the State, as with most of the other concepts in the *Notebooks*, any restricting of the discussion to passages where he discusses hegemony directly can be misleading. If taken out of context of the whole of his thought, it is quite possible to obscure the kind of relationship which he is trying to portray between the different dimensions of reality, the economic, political, and cultural. Involved in an understanding of hegemony and therefore of the State is his concept of political society, civil society, the revolutionary process, and the peculiarly Gramscian notion of the historical bloc. And very importantly, the revolutionary party is directly concerned since Gramsci's view of the State as including hegemony transforms the area of activity which is considered political. Referring to Marxism and to Lenin's work, Gramsci argues

> that not only the philosophy of praxis does not exclude ethical-political history but that on the contrary *its most recent phase of development* consists precisely in the vindication of the moment of hegemony as *essential to its conception of the State* and in the 'exploitation' of the cultural factor, of cultural activity, of a cultural front which is as necessary as the merely economic and merely political ones. *Q*, p. 1224. [My emphasis.]

We can begin to elaborate Gramsci's concept of hegemony by examining the way in which he describes the basis of the supremacy of a class:

> the supremacy of a social group manifests itself in two ways, as 'domination' and as 'intellectual and moral leadership'. A social group dominates antagonistic groups, which it tends to 'liquidate', or to subjugate perhaps even by armed force; it leads kindred and allied groups. A social group can, and indeed must, already exercise 'leadership' before winning governmental power (this indeed is one of the principal conditions for the winning of such power); it subsequently becomes dominant when it exercises power, but even if it holds it firmly in its grasp, it must continue to 'lead' as well. *SPW*, pp. 57-8.[3]

In this passage Gramsci presents us with a totality constituted by the unity of two concepts: direction and dominance. The relationship between these two concepts suggests three things. First of all, dominance is exerted over the enemy and direction over allies. Turned around, to the extent that a group is able to assert its direction over a second group, this latter can be considered an ally rather than an enemy. Secondly, direction is a precondition for the conquest of the State apparatus in the narrow sense of government power. And thirdly, once State power has been achieved, the two aspects of the supremacy of a class, both direction and dominance, are continued. Yet, while supremacy of a class *appears*, shows itself, in two ways, as we shall see these two moments or manifestations of its rule are never completely separated, and are, we would argue, fundamental in Gramsci's very vision of politics as such.[4] The relationship between these two moments within what he calls a 'dual perspective' in political action and state life (*SPN*, p. 149) can be described as an oppositional couple. This double or dual perspective, which is extremely important in his thought, may be presented on various levels which can be reduced theoretically to

> two fundamental levels, corresponding to the dual nature of Machiavelli's Centaur — half-animal and half-human. They are the levels of force and of consent, authority and hegemony, violence and civilisation, of the individual moment and of the universal moment "Church' and 'State'), of agitation and of propaganda, of tactics and of strategy, etc. *SPN*, pp. 169-70.[5]

A dialectical view of the nature of politics itself is revealed here. According to Gramsci, politics contains *within* itself the contradiction which will eventually be resolved in what Gramsci calls 'regulated society' in which politics can disappear. The political is not defined by, it cannot be understood in terms of, only one of its attributes, of force or consent. It is *both* force *and* consent, authority *and* hegemony, violence *and* 'civiltà'.[6] We shall see how he distinguishes between the two aspects yet never separates them completely.

Gramsci has constantly before him this dual perspective when he discusses the State, and it affects the way in which he situates it in the superstructure. The traditional Marxist schematic of a political superstructure which is contingent to but occupying a different theoretical space from an ideological superstructure appears more complex in Gramsci so that institutions like the State machinery or, for example, the Church,[7] occupy two spaces at one time; they can have meaning *both* in terms of political society *and* civil society so that any division is purely methodological.[8] Gramsci's double perspective redefines politics and the State and this redefinition will be fundamental to any understanding of the party and its tasks.

Gramsci, in fact, works with *two* main definitions of the State, one limited and one extended or enlarged, both of which were elaborated in prison in the same period.[9] The ranking of these definitions can only come from placing them within a whole problematic. In this case Gramsci's extended definition is the dominant one:

> it should be remarked that the general notion of State includes
> elements which need to be referred back to the notion of civil society
> (in the sense that one might say that State = political society + civil
> society, in other words hegemony protected by the armour of
> coercion). *SPN*, pp. 262-3.[10]

Yet, at the same time Gramsci makes methodological distinctions in
order to describe different aspects of reality.

> What we can do, for the moment, is to fix two major superstructural
> 'levels': the one that can be called 'civil society', that is the en-
> semble of organisms commonly called 'private', and that of 'political
> society' or 'the State'. These two levels correspond on the one hand
> to the function of 'hegemony' which the dominant group exercises
> throughout society and on the other hand to that of 'direct domina-
> tion' or command exercised through the State and 'juridical' govern-
> ment. *SPN*, p. 12.[11]

This second view indicates that Gramsci is conscious of the problem of
delineating the differences or boundaries between civil and political
society.[12] The differences in Gramsci's two definitions of the State are
thus more of emphasis than of essence. In the first Gramsci talks about
the 'general notion of the State' in which there are elements of civil
society. This would indicate an overlap or coincidence of two areas which
none the less have certain essential differences. In the second description
of two superstructural plans, he uses the term 'direct domination' which
would imply that there is also an *indirect* domination in civil society.
The State and the 'juridical government' is the expression of the direct
domination. Here the State and its legal apparatus appears in a restricted
definition.

It is important to note that the extended notion of the State is
firmly rooted in a certain historical period. Gramsci uses the concept
of hegemony to describe a *modern* State, and it is indeed an integral part
of the very definition of a modern State and arises from the development of modern society.[13] It was not part of ancient or feudal society.

> In the ancient and mediaeval State alike, centralisation, whether pol-
> itical-territorial or social . . . was minimal. The State was, in a certain
> sense, a mechanical bloc of social groups . . . The modern State sub-
> stitutes for the mechanical bloc of social groups their subordination
> to the active hegemony of the directive and dominant group. *SPN*, p. 54.

In terms of the strategy of the revolutionary party, which will be discussed below, the relationship between civil society and the State is a crucial one and is related directly to either the modern or feudal characteristic of a specific State. Without discussing here the strategic aspects, in this context it will be useful to consider another well known passage in which Gramsci writes,

> In Russia the State was everything, civil society was primordial and gelatinous; in the West, there was a proper relation between State and civil society, and when the State trembled a sturdy structure of civil society was at once revealed. The State was only an outer ditch, behind which there stood a powerful system of fortresses and earthworks. *SPN*, p. 238.[14]

We shall return to this passage. Here we would argue that it is the *non-modern* attributes of the Russian State, the fact that it did not represent the organisation of masses in a modern way but resembled rather 'in a certain sense, a mechanical bloc of social groups' which resulted in a lack of a developed civil society to act as a further fortification as in the West where the State is but what we might call the first appearance of the whole reality.[15] Thus the definition of the State as force plus hegemony depends on the development of the area of civil society. Although the Russian State was, in Lenin's terms, 'the weakest link' in the imperialist chain, its pre-modern nature meant that it was not the internal political correspondent of the organisation of capitalism in the imperialist system. The relatively backward nature of the development of the political sphere in Russia is a point of reference which must be taken into account when considering the limits of Lenin's analysis in *State and Revolution*, which does not address the problem of the extended state.

Because of his extended definition of the State Gramsci is often considered a theorist of the superstructure.[16] While it is true that he developed this hitherto relatively neglected area of Marxist theory, it must not be forgotten that this was both implicitly and explicitly within a problematic which related the superstructure to an economic base or a dimension of reality expressed in terms of the conditions of production. The reproduction of these conditions had to be provided for by the political and ideological superstructure. Gramsci had maintained since his writings in the *Ordine Nuovo* that the relationship between State and economy or State and society had changed.[17] Thus when Gramsci discusses the terms 'ethical State' and 'civil society' and says that the 'ethical' or 'civil' aspect of the State is one of its most important functions,[18] it is in terms of a relationship to the potential presented by the development of the forces of production.

Thus each moment of hegemony represents a certain relationship between class forces, and in any given moment certain compromises are both possible and necessary:

> every State is ethical in as much as one of its most important functions is to raise the great mass of the population to a particular cultural and moral level, a level (or type) which corresponds to the needs of the productive forces for development, and hence to the interests of the ruling classes. *SPN*, p. 258.

The ethical function of the State is extended beyond

> the school as a positive educative function, and the courts as a repressive and negative educative function which are the most important State activities in this sense: but, in reality, a multitude of other so-called private initiatives and activities tend to the same end — initiatives and activities which form the apparatus, of the political and cultural hegemony of the ruling classes. *SPN*, p. 258.

Thus even activities which are ostensibly private have a political meaning and therefore are in turn a part of the provision of the conditions under which a dominant mode of production can exist and expand.[19]

The way in which Gramsci links the two spheres of reality, the so-called base and superstructure, has great consequence for an understanding of the problems involved with the building of socialism. This is quite explicit when he writes:

> In reality, the State must be conceived of as an 'educator', in as much as it tends precisely to create a new type or level of civilization. Because one is acting essentially on economic forces, reorganising and developing the apparatus of economic production, creating a new structure, the conclusion must not be drawn that superstructural factors should be left to themselves, to develop spontaneously, to a haphazard and sporadic germination. *SPN*, p. 247.[20]

Here Gramsci reveals a view of the uneven development of areas of the superstructure which does not develop automatically and spontaneously following changes in the economic structure. Yet development of the superstructure is nonetheless related, even if in a highly mediated way, to the economic sphere. The roots of the hegemony of a class are in the organisation of the economy. He explains:

> Undoubtedly the fact of hegemony presupposes that account be taken of the interests and the tendencies of the groups over which hegemony is to be exercised, and that a certain compromise equilibrium should be formed — in other words, that the leading group should make sacrifices of an economic-corporate kind. But there is also no doubt that such sacrifices and such a compromise cannot touch the essential; for though hegemony is ethical-political, it must also be economic, must necessarily be based on the decisive function exercised by the leading group in the decisive nucleus of economic activity. *SPN*, p. 161.

But in any compromises which are made, the essential economic function of the directing class remains. A precise understanding of the relationship of different groups which are allied under the hegemony of the dominant class is necessary for the party so that it can formulate its tactics bearing in mind the ethical and cultural *form* of the hegemony of its opponents but also the economic consequences which provide the limits or boundaries of compromises by the 'leading group'. This is crucial in order to understand the economic contradictions which may arise between allied groups, contradictions which must form an important element in a strategy by a revolutionary party which seeks to help establish the hegemony of another class. The existence of such economic limits also indicates potential economic contradictions between the working class and its allies. Gramsci's perspective is made richer if we connect this discussion to his writings in the *Ordine Nuovo* period where he analysed the changed relationship between the political and economic spheres and to his notes on the passive revolution discussed below and Americanism and Fordism, where these themes are developed further. The modes of hegemony of a class are related to the way in which masses of people are organised in the economy and the way in which these organised masses relate to the State. In the modern period, the relationship between economics and politics cannot be comprehended through a schematic use of the metaphor of base and superstructure.

While the economic sphere is thus a fundamental aspect of Gramsci's problematic, it is the realm of politics with its area of hegemony which according to Gramsci represents the moment of the highest historical development of a class. And here the achievement of State power, and the consequences it brings for the possibility of an extension and a full development of that hegemony already partially in existence, has a special significance. The State in all its aspects, that is, extended to include the area of hegemony, gives both prestige to the class which has founded it[21] and represents the historical unity of the ruling class in a concrete form, which 'results from the organic relations between State or political society and "civil society".' (*SPN*, p. 52.)

The achievement of State power can only come after the establishment of a certain hegemony in society, and this means that any class which is to reach its highest level of historical development as represented by the foundation of its own State must have already developed beyond an economic-corporative stage, or a primitive development of class-consciousness, to a political one which is defined by the ability of a class to establish its hegemony in society as a whole. Highly significant in terms of the way in which Gramsci defines the political and therefore the area of political activity by the party is the way in which he describes the different levels or moments in the development of a political class consciousness.

The first and most primitive moment, the economic corporative one, is when members of the same category feel a certain solidarity toward each other but not with other categories of the same class. In a second moment or level of class-consciousness there are certain implications for the State:

> A second moment is that in which consciousness is reached of the solidarity of interests among all the members of a social class—but still in the purely economic field. Already at this juncture the problem of the State is posed—but only in terms of winning politico-juridical equality with the ruling groups: the right is claimed to participate in legislation and administration, even to reform these—but within the existing fundamental structures. *SPN*, p. 181.

What is interesting here is that while this second moment does involve the State arena, it is not of itself a moment of truly political activity by the subaltern class. The political development of a class is conceived of by Gramsci as taking place *only* when that class sees its role in terms of establishing its hegemony in society.

> A third moment is that in which one becomes aware that one's own corporate interests, in their present and future development, transcend the corporate limits of the purely economic class, and can and

must become the interests of other subordinate groups too. This is the most purely political phase, and marks the decisive passage from the structure to the sphere of the complex superstructures; it is the phase in which previously germinated ideologies become 'party', come into confrontation and conflict, until only one of them, or at least a single combination of them, tends to prevail, to gain the upper hand, to propagate itself throughout society—bringing about not only a union of economic and political aims, but also intellectual and moral unity, posing all the questions around which the struggle rages not on a corporate but on a 'universal' plane, and thus creating the hegemony of a fundamental social group over a series of subordinate groups. *SPN*, pp. 181-2.

This phase is political not because the object of the struggle is the State in a narrow sense but because the struggle is manifest not only in the realm of the economic or in the area of the present State machinery but it concerns the full range of human activity. The *political* struggle of the class and its party is one which is conducted in terms of establishing an alternative hegemony. It is thus conducted on the intellectual and moral fronts as well as the economic and strictly political. Consequently, in the context of this struggle for hegemony all of these areas of society acquire a *political* significance. It is not the site of the struggle which makes it political or not. A struggle in the economic arena may be political if it is part of an overall strategy aimed at the establishment of the hegemony of a class, while a class may act within the political arena but in a non-political way. It is the way in which questions are posed, in a 'universal' rather than a corporative manner which makes the struggle political or not. This influences the very view of the State.

It is true that the State is seen as the organ of one particular group, destined to create favourable conditions for the latter's maximum expansion. But the development and expansion of the particular group are conceived of, and presented, as being the motor force of a universal expansion, of a development of all the 'national' energies. In other words, the dominant group is coordinated concretely with the general interests of the subordinate groups, and the life of the State is conceived of as a continuous process of formation and superseding of unstable equilibria (on the juridical plane) between the interests of the fundamental group and those of the subordinate groups—equilibria in which the interests of the dominant group prevail, but only up to a certain point, i.e. stopping short of narrowly corporate economic interest. *SPN*, p. 182.

Thus Gramsci goes beyond a view of the State as an *instrument* of a class. The State is a class State in that it creates conditions under which a certain class can develop fully, but it acts in the name of universal interests within a field of constantly changing equilibria between the dominant class and subaltern groups. The interests of the subordinate groups must have some concrete and not simply ideological weight; otherwise the interests of the dominant class would be merely economic-corporative. The definition of the highest development of a class consists in its ability to represent universal interests. In these and other notes Gramsci transforms the notion of politics so that it can comprehend a *national-popular* dimension. Politics can no longer be reduced, within Gramsci's problematic, to the immediate economic-corporative interests of a class. The way in which the proletarian State will differ from the bourgeois State in this respect, is that it is able to create the conditions under which the objective interests of all sectors of society can eventually coincide, as class divisions are progressively overcome, while the bourgeoisie, whatever its beliefs and intentions, inevitably cannot reconcile the fundamental conflict within it, between capital and labour, because of the very nature of bourgeois society. Thus the range of its universalistic function has objective limits which it cannot surpass.[22]

Yet, in considering the highest development of a class in terms of its political or hegemonic moment, in no way is development to this stage inevitable according to Gramsci. Both in terms of the bourgeoisie and the proletariat the achievement of this stage can be delayed, or be immature, or contorted. This will become clear when we discuss Gramsci's critique of the Italian bourgeois revolution, his concept of the passive revolution, and his criticism of economism. It is precisely because this development is not automatic that the party is given a crucial role.

3. The Historical Bloc

Any discussion of Gramsci's view of hegemony and the State must include his concept of the historical bloc. A considerable literature exists on this aspect of his work[1] so that it is somewhat surprising to learn that an explicit discussion occupies a very small amount of space in the *Notebooks*.[2] While it is not possible here to discuss the manifold consequences of these various interpretations of the meaning of the whole of Gramsci's thought, it can be argued that the *two* ways in which Gramsci uses this concept, which, as will be shown have a common core, focus on certain central issues in his problematic which are of consequence for the revolutionary party.

In the great majority of cases Gramsci uses historical bloc with regard to the relationship of the structure to the superstructure and in this context the concept is part of Gramsci's double-fronted battle against a Crocean idealist distortion of the Marxist dialectic on the one hand and of an economistic deviation on the other. These two objects of Gramsci's criticism converge in their reduction of the dialectic to one or other of the fundamental aspects of reality, either the ethical-political or the economic. Gramsci re-examines the terrain of the superstructures and most particularly the ideological area within Marx's problematic to argue against both distortions. This is the first context in which he uses the concept of historical bloc. It represents what Gramsci calls 'the unity of the process of the real.' (*Q*, p. 1300) 'Structures and superstructures', Gramsci wrote, 'form a "historical bloc". That is to say the complex, contradictory and discordant *ensemble* of the superstructures is the reflection of the *ensemble* of the social relations of production.' (*SPN*, p. 366.)[3] The contradictory and discordant whole of the superstructures is the reflection of the *contradictory* nature of the social relations of production. The superstructures are not the single expression of a single contradiction in the economic base.

Rather than revaluate the area of the superstructures at the cost of devaluing the structure, which, Gramsci argues must be 'conceived in an ultra realistic way' (*Q*, p. 1300) the proper understanding of the 'vital and necessary relationship' (*Q*, p. 1321[4]) between the two, the confirmation that ideologies have the 'same energy as a material force ' (*SPN*, p. 377) reinforces

the conception of *historical bloc* in which precisely material forces are the content and ideologies are the form, though this distinction between form and content has purely didactic value, since the material forces would be inconceivable historically without form and the ideologies would be individual fancies without the material forces. *SPN*, p. 377.

This is but a small part of a very large aspect of Gramsci's work in prison. His intervention in order to refound a correct understanding of the Marxist dialectic is rooted in his notes on Croce and Bukharin as well as those on economism. A full discussion of their implications would take us too far afield from his concept of the party. Suffice it to say that this area of his writings has great significance for the theoretical work of the party and ultimately its analysis of social reality and the conjuncture.

The historical bloc is, in fact, the site of the joining together of two levels of analysis, the first theoretical in which the concept helps to describe the relationship between two areas of abstract reality, the structure and the superstructure, and the second concrete in the description of the linking of these two areas in real society. This second use of the concept by Gramsci is more immediately a part of the analysis of the concrete social formation, and its very use implies a different-iated analysis. Here the historical bloc has to do with the way in which various classes and factions of classes are related in a situation in which implicitly one mode of production is dominant but articulated with other modes of production. In addition, what must be emphasised is that the way in which a given historical bloc is articulated is organically related to the ability or not of a new, progressive class to construct an alternative historical bloc. Moreover, since the historical bloc is specific to the national context, although in an international conjuncture, a special emphasis is placed on the national dimension as the basic unit to be analysed.

Having said that the historical bloc describes the way in which different social forces relate to each other, it must also be pointed out that an historical bloc is not to be reduced to a mere political alliance since it assumes a complex construction within which there can be sub-blocs such as, for example, an agrarian bloc, a complex formation in its own right, and an industrial bloc, each of these containing different elements and potential contradictions. The historical bloc can produce *various pol-itical* blocs made up of different combinations of political allies which none the less maintain the general configuration of the fundamental historical bloc. Thus the political representation of a concrete historical bloc varies so that there is never a complete reflection of the forces that make up the historical bloc. For example, there can be a variety of government coalitions and indeed a variety of State forms, as there were in Italy from the Risorgimento until the 1930s in a society in which the fundamental historical bloc described by Gramsci in *Some Aspects of the Southern Question* remains basically the same. Yet we must qualify this in that while the historical bloc remains *basically* the same, it does change as new elements develop, such as finance capital, and some dis-appear or diminish or are articulated differently, such as feudal agricul-tural production. The important point is that changes in the political bloc do not necessarily and indeed hardly ever represent in a one to one way changes in the historical bloc as a whole. What is provided for in Gramsci's exposition is the disjuncture between the dominance on the economic level of one mode of production and the dominance at the political level of one or a combination of forces which may or may not directly reflect this economic dominance.

Social forces can be more or less integrated in the historical bloc as a whole, such as the peasants or the industrial workers and may or may not participate in the political bloc. As the concrete form of the organic linking together on the theoretical level of the structure and the super-structure, the historical bloc is just as 'contradictory and discordant' as the superstructure is, the superstructure itself as a particular type of re-flection of the contradictory nature of the social relations and different modes of production. The historical bloc represents the *dominance* of one class which 'leads' its allies, and is dominant over its enemies. Its chief class enemy may be attempting to organise an alternative historical bloc by attracting certain social forces over to its side and consequently weakening the present historical bloc.

The very fact that Gramsci uses a variety of terms, sometimes in an almost interchangeable way, for what in English is usually subsumed under the category 'ruling class' ('gruppo dirigente', 'classi dirigenti', 'gruppi dominanti', 'classi dominanti',)[5] indicates both the dual nature of that rule and the complexity of the group which is actually involved in governing. In this group there will be elements of social forces in the dominant (and directing) political bloc, and the ruling group or class will manifest the contradictory nature of the bloc it represents. This has particular consequences when it is a matter of analysing the various political parties in a society and the nature of their representation of different social forces.

According to Gramsci, the 'necessary' concrete form of the concrete historical bloc which exists in society at any point in time is defined by the 'moment of hegemony and of consent'(Q, p. 1235) just as Gramsci defined the modern State by its ability to form an organic bloc of classes based on the hegemony of the ruling class, the very nature of an historical bloc is bound up with the extent of the hegemony of the dominant class. Thus a class can find relative unity in any number of different forms of State some of which are not fully 'integral' or extend-ed in that they do not successfully embrace the area of hegemony or enjoy a fully developed civil society. An example is the State which arose out of the Italian Risorgimento or the State produced by the Russian Revolution. To the extent that a State is successful in developing this area of hegemony, a class can build an organic historical bloc. A class can in fact organise itself in a State which only barely goes beyond the bounds of an economic-corporative development, but it is only when this state has developed the area of hegemony that it is an extended or integral State, and only then can it represent a fully developed and maximally extended historical bloc. The social and historical base of the State in this case will be much stronger.[6]

It can be argued that a State which has a relatively limited rather than an integral or fully hegemonic existence can endure so long as there is no imminent alternative historical bloc. The historical bloc must in fact be seen to be the result of a relation of forces.[7] Both the existence or non-existence of a fully extended historical bloc underpinning the State and the creation or not of an alternative depend on the ability of the political forces of the fundamental classes[8] in society to fulfill the highest political expression of those classes in the form of the State including a widespread hegemony in society and backed by a solid historical bloc.[9] This can only be done if the concrete articulators of any such bloc, of the hegemony which produces the cohesion of such a bloc, are developed. These articulators are the intellectuals and a whole range of institutions, which will be discussed below.

The consequence of this range of possibilities, in addition to demonstrating a non-mechanistic view of the relationship of the various political forms in society to the economic structure, has important consequences for the analysis of real political phenomena. Thus, while the bourgeoisie may find an effective unification in fascism or the proletariat in a régime which lacks socialist democracy and a relationship of hegemony with the mass of the population, neither of these can be considered integral States in the Gramscian sense, neither have surpassed more than minimally the economic, coercive functions of a State which enjoys a restricted positive hegemony. Here we can return to Gramsci's two concepts of the State, and we have an explanation of why he thinks, indeed must think, two concepts, one limited to the legal coercive area of the State apparatuses, and one extended to include the apparatuses of hegemony. These two definitions must be understood as two poles within which a State can exist. The restricted notion cannot imply a complete absence of hegemony while extended notion necessarily includes the existence of the coercive apparatus of the State machinery.[10]

The historical bloc in implying necessarily the existence of hegemony also implies that in order to create a new historical bloc alternative to the existing one, the new, progressive class must create its own hegemonic apparatuses. The way in which the working class is able to do this, according to Gramsci, is through the party. The extent to which this is in fact possible before the establishment of its own State will be discussed below. In this context, however, Gramsci indicates in his writings on the historical bloc, the conditions under which an organic historical bloc can be built, conditions which have important implications for the way in which the party conducts its activity. We shall develop this more fully, but we must anticipate our discussion somewhat because here we reach the common core in his two uses of the term historical bloc — as the *organic* link both between the structure and the superstructure, and between the different elements in the concrete historical bloc. In order for this link to be organic in the real world, it must be based on a hegemony established in a particular way, by the articulators of hegemony, the intellectuals, who must have a certain relationship with the mass of the people. Intellectuals must, if they are to fulfill their function (a function which will be fully discussed below), feel

> the elementary passions of the people, understanding them and therefore explaining and justifying them in the particular historical situation and connecting them dialectically to the laws of history and to a superior conception of the world, scientifically and coherently elaborated — i.e. knowledge. One cannot make politics-history without this passion, without this sentimental connection between intellectuals and people-nation. In the absence of such a nexus the relations between the intellectual and the people-nation are, or are reduced to, relationships of a purely bureaucratic and formal order; *SPN*, p. 418.

And purely formal and bureaucratic relationships are not hegemonic ones, according to Gramsci. Hegemony can only be established

> If the relationship between intellectuals and people-nation, between the leaders and the led, the rulers and the ruled, is provided by an organic cohesion in which feeling-passion becomes understanding and thence knowledge (not mechanically but in a way that is alive), then and only then is the relationship one of representation. Only then can there take place an exchange of individual elements between the rulers and ruled, leaders [*dirigenti*] and led, and can the shared life be realised which alone is a social force — with the creation of the 'historical bloc'. *SPN*, p. 418.

This then is the only basis on which a *representative* relationship can be established, when an organic historical bloc can be established. And extended to the party as the 'collective intellectual'[11] of the working class, this has great consequences for its relationship to the class and to the rest of the population. This will be discussed in a later section.

4. The Lessons of the Italian Bourgeois Revolution

Although historical developments in Italy and in the world in general while Gramsci was in prison were extremely important for his work and form the context of much of his prison writing,[1] earlier historical periods in Italian history also provided a focus for his studies, in particular the period of the development of the communes in Italy and the Risorgimento. An examination of the process of the establishment of a nation-state in Italy, which coincided, in Marxist terms, with the Italian bourgeois revolution, was undertaken by Gramsci for two main reasons. The first was in order to understand better the contemporary Italian situation, the context within which fascism was established and within which a party of the Italian working class had to work. This is the aspect which is emphasised in certain pre-prison writings, such as the 'Theses of Lyons', which consider Italian historical development. In prison, out of the direct political struggle, a second aspect comes to dominate, that is, the endeavour to abstract certain lessons from the process of the Italian bourgeois revolution which the Italian proletariat could learn in order to accomplish its own revolution successfully by building an organic historical bloc to replace the rather faulty creation of the bourgeoisie.[2]

Implicit here is the idea that at least certain aspects of the bourgeois and the proletarian revolutions are symmetrical, an idea which marks a change and development of Gramsci's position from an earlier period. An index of this change is his definition of and attitude toward Jacobinism, and it is important because it also marks a substantial change in his view of the role of the revolutionary party.

Thus we must return to his early articles on the events in Russia. In his first writings on the Russian Revolution he discounts the charge by certain newspapers that the revolution is Jacobin.[3] What is interesting is that in these early writings he equates Jacobinism with the bourgeois revolution *tout court*, and while he recognises the achievements of the French Revolution, he maintains that it is something fundamentally and completely different from the proletarian revolution both in terms of its authoritarian nature[4] and its utopian vision.[5] As we suggested earlier, counterposed to this is a vision of the Russian Revolution as profoundly libertarian[6] and of the Bolsheviks as realists.[7] What is missing in this view is, on the one hand, a differentiated analysis of the bourgeois revolution and, on the other, a clear understanding of the role of the revolutionary party in the proletarian revolution. As these two elements in his ideas develop, his definition and understanding of Jacobinism changes and so does his attitude to it. Jacobinism comes to be identified with that segment of the bourgeoisie which pushes the revolution to fulfill its full historical potential by articulating an hegemony based on an organic link with the mass of the people, in the case of France between the urban bloc and the peasant masses, thus going beyond the economic-corporative interests of the bourgeoisie. Whatever the merits of this as an interpretation of real history, which is not the object of our concerns here, the establishment of an historical bloc under the hegemony of the bourgeoisie, the bourgeois revolution, comes to provide in Gramsci's eyes certain concrete lessons for the proletariat. His criticism of the main weakness of the Italian bourgeois revolution is that it lacked 'an effective *Jacobin* force'. (*SPN*, p. 131.)[8]

The important 'principles of historical research' (*SPN*, p. 53) which Gramsci says may be learnt from a study of the Italian Risorgimento come from an examination of the process whereby the 'moderates', or the groups under the leadership of Cavour and Piedmont, succeeded in establishing their hegemony over the rival political blocs contending for dominance, notably the 'Action Party' or those groups influenced by Garibaldi and Mazzini. Yet, while the moderates succeeded in establishing their political leadership, the extent of their hegemony in society as a whole remained limited and the resultant historical bloc was extremely weak. The Italian bourgeoisie, he wrote,

> said that they were aiming at the creation of a modern State in Italy, and they in fact produced a bastard. They aimed at stimulating the formation of an extensive and energetic ruling class, and they did not succeed; at integrating the people into the framework of the new State, and they did not succeed. *SPN*, p. 90.

For the hegemony of the ruling groups to be extended throughout Italian society so that the mass of the population, the peasants in this case, would be wedded to new historical bloc, the question of an agrarian reform and ultimately that of the position of the Church had to be resolved. The fact that the Italian nation-state was founded on the basis of the limited hegemony of its ruling class at the same time affected and was the result of both the mode of its historical change and the content of that change.

The issue here is not the historical merits or failings of Gramsci's analysis, about which there exists a good deal of debate.[9] We are interested in those theoretical principles which he abstracts from the process which he thinks may be of use to the proletariat and in particular its political party. In what is a highly differentiated analysis of a social reality which is inherently complex, Gramsci specifies the different aspects of the struggle waged by the moderates:

> these forces took power and united in the modern Italian State, in struggle against specific other forces and helped by specific auxiliaries or allies. In order to become a State, they had to subordinate or eliminate the former and win the active or passive assent of the latter. *SPN*, p. 53.[10]

The development of the moderates 'from subaltern groups to hegemonic and dominant groups' depended on their ability to acquire '1. autonomy *vis-à-vis* the enemies they had to defeat, and 2. support from the groups which actively or passively assisted them.' (*SPN*, p. 53.) Thus a social force must both maintain its autonomy in order to defeat its enemies and at the same time create its hegemony in order to have the active or at least passive help of other social forces.

The great attribute of the moderates, according to Gramsci, was that they were able to absorb gradually but continuously,

> the active elements produced by allied groups—and even of those which came from antagonistic groups and seemed irreconcilably hostile. In this sense political leadership became merely an aspect of the function of domination—in as much as the absorption of the enemies' *élites* means their decapitation, and annihilation often for a very long time. *SPN*, p. 59.

The relationship between the two poles of political activity, 'domination' and 'leadership' is apparent here. In the Italian context this resulted in the transformism of Italian parliamentary politics, Gramsci said, but he also had something else in mind. From the time of his earliest militancy in the PSI he had fought to overcome a situation in which the working class was unable to maintain its political autonomy because Giolitti's policies represented only the most skillful of a variety of attempts to decapitate politically the working-class organisations. This concern reappeared

in different periods of his work,[11] and in prison it is one of the main
reasons he argues for the necessity of a revolutionary party to establish
its hegemony. As he continues in the above passage,

> It seems clear from the policies of the Moderates that there can, and
> indeed must, be hegemonic activity even before the rise to power,
> and that one should not count only on the material force which
> power gives in order to exercise an effective leadership. *SPN*, p. 59.

This hegemonic activity should serve to attract intellectuals, as part of
the influence on other social forces, because, as we shall see, it is intellectuals who are the organisers of the hegemony of any class. But the
methods by which a particular social force is able to accomplish its
hegemony depends on its position in society. During the Risorgimento
the moderates were able to attract intellectuals in a particular way because
they

> were a real, organic vanguard of the upper classes, to which econ-
> omically they belonged. They were intellectuals and political organ-
> isers, and at the same time company bosses, rich farmers or estate man-
> agers, commercial and industrial entrepreneurs, etc. . . . the Moderates
> exercised a powerful attraction 'spontaneously', on the whole mass of
> intellectuals of every degree who existed in the peninsula, in a 'diffused'
> 'molecular' state. *SPN*, p. 60.

The Partito d'Azione, on the other hand, could not count on being
a 'spontaneous' vanguard because it was situated differently in society.
In order for it to establish an alternative hegemony it needed to organise politically around a political programme based on attracting different
social forces, particularly the peasants.[12] Its strategy, therefore, needed
to have both a different political content and a different political *form*.
There is a parallel here with the working class in bourgeois society.
Because this class is intrinsically in a different position from the bourgeoisie, it can be argued that it cannot spontaneously counterpose an
alternative hegemony. This can only be done through the formation of
a revolutionary vanguard organised politically.[13] The political organisation of certain social forces, therefore, can be directed toward political ends in the narrower sense because these forces can depend on
their hegemonic influence being exerted spontaneously, but the political
organisation of the working class must act on a variety of fronts, political
in the widest sense.

5. The Conquest of Hegemony by a Subaltern Class

Because of particular difficulties faced by the working class in achieving its hegemony in bourgeois society, the relationship between the development of this proletariat hegemony and its final culmination in the form of State power is also a particular one. The hegemony which any class can establish before having State power is limited. It must represent the *most* hegemonic force available, and therefore the hegemony of the current ruling class must be in crisis.[1] But the new, post-revolutionary State itself, in the restricted sense, will provide the new ruling class with the ability to develop its hegemony fully and to become 'really autonomous and hegemonic' (*SPN*, p. 388) because the State can be used to provide the means to push forward this hegemony to its fullest possible extension. The benefits, as it were, of achieving State power are all the greater for the proletariat because it is that much more difficult in bourgeois society for it to develop its own autonomous and hegemonic culture.

Gramsci points out that this was one of the historical difficulties of Marxism which had to relate on the one hand to the very low cultural level of the masses and at the same time serve to combat the ideas of the cultured classes. For the working class,

> creating a group of independent intellectuals is not an easy thing; it requires a long process, with actions and reactions, coming together and drifting apart and the growth of very numerous and complex new formations. It is the conception of a subaltern social group, deprived of historical initiative, in continuous but disorganic expansion, unable to go beyond a certain qualitative level, which still remains *below the level of the possession of the State and of the real exercise of hegemony over the whole of society* which alone permits a certain organic equilibrium in the development of the intellectual group. *SPN*, pp. 395-6. [My emphasis.]

Gramsci says this in the context of a discussion of the 'fate' of Marxism in Europe in the period of the Second International, and it may be that as the cultural level of the masses is raised, both by changes in bourgeois society itself, such as an expanded educational system, and by the activities of the revolutionary party, the difficulties faced by the working class in this direction would decrease. Yet, in the early 1930s the problems of building an alternative hegemony seemed very great indeed, and the fact that the first socialist state was being created in Russia where 'civil society was primordial and gelatinous'(*SPN*, p. 238) meant that while the Bolsheviks may have been able to achieve State power more easily because the previous ruling class did not enjoy an extended hegemony in the modern sense, the task of building their hegemony was all the greater after State power had been achieved.

Thus State power *per se*, the State understood here in the restricted sense, can have even more importance for the development of the hegemony of the working class in certain circumstances than previously it did for the bourgeoisie. Precisely to the extent that this State power is something more, that it represents a

> movement to create a new civilisation, a new type of man and of citizen, it must serve to determine the will to construct within the husk of political society a complex and well-articulated civil society, in which the individual can govern himself without his self-government thereby entering into conflict with political society — but rather becoming its normal continuation, its organic complement. *SPN*, p. 268.

The historical task of the proletariat is to create a society in which politics in its narrow sense decreases and in which politics in its widest sense, including civil society or 'self-government' becomes the norm. To the extent that this has been less possible before the seizure of power, State institutions may have to assume a particular weight in creating the apparatuses of civil society, of hegemony, of consent which will eventually expand to fill the whole terrain of politics.

> For some social groups, which before their ascent to autonomous State life have not had a long independent period of cultural and moral development on their own . . . a period of statolatry is necessary and indeed opportune. This 'statolatry' is nothing other than the normal form of 'State life', or at least of initiation to autonomous State life and to the creation of a 'civil society' which it was not historically possible to create before the ascent to independent State life. However, this kind of 'statolatry' must not be abandoned to itself, must not, especially, become theoretical fanaticism or be conceived of as 'perpetual'. It must be criticised, precisely in order to develop and produce new forms of State life, in which the initiative of individuals and groups will have a 'State' character, even if it is not due to the 'government of the functionaries' (make State life become 'spontaneous'). *SPN*, pp. 268-9.[2]

Gramsci reformulates part of Lenin's argument in *State and Revolution* based on an expanded notion of the State. The moment of 'smashing the State machinery' does not disappear but the specific significance of State power becomes relative to other factors such as the existence or not of a civil society to bolster the position of the ruling class, and the ability of the working class to create its own hegemony and its own civil society. As an object of the struggle of the working-class, State power is only one step in the process of building a new civilisation in which State coercion will no longer be necessary. But, and this is the crucial point in Gramsci's problematic, there is no 'before' and 'after' in the struggle in the sense that the process of building a new and alternative hegemony or civil society begins before the moment of State power and continues afterward. Taking up themes from his earlier writings, in the *Notebooks*, Gramsci aims to overcome the implicit Second International view of the fall of capitalism and the building of socialism as two separate stages in which the working class, whether in a reformist or a Kautskyian version, can do nothing under capitalism to build a completely new society. In Gramsci's view the political struggle before attaining State power is a struggle for something qualitatively different from bourgeois society. In that sense it is not simply a struggle for reforms which make the present society *evolve* into socialism because the moment of State power, since it provides the class with the maximum potential for hegemonic expansion, is viewed as existing at a qualitatively higher level than previous moments.[3] It is this positive, creative function of the working-class movement in constructing elements of socialism still under capitalism plus the fact that the new State is a new *type* of political power that separates Gramsci's ideas from the underlying problematic of Second International Marxism. While it is true that Kautsky as well as Bernstein maintained that the achievement of reforms played an important role, there is no perspective in the thought of the Second International of the ability of the working class to intervene in such a way that the nature of political power itself would begin to change. In Gramsci's view the socialist State is different because it will allow the working class to create a new mode of production, which for the first time does not imply class divisions, and most importantly a new culture for a socialist man, in which the coercive moment of politics will eventually disappear. Its object is thus fundamentally different from any previous State and it must have a form and a political content suitable to this object.

The two moments of destruction and construction are organically linked at all times in Gramsci's vision of politics and the revolutionary process is portrayed as a struggle by the working class both before and after the revolution; indeed the very meaning of revolution or transformation of a social formation takes on a new dimension. The object of Gramsci's work is the period of transition during which the proletariat is viewed as a class belonging both to capitalist society and potentially a socialist society. It is faced by an opposition, on the other hand, the bourgeoisie, which has an historical role only in the present society.[4]

With regard to the general approach of the Comintern, Gramsci's great originality is that he analysed the way in which the changed relationship between State and society in advanced capitalism provides the possibility for a transformation of politics. We are anticipating the development of our argument somewhat but we would note that the tendency to relegate concrete questions of the nature of socialist political power to a period *after* the socialist revolution is a severe limit of the theoretical and strategic perspectives of both Second *and* Third International Marxism. Gramsci provides indications for rethinking the relationship between the development of a full socialist democracy and changes in capitalism. By posing the question of the *transformation* of politics, he answers those critics of Marxism who maintain that politics in some form can never disappear.

The achievement of State power, then, although only one moment of the revolutionary process, is a crucial step for Gramsci in the building of a new society. The State apparatuses provide the structures for the fullest expansion of the hegemony of a class since only 'after the creation of the new State does the cultural problem impose itself in all its complexity and tend towards a coherent solution' (*SPN*, p. 398). A coherent solution to the cultural problem entails, among other things, the creation of a new *Weltanschauung* which for Gramsci is indeed part of the very definition of the founding of a new State.[5] If the State is to be underpinned by an organic historical bloc, this new *Weltanschauung* must not, however, be restricted to a small *élite* but must be extended to the mass of the population, a cultural reform which Gramsci compares to the Protestant Reformation. In the founding of a new State by the working class, it is Marxism which will provide the theoretical tools for the creation of such a fundamental change in the way in which both different types of intellectuals and the mass of the population will view the world,[6] a transformation rooted in changes in the social relations of production.

Perhaps most significant of all are the indications by Gramsci of the way in which a new culture must be developed once the acquisition of State power gives a class the full potential to do so. Gramsci stresses that the creation of a new culture does not take place spontaneously but must be part of a concerted effort to create new superstructures and new social relations.[7] The revolutionary party thus has a very important task in this regard after the revolution. Yet, and this is also of great consequence, the cultural struggle is waged in different ways in different moments of the revolutionary process and therefore the cultural battle must avoid any schematism by being rooted in an understanding of the complexity of different phases of this process. Once State power is achieved, the full range of superstructures must be extended, with the aid of tools provided by a still higher development in the field of theory, a development required by the new tasks confronting the working class movement.[8]

Gramsci is arguing against a spontaneist and economistic view of the building of socialism. He specifies that no cultural reform is possible without an economic reform which he describes as the concrete mode in which every intellectual and moral reform presents itself, and the content and form of the new superstructures must be developed in reference to the new social relations of production.[9] But the creation of new superstructures which will form an 'historic bloc' with the economic base cannot be left to a spontaneous sporadic occurrence,[10] or the new superstructures which will form an 'historic bloc' with the economic base cannot be left to a spontaneous sporadic occurrence,[10] or the cultural hegemony has not been able to expand fully and whose struggle on the cultural level has been a predominantly critical one will now be able to move forward to an even more positive, creative stage. But the content and form of this stage cannot be predetermined before the problem is *real* or concrete; no blueprints can be drawn before the concrete possibilities appear.

It is true that no type of State can avoid passing through a phase of economic-corporate primitivism, it may be deducted that the content of the political hegemony of the new social group which has founded the new type of State must be predominantly of an economic order: what is involved is the reorganisation of the structure and the real relations between men on the one hand and the world of the economy or of production on the other. The superstructural elements will inevitably be few in number, and have a character of foresight and of struggle, but as yet few 'planned' elements. Cultural policy will above all be negative, a critique of the past; it will be aimed at erasing from the memory and at destroying. The lines of construction will as yet be 'broad lines', sketches, which might (and should) be changed at all times, so as to be consistent with the new structure as it is formed. *SPN*, pp. 263-4.

In the first instance the new State founded by the working class will be founded on consent which is as widespread as possible but its hegemony is necessarily limited. After taking State power, the cultural struggle, which existed before but which cannot develop fully before the moment of State power, must move forward alongside the changes in the economic base so that the area of hegemony can expand to the fullest degree possible and weld together a new historical bloc based on a new *Weltanschauung*. This in turn will actually provide the conditions for the complete transformation of the economic base as the relationship between State and society, and State and economy, already changing in the period of monopoly capitalism, according to Gramsci, is transformed. Thus Gramsci gives a particular meaning to the moment of State power within what is a *process* of revolution which begins before and continues afterward. The binomial destruction-construction is always present within his vision, and the very meaning of revolution or the transformation of a social formation takes on a new dimension.

6. The Organisers of Hegemony: the Intellectuals

While Gramsci's interest in intellectuals may seem an obvious extension of an interest in culture which goes back to his earliest political activities in Turin, his investigation of intellectuals in prison is on a higher level of theoretical generalisation, remaining, however, intimately linked to the study of the concrete Italian historical bloc.[1] In this study, which Gramsci had begun in *The Southern Question*, Gramsci analysed the way in which the political rule and the hegemony of a class in an historical bloc was concretely articulated, was concretely organised.[2] Gramsci examined the question of the role of the intellectuals as part of his attempts to understand the real unity of base and superstructure. The connecting fibres within and between areas of social reality are provided, according to Gramsci, by the intellectuals, defined in a particular way, implying a particular notion of intellectual.

By 'intellectuals' must be understood not those strata commonly described by this term, but in general the entire social stratum which exercises *an organisational function* in the wide sense — whether in the field of production, or in that of culture, or in that of political administration. They correspond to the NCOs and junior officers in the army, and also partly to the higher officers who have risen from the ranks. *SPN*, p. 97. [My emphasis.]

The intellectuals therefore have a role in all levels of society, not merely in spheres which are explicitly cultural, in the economic base and in both civil society and political society in the restricted sense.

In this analysis we find a very special definition of intellectual and at the same time discover that for Gramsci the various apparatuses of society can serve a multitude of functions. The *methodological*, rather than *real*, differentiation between civil and political society becomes clearer. The State apparatuses in the extended sense provide the site of both the element of coercion and also of that of hegemony. The area of culture in civil society is perhaps more obvious while the terrain of production can be the direct source of elements of the superstructure. Ideologies, as furthered and embodied in the hegemonic apparatuses, organise society.[3]

Gramsci established a particular framework for the discussion of the intellectuals in order to highlight the mystification of their role by such thinkers as Croce, who, he argued, continued a tradition going back to Plato and culminating in Hegel. This tradition assigned a special social position to the intellectuals who are presented as a new kind of 'State aristocracy'.[4] In this idealist view the intellectuals were considered to exist above and outside the realm of the relations of production. Gramsci was concerned to determine the nature of what was a very real but also a very mediated relationship.[5] At the same time, his work was also aimed against the lack of comprehension in the socialist movement, based on an economistic interpretation of reality, of the social and political roles of intellectuals.

The answer to the question whether the intellectuals are 'an autonomous and independent social group' or whether 'each group (has) its own particular specialized category of intellectuals' (*SPN*, p. 3) is to be found, according to Gramsci, not by the intrinsic nature of intellectual activities *per se* but from the position these activities occupy 'in the ensemble of the system of relations in which these activities (and therefore the intellectual groups who personify them) have their place within the general complex of social relations'. (*SPN*, p. 8.) Gramsci explains that a worker is defined as such not because he might undertake predominantly manual labour but because whatever labour he undertakes, and he maintains that there is always some component of mental labour, it is within certain conditions and certain social relations. On the other hand, the capitalist, he says, may either personally embody and carry out certain intellectual functions or hire someone else to furnish those which he needs. The fact remains that his role is not defined by these but by his place in the social relations of production. It is in this sense that 'all men are intellectuals . . . but not all men have in society the function of intellectuals.' (*SPN*, p. 9.) On the one hand Gramsci attempts to demystify intellectual activity *per se* and on the other he assigns it a specific place and importance within the complex of social relations, thus arguing both against an idealist tradition and an economistic one.

What then is the position of the intellectuals 'in the general complex of social relations'? They occupy, in fact, a variety of positions which are different 'distances' from the economic base. However involved they may be in the world of production (such as technicians or managers), their relationship, unlike that of either the capitalist class or the proletariat, is always mediated to a greater or lesser extent. Within the realm of the superstructure, the intellectuals perform 'organisational and connective' (*SPN*, p. 12) functions within *both* the area of civil society or hegemony *and* the area of political society or the State.

> The intellectuals are the dominant group's 'deputies' exercising the subaltern functions of *social hegemony and political government*. These comprise:
>   1. The 'spontaneous' consent given by the great masses of the population to the general direction imposed on social life by the dominant fundamental group; this consent is 'historically' caused by the prestige (and consequent confidence) which the dominant group enjoys because of its position and function in the world of production.
>   2. The apparatus of state coercive power which 'legally' enforces discipline on those groups who do not 'consent' either actively or passively. This apparatus is, however, constituted for the whole of society in anticipation of moments of crisis of command and direction when spontaneous consent has weakened. *SPN*, p. 12. [My emphasis.]

Posing the problem in this way does indeed have 'as a result a considerable extension of the concept of intellectual, but it is the only way which enables one to reach a concrete approximation of reality'. (*SPN*, p. 12.) Not only is the word intellectual applied within civil society to such groups as school teachers or journalists as well as to university professors but also to a whole range of positions in political society from the lowest state official, perhaps the clerk in the local government office, to the highest civil servant. By defining intellectuals in terms of 'the entire social stratum which exercises an organisational function in the

wide sense – whether in the field of production, or that of culture, or in
that of political administration' (*SPN*, p. 97) all these strata must be included.

The other attribute which the different types of intellectuals have in
common, in addition to the kind of functions they perform in different
positions in society, is the fact that they find themselves in a mediated
relationship to the world of production, in Gramsci's terms, and as we
shall see in a moment, in different kinds of relationships to the different
classes in society. It is this relative autonomy which links them together
and which has particular political consequences for it represents an area
of potential political space within which a revolutionary party can work
if it has a strategy which takes account of these strata. It is significant
that Gramsci does not use the term petty bourgeoisie in this regard, differentiating these groups from those engaged in the petty bourgeois
mode of production.

An outstanding feature of Gramsci's analysis of the role and position
of intellectuals in modern society is its complexity and its constant reference to an examination of a concrete reality. This complexity can
only be rendered by a multi-dimensional analysis. The first dimension
refers to a type of categorisation which can be applied to any social
reality. But even at this level of abstraction, when Gramsci speaks of
'organic' and 'traditional' intellectuals, he is very conscious of the
dangers of schematisation and the need for a concrete historical analysis.[6]
The second dimension concerns the differences in the position of urban
and rural intellectuals. Although this discussion is presented in the *Notebooks* in general terms, it is rooted very much in an examination of the
Italian social formation, and his discussion of other historical examples
is almost entirely in terms of the organic-traditional dimension. When
we attempt to join these two dimensions together, the picture is indeed
complex.

In terms of theoretical differentiation, the most important of the
variety of forms of intellectuals are the organic and the traditional.
Organic intellectuals are the more directly linked to the dominant mode
of production.

> Every social group, coming into existence on the original terrain
> of an essential function in the world of economic production, creates
> together with itself, organically, one or more strata of intellectuals
> which give it homogeneity and an awareness of its own function not
> only in the economic but also in the social and political fields. The
> capitalist entrepreneur creates alongside himself the industrial tech-

nician, the specialist in political economy, the organisers of a new culture, of a new legal system, etc. *SPN*, p. 5.

While some of these organic intellectuals, such as the industrial technicians, provide services for a single or a few capitalists within the productive sphere, and in this sense their activities remain within the realm of the economic-corporative needs of the capitalist class, this class must at the same time select other intellectuals with

> the capacity to be an organiser of society in general, including all its complex organism of services, right up to the state organism, because of the need to create the conditions most favourable to the expansion of their own class; or at the least they must possess the capacity to choose the deputies (specialised employees) to whom to entrust this activity of organising the general system of relationships external to the business itself. *SPN*, pp. 5-6.

What are the elements here which define certain groups of intellectuals as organic? First of all, they belong as a category to the same historical time as a new class which creates and elaborates them. Secondly, these intellectuals give this class 'homogeneity and an awareness of its own function not only in the economic but also in the social and political fields'. (*SPN*, p. 5.) That is, they perform a particular function in all areas of social reality.[7] Yet, a few paragraphs further on in the same note in a passage which was added to the original and which indicates further elaboration on his part,[8] Gramsci also writes:

> It should be possible to measure the 'organic quality' [*organicità*] of the various intellectual strata, their degree of connection with a fundamental social group, establishing a gradation of their functions and of the superstructures from the bottom to the top (from the structural base upwards). *SPN*, p. 12.[9]

This follows a sentence which explains that the relationship between intellectuals and the world of production, 'is not as direct as it is with the fundamental social groups but is, in varying degrees, "mediated" by the whole fabric of society and by the complex of superstructures, of which the intellectuals are, precisely, the "functionaries".' (*SPN*, p. 12.)

Reflecting the changes in the relationship between structure and superstructure in the period of monopoly capitalism this passage implies that there is a range of 'organicity' depending on where in the super-

structure the intellectual finds himself. Whereas the capitalist class and
the proletariat, 'the fundamental classes', are related directly to the
mode of production, the function of the intellectuals is always considered superstructural even though it may be relatively nearer or farther
from the structural base. Gramsci adds here a syncronic view to what
was previously a diachronic one. In this second schema, it is not the
historical time which indicates the organic nature of an intellectual but
his function and its place in the superstructure. In what may not overcome what seems to be a contradiction in Gramsci's concept, we shall
consider in a moment how this schema relates to the second important
form in which intellectuals appear in a concrete social formation, as
traditional intellectuals.

Yet, before moving on to this, there is still another dimension to
Gramsci's discussion which may help to clarify his position. Although
it is often overlooked, Gramsci assigns as much an *organisational* function
as an *ideological* one in any narrow sense to the intellectuals. Or, in other
terms, he stresses the organisational aspect of ideology. At the same time
this function is seen as a *technical* one. The influence of the *Ordine
Nuovo* period and Gramsci's interest in the varied aspects of the world
of production as an economic sphere which is never simply reduced to
the economic but also embodies aspects of the superstructure is apparent
both when he discusses the organic intellectuals of the capitalist class
and the organic intellectuals to be created by the proletariat. Thus, for
example, the capitalist himself, or someone in his stead, must have 'a
certain directive and technical (i.e. intellectual) capacity'. (*SPN*, p. 5.)
In fact Gramsci actually defines the organic intellectuals in terms of
organisational activity and technical specialisation. In a sentence which
portrays intellectual functions as a result of the division of labour, rather
like workers or technicians, Gramsci explains:

> It can be observed that the 'organic' intellectuals which every new
> class creates alongside itself and elaborates in the course of its develop-
> ment, are for the most part 'specialisations' of partial aspects of the
> primitive activity of the new social type which the new class has
> brought into prominence. *SPN*, p. 6.

Organic intellectuals are specialists who fulfill technical, directive, organisational needs.

This particular description of the organic intellectuals must be connected to another note in which Gramsci discusses the kind of organic
intellectuals which must be produced by the working class. The difference

between intellectuals and non-intellectuals, he says, is not an intrinsic one but depends on their 'immediate social function',

> that is, one has in mind the direction in which their specific profes-
> sional activity is weighted, whether towards intellectual elaboration
> or towards muscular-nervous effort. This means that, although one
> can speak of intellectuals, one cannot speak of non-intellectuals,
> because non-intellectuals do not exist. But even the relationship
> between efforts of intellectual-cerebral elaboration and muscular-
> nervous effort is not always the same, so that there are varying
> degrees of specific intellectual activity. There is no human activity
> from which every form of intellectual participation can be excluded:
> *homo faber* cannot be separated from *homo sapiens. SPN*, p. 9.

It is on the basis of recognising this that the organic intellectuals of the working class must be formed. But, here, Gramsci argues for a fundamental change in the nature of these intellectuals compared to the organic intellectuals of the bourgeoisie, and this change has to do with the relationship to the world of production.

> The problem of creating a new stratum of intellectuals consists
> therefore in the critical elaboration of the intellectual activity that
> exists in everyone at a certain degree of development, modifying its
> relationship with the muscular-nervous effort towards a new equili-
> brium, and ensuring that the muscular-nervous effort itself, in so far
> as it is an element of a general practical activity, which is perpetually
> innovating the physical and social world, becomes the foundation of
> a new and integral conception of the world. *SPN*, p. 9.[10]

The new intellectual performs ideological and organisational functions based on a practical intervention to change the real world. It is this con-crete activity which is the foundation of the elaboration of a philosophy which is a new and integral conception of the world. A new type of training is necessary for a new type of organic intellectual.

> The traditional and vulgarised type of the intellectual is given by the
> man of letters, the philosopher, the artist. Therefore journalists, who
> claim to be men of letters, philosophers, artists, also regard themselves
> as the 'true' intellectuals. In the modern world, technical education, close-
> ly bound to industrial labour even at the most primitive and unqualified
> level, must form the basis of the new type of intellectual. *SPN*, p. 9.

He goes on to describe the new intellectuals.

> The mode of being of the new intellectual can no longer consist in eloquence, which is an exterior and momentary mover of feelings and passions, but in active participation in *practical life, as constructor, organiser, 'permanent persuader' and not just a simple orator* (but superior at the same time to the abstract mathematical spirit); from technique-as-work one proceeds to technique-as-science and to the humanistic conception of history, without which one remains 'specialised' and does not become *'directive' (specialised and political). SPN*, p. 10. [My emphasis.]

The organic intellectuals of the working class have a quite different relationship to the world of production, and the relationship between the concrete needs of a class and their theoretical elaboration of these needs is completely changed in comparison with the functioning of previous organic intellectuals. While the nature of the development from 'technique-as-work' to 'technique-as-science' is not elaborated here, it is only when the higher form is reached that a *hegemonic* expression is achieved, that is, the organic intellectual becomes '"directive" (specialised and political)'. This can also be related to Gramsci's concept of the historical bloc, for the link between base and superstructure is made organic by the activity of the intellectuals. And in this sense, the 'closer' to the sphere of production, the more organic are the function of the intellectuals.

Gramsci's argument here is not that the capitalist class does not have organic intellectuals closely involved in the sphere of production. Indeed, as we shall see in a moment, the industrial technicians are examples of organic intellectuals of the bourgeoisie. Nor, in following this line of discussion, do we reject the organic relationship between, say, intellectuals in the State machine or the upper echelons of the academic world. Gramsci is still arguing that these functions are organic. But the nature of the link is different for the bourgeoisie and the proletariat. What we can infer here is that the relationship between the organic intellectuals of the proletariat in the various realms of the superstructure and the economic base must be a *more* organic one throughout than is the case for the bourgeoisie. While the precise formulation of the relationship of 'technique' to 'science' may be criticised, the nature of the 'organicity' of the new intellectuals which Gramsci is describing can still stand as an indication of the type of organic intellectuals which the proletariat needs. We shall return to his point when we discuss the elaboration of organic intellectuals by the revolutionary party.

We now turn to another category of intellectuals which Gramsci discusses, the traditional intellectuals.

> every 'essential' social group which emerges into history out of the preceding economic structure, and as an expression of a development of this structure, has found (at least in all of history up to the present) categories of intellectuals already in existence and which seemed indeed to represent an historical continuity uninterrupted even by the most complicated and radical changes in political and social forms. *SPN*, pp. 6-7.

An example of this traditional intellectual was the clergy which had been organically linked, Gramsci argues, to the aristocracy,[11] or philosophers like Croce and Gentile who appeared part of an intellectual tradition unconnected with a particular mode of production or indeed a single social formation. What marks these groups of intellectuals as traditional is the fact that they belong to a different historical time from the organic intellectuals created by the new class. Some of the traditional intellectuals had an earlier organic link with a previous dominant class, and they *appear* to be part of an historical continuity.

Yet, according to Gramsci, both the clergy and Croce and Gentile have a very real function with regards to a concrete historical bloc in which the capitalistic mode of production is dominant.[12] The fact that functions organic to one class can be undertaken by intellectuals who were organic to a previous dominant class or who *appear* in this universalistic form as traditional intellectuals has important consequences for their *political* role.[13] If we connect this with the range of organicity related to the proximity in a schematic sense to the structure, we can better understand the *appearance* of neutrality of the superstructures. A category of intellectuals may have a history as organic to one class, such as the feudal aristocracy. If this class still exists in the sense that the feudal mode of production survives, albeit in a subordinate rather than dominant form, these intellectuals can still provide an organic function in terms of the feudal class. At the same moment, these intellectuals can appear as traditional *vis à vis* a new dominant class. To the extent that this new class 'wins them over'[14] they can serve a different, organic function for the new dominant class. In an argument related to the theme of passive revolution, the task of the working class in this regard is qualitatively new. The working class must transform the very mode of existence of these intellectuals as it wins them to a new type of society. It cannot simply instrumentalise them.

But how does this apply to a 'real historical process'? When we examine a concrete social reality, a concrete historical bloc, we find that 'the elaboration of intellectual strata in concrete reality does not take place on the terrain of abstract democracy but in accordance with very concrete historical processes' (*SPN*, p. 11) and we reach a second, particularly Italian dimension to Gramsci's discussion in the *Notebooks*, the different position of urban and rural intellectuals.[15] In the Italian situation this coincides with geographical and economic differences. Gramsci is interested in the different types of intellectuals produced by the bourgeoisie in the northern industrial cities and by the southern 'rural bourgeoisie', some of whom may live in cities in the south but who are part of a very different tradition.[16] This concrete analysis is rooted in Gramsci's earlier works, best exemplified by *Some Aspects of the Southern Question*, and demonstrates his sensitivity to the manifold political nuances of the large variety of social and economic strata in an extremely differentiated social reality. The different political roles which intellectuals have depend on their very different social positions within a particular social structure. The political consequences of these differences are extremely important for a political party which is trying to create a strategy and tactics. In his concrete analysis of a concrete situation Gramsci is seeking to discover the specificity of the complex position of different strata within a concrete historical bloc in order to avoid facile and undialectical generalisation.

With regard to the northern cities, Gramsci notes:

> Intellectuals of the urban type have grown up along with industry and are linked to its fortunes. Their function can be compared to that of subaltern officers in the army. *They have no autonomous initiative* in elaborating plans for construction. Their job is to articulate the relationship between the entrepreneur and the instrumental mass and to carry out the immediate execution of the production plan decided by the industrial general staff, controlling the elementary stages of work. *SPN*, p. 14. [My emphasis.]

The fact that these strata perform their intellectual functions so close to an economic base, to a base which is part of the capitalistic mode, and that they have 'no autonomous initiative' in the course of their duties is of political consequence as we shall see in a moment.

The situation of the southern rural intellectuals[17] is much more complicated.

Intellectuals of the rural type are for the most part 'traditional', that is they are linked to the social mass of country people and the town (particularly small-town) petite bourgeoisie, *not as yet elaborated and set in motion by the capitalist system.* This type of intellectual brings into contact the peasant masses with the local and state administration (lawyers, notaries, etc.). Because of this activity they have *an important politico-social function*, since professional mediation is difficult to separate from political. *SPN*, p. 14. [My emphasis.]

There are several different elements here. These intellectuals are considered traditional from a particular point of view, from the point of view of the dominant, capitalistic mode of production. They are still linked to a world which is pre-capitalist. In this terrain they weld together a sub-bloc which has its own particular coherence.[18] Although they are traditional *vis à vis* the dominant bloc, they can at the same time have *organic* links to surviving pre-capitalist modes and classes. They live, as it were, in two different historical times.

This becomes clearer when we consider that in Italy there is yet another dimension: 'in Italy the rural bourgeoisie produces in particular state functionaries and professional people, whereas the urban bourgeoisie[19] produces technicians for industry.' (*SPN*, p. 12.) The central state machinery is predominantly populated by intellectuals produced in the south. These intellectuals perform functions within the political superstructure which exists in an historical bloc made up of different sub-blocs one of which is dominant at the economic level, the northern industrial bloc. Therefore, in what is a very mediated way, among their functions, these intellectuals produced by the southern rural bourgeoisie supply the capitalist class at the level of the State machinery, 'the capacity to be an organiser of society in general, including all its complex organism of services, right up to the state organism, because of the need to create the conditions most favourable to the expansion of their own class'. (*SPN*, pp. 5-6.) The position of these intellectuals is multi-faceted because they also serve to bind together the whole historical bloc.

There is a further aspect to the position of some traditional southern intellectuals:

Over and above the agrarian bloc, there functions in the South an intellectual bloc which in practice has so far served to prevent the cracks in the agrarian bloc becoming too dangerous and causing a landslide. Giustino Fortunato and Benedetto Croce are the exponents of this intellectual bloc, and they can thus be considered as the most active reactionaries of the whole peninsula. *PWII*, p. 459.

This hegemonic role with regards to the southern agrarian bloc had, in the case of Croce, consequences for the historical bloc as a whole. Not only did he help to prevent the crumbling of the southern bloc, but he helped to weld it to the rest of the historical bloc through his mediating influence on young, radical southern intellectuals.

In this sense, Benedetto Croce has fulfilled an extremely important 'national' function. He has detached the radical intellectuals of the South from the peasant masses, forcing them to take part in national and European culture; and through this culture, he has secured their absorption by the national bourgeoisie and hence by the agrarian bloc. *PWII*, p. 460.

Another important element in this already extremely complex picture of the position of the various intellectual strata in Italy has to do with their relationship to what Gramsci calls 'the instrumental mass', the peasants in the south and the working class in the north. The southern intellectuals have a very real political influence over the peasants which comes partly from their professional activities and partly from their higher standard of living so that they serve as a model for the social aspirations of the peasantry.

One can understand nothing of the collective life of the peasantry and of the germs and ferments of development which exist within it, if one does not take into consideration and examine concretely and in depth this effective subordination to the intellectuals. Every organic development of the peasant masses, up to a certain point, is linked to and depends on movements among the intellectuals. *SPN*, pp. 14-15.

The relationship between the urban intellectuals and the working class with which they are in contact is quite different.

Factory technicians do not exercise any political function over the instrumental masses, or at least this is a phase that has been superseded. Sometimes, rather, the contrary takes place, and the instrumental masses, at least in the person of their own organic intellectuals, exercise a political influence on the technicians. *SPN*, p. 15.[20]

The political subordination of the peasants is part of the extreme difficulty this class has in developing an organic, autonomous role.[21] On the other hand, the working class can itself exercise an autonomous political influence on the intellectuals of the industrial north through the creation of their own organic intellectuals, with the help of their political party. The struggle of the working class to establish its hegemony takes place on a terrain which is more favourable. The activities of the party in establishing this hegemony in the nation as a whole will, however, have to take account of all facets of this very complex social reality, one part of which has to do with the particular type of subordination of the peasantry.

7. Intellectuals and the Political Party

The most interesting problem in this context according to Gramsci is 'the modern political party, its real origins, its developments and the forms it takes'. (*SPN*, p. 15.) Gramsci is careful to distinguish the way in which the role of the political party is different for the different classes in society. In a passage which he added when he redrafted an earlier version,[1] he wrote:

> The political party for some social groups is nothing other than their specific way of elaborating their own category of organic intellectuals directly in the political and philosophical field and not just in the field of productive technique. These intellectuals are formed in this way and cannot indeed be formed in any other way, given the general character and the conditions of formation, life and development of the social group. *SPN*, p. 15.

Just as the Partito d'Azione could only have exercised a hegemonic influence over large numbers of intellectuals through a political party so the working class can only develop its organic intellectuals in the philosophical and political fields through its political party. In the field of production it is able to create certain categories of intellectuals,[2] but it must have a political party if it is to form intellectuals who are trained for the various areas of an alternative superstructure. Implicit here is a recognition of one of the limits of the problematic of the factory council period, in that Gramsci specifies that the working class is able to do so much but no more within the productive sphere in developing an alternative hegemony. An important aspect of the development in his ideas on the revolutionary party in prison is that he portrays much more clearly the *specific* role of the party in articulating the hegemony of the working-class movement. Whereas the origins of the concept of the hegemonic task of the working class can be found in Gramsci's articles in the *Ordine Nuovo*, and a certain further development of his ideas on the need for the party to create an adequate strategy is evident in 1923-6, in the *Notebooks* the crucial role of the party in developing the organic intellectuals of the working-class movement comes to the fore. It is linked to earlier themes by Gramsci's insistence that the link between the proletariat's organic intellectuals and the masses must be qualitatively new, a dimension of Gramsci's work which is related to his discussion of the passive revolution which we consider below. It is not accidental, we would argue, that the discussion of the intellectuals in prison is so rooted in the relationship between the predominantly industrial north and the agrarian south for it is part of Gramsci's attempt to resolve what were both theoretically and practically unresolved problems of the relationship between workers and peasants in the *Ordine Nuovo* period as we suggest above.

In prison Gramsci insists that for *all* classes

> The political party . . . is precisely the mechanism which carries out in civil society the same function as the State carries out, more synthetically and over a larger scale, in political society. In other words it is responsible for welding together the organic intellectuals of a given group—the dominant one—and the traditional intellectuals. The party carries out this function in strict dependence on its basic function, which is that of elaborating its own component parts— those elements of a social group which has been born and developed as an 'economic' group—and of turning them into qualified political intellectuals, leaders and organisers of all the activities and functions inherent in the organic development of an integral society, both civil and political. *SPN*, pp. 15-16.

In order to understand what Gramsci means here we must extract the various elements found in this passage. Earlier he had written,

> One of the most important characteristics of any group that is developing towards dominance is its struggle to assimilate and to conquer 'ideologically' the traditional intellectuals, but this assimilation and

conquest is made quicker and more efficacious the more the group in question succeeds in simultaneously elaborating its own organic intellectuals. *SPN*, p. 10.

The way in which this is done is different for the different classes in society because of their different relationship to the State. For a class which is already dominant, economically, culturally and politically, the State apparatus welds together this class's organic intellectuals and traditional intellectuals. Not all classes have the 'use' of the State apparatus in this sense. While the dominant class is served by *both* the State in the political sphere *and* the political party in the sphere of civil society, other classes can weld together their own organic intellectuals and traditional intellectuals *only* in civil society where the 'mechanism' or apparatus for doing this is the political party. The party can succeed in this task to the extent that it can elaborate organic intellectuals and help the working class to develop an alternative hegemony involving a transformation of the mode of existence of intellectuals in society as a whole. It is on this basis that it will 'win over' the traditional intellectuals and transform their relationship with the masses.

This fits closely with another order of problems which we have already discussed, for what a party is doing in civil society is either helping to maintain the realm of hegemony of a dominant class parallel to the hegemony established by the State in political society or, in the case of the working class under capitalism, it is fighting for an alternative hegemony without the aid of State apparatus. Thus for the working class the party is the mechanism both for the elaboration of its own organic intellectuals prepared in the ideological and political fields, and it is the mechanism for the establishment of hegemony before it reaches State power. Once it has achieved State power the working class will be able to extend its hegemony as it transforms the State apparatuses. In the meantime it is through the political party that the working class can develop beyond a purely economic-corporative position.

In a statement which both echoes some of his arguments against Bordiga and casts a new light on the Leninist statement that the party must bring theory to the proletariat from the outside, Gramsci explains that however strange it might seem, *all* members of a political party must be considered intellectuals. Even though there will be different levels, what is really important is

the function, which is directive and organisational, i.e. educative, i.e. intellectual. A tradesman does not join a political party in order to do business, nor an industrialist in order to produce more at lower cost, nor a peasant to learn new methods of cultivation . . .

For these purposes, within limits, there exists the professional association, in which the economic-corporative activity of the trades-man, industrialist or peasant is most suitably promoted. In the pol-itical party the elements of an economic social group get beyond that moment of their historical development and become agents of more general activities of a national and international character. *SPN*, p. 16.

The worker who enters the revolutionary party will overcome the limits of his existence in the economic sphere. He will in the Gramscian sense become an intellectual and no longer simply be defined as a producer of surplus value. The party joins together intellectuals who are also work-ers with intellectuals who outside the party come from a variety of pos-itions in society. All of them function as intellectuals within the party so that all of them become something other than simply defined by their individual class background. A function which Gramsci had earlier attributed to the factory council is now given to the party.

Although all members of all parties are intellectuals in the broadest sense, the new intellectuals of the revolutionary party will be different from other intellectuals. As we have suggested above, these new intellect-uals must be able to relate their activities to the concrete situation of the working class in the work place which must be their point of depart-ure.[3] This was the method of the *Ordine Nuovo*. When Gramsci argues that the mode of existence of the new intellectuals will no longer consist in eloquence but in being rooted in the world of production,[4] he indicates the way in which changes in the organisation of knowledge, which will form the basis of a new socialist society, are related to changes in capital-ism. Thus the new intellectual is more than a 'theoretician' although it could be argued that as he also talks about different levels of intellect-uals within the party, it can be assumed that there will be theoretical activity at some level.[5] But he does not specify this. The organic intel-lectual of the working class is a builder, an organiser, a permanent per-suader so that he is able to engage in all aspects of the struggle. He is aware of the complexities of production, he is able to wage the cultural struggle for hegemony, and he is also able to prepare the political struggle which will culminate in the seizure of power. These attributes, developed before the revolution, will serve after the revolution as the tasks of the organic intellectuals continue in all these areas, from the organisation of socialist production to the building of a new culture.

This is the second aspect, for once again the creation of a new intellectual is not left until the seizure of power and the socialisation of the
means of production but already begins in the heart of the old society.[6]

8. The Modern Prince

Understanding society in terms of hegemony, the historical bloc, theoretical and concrete, and the intellectuals in the Gramscian sense informs
the party of its task and the type of organisation needed to fulfill it.
These concepts are used to articulate the complex object of the party:

> In the modern world, a party is such — integrally, and not, as happens,
> a fraction of a larger party — when it is conceived, organised and led
> in ways and in forms such that it will develop integrally *into a State*
> (an integral State, and not into a government technically understood)
> and into a conception of the world. *SPN*, p. 267. [My emphasis.]

Gramsci is very specific about this object, which is not successfully
fulfilled by all parties — the establishment of an integral State, a State
which has a fully developed hegemony in civil society encompassing the
mass of the population and thereby cementing together a strong historical bloc. The example of the successful achievement of this object in a
particular historical period is the French State produced by the French
Revolution in which there was decisive force — Jacobinism. Whereas in
his early writings Gramsci emphasised the élitist and authoritarian nature
of Jacobinism the aspect which Gramsci stresses above all else in the
Notebooks is the popular nature of the hegemony established by the
Jacobins, 'Which in other nations awakened and organised the national-
popular collective will, and founded the modern States'. (*SPN*, p. 131.)
This change in interpretation of Jacobinism parallels his new understanding of the nature of the modes of constitution of the rule of the bourgeoisie, a rule which is most progressive and most expansive when it rests
on an organised national collective will.

Although expressed in an idealist style reminiscent of his early writings, Gramsci specifies that he intends a particular definition of a collective, political will, 'will as operative awareness of historical necessity, as
protagonist, of a real and effective historical drama'. (*SPN*, p. 130.) This
is organised, collective human activity intervening in the historical process
where certain material conditions exist. He specified further,

An historical act can only be performed by 'collective man', and this presupposes the attainment of a 'cultural-social' unity through which a multiplicity of dispersed wills, with heterogeneous aims, are welded together with a single aim, on the basis of an equal and common conception of the world. *SPN*, p. 349.

None the less collective will is a rather vague term which we shall try to clarify by examining the way in which Gramsci uses it and the way in which it fits in his whole system of thought.

For Gramsci, Machiavelli's *Prince* symbolises precisely 'the process whereby a given collective will . . . is formed'. (*SPN*, p. 125.)[1] What is interesting here is not so much Gramsci's interpretation of Machiavelli *per se*,[2] but the way in which Gramsci finds in Machiavelli the recognition of the need for a popular basis for the foundation of a modern nation-state.[3] Gramsci finds that the aim of Machiavelli's work is parallel to his own.

One may therefore suppose that Machiavelli had in mind 'those who are not in the know', and that it was they who he intended to educate politically. Who therefore is 'not in the know'? The revolutionary class of the time, the Italian 'people' or 'nation'.

It seems clear that Machiavelli wished to persuade these forces of the necessity of having a leader who knew what he wanted and how to obtain it, and of accepting him with enthusiasm even if his actions might conflict or appear to conflict with the generalised ideology of the time — religion.

This position in which Machiavelli found himself politically is repeated today for the philosophy of praxis. *SPN*, pp. 135-6.

It is because of the nature of this process of educating 'those not in the know'[4] and thus creating a collective will and founding a new State that Gramsci argues that in the present period the form of the 'leader' of the 'modern prince' is specifically the revolutionary party,[5] not a trade union as the syndicalists would have it, nor a charismatic figure such as Mussolini. In a two-pronged argument, which contains within it his concept of revolutionary change, Gramsci argues that the activity of a trade union is necessarily 'a "passive activity", so to speak, of a negative and preliminary kind . . . an activity which does not envisage an "active and constructive" phase of its own'. (*SPN*, p. 127.) In fact, it is implicit in Gramsci's argument that even the negative aspect is illusory unless it is understood as an integral part of a process of construction, a

theme going back to his earlier writings. Here Gramsci's argument intersects with his view of revolutionary change as a dialectical process of
destruction-construction, 'destruction and negation cannot exist without
an implicit construction and affirmation . . . as a party programme'.
(*SPN*, p. 129.)

One of the most important unifying concepts in the whole of his
work this is also the prime element in his arguing that a charismatic
leader cannot bring about a revolutionary transformation of society
because he would not be able to organise a new collective will on which
a new State, and new social and national structures, would be based but
could only act in an immediate, limited way to restore the lost cohesion
of an old social order.[6] Specifying this constructive function and thus
differentiating his use of the term 'myth' from that of Sorel, Gramsci
writes:

> The modern prince . . . cannot be a real person, a concrete individual.
> It can only be an organism, a complex element of society in which a
> collective will, which has already been recognized and has to some
> extent asserted itself in action begins to take concrete form. History
> has already provided this organism, and it is the political party – the
> first cell in which there come together germs of a collective will tend-
> ing to become universal and total. *SPN*, p. 129.

Gramsci's concept of a collective will embodied by the revolutionary
party, as opposed to a trade union or a single person, is, it could be argued
a dialectical one. As 'operative awareness of historical necessity' (*SPN*,
p. 130) it is based on material conditions and is already partially in
evidence. It is the political party which represents both the partial existence
of the collective will and its potential of becoming 'universal and total'. It is
'at one and the same time the organiser and the active, operative expression' (*SPN*, p. 133) of this collective will. The relationship of its remaining
merely a potential and its becoming a real historical force depends on the
ability of the party to help the working class to represent the universal
interests of the whole of society.

A condition for the full development of this collective will is, in
Gramsci's view, an intellectual and moral transformation of society. This
is one of the prime tasks of the party.

> The modern Prince must be and cannot but be the proclaimer and
> organiser of an intellectual and moral reform, which also means creat-
> ing the terrain for a subsequent development of the national-popular

collective will towards the realisation of a superior, total form of
modern civilisation. *SPN*, pp. 132-3.

The revolutionary party thus has as its object the creation of the possibility, or the terrain, for the highest development of human activities,
and it is the revolutionary party which, through its political initiative in
a concrete situation, must encompass the full range of these activities.[7]
A fundamental aspect of this intellectual and moral reform is a changed
relationship between the State and the mass of the population in an
extension and redefinition of the concept of democracy, a theme which
we will discuss below.

We can now understand that by collective will Gramsci means the
potential to create a new State and a new historical bloc bound together
by a broadly extended hegemony, which is manifested in a fundamental
change in the world view of the mass of the population and their relationship to the State. This is what the Jacobins accomplished and Machiavelli
failed to achieve, according to Gramsci, and it is the objective of the
revolutionary party.

This brings us to another aspect of Gramsci's interest in Machiavelli.
Gramsci and Machiavelli, unlike many other political theorists, are both
primarily concerned with the problem of how to establish a new State
rather than defining in any detail the exact configuration of this State.
Their work focuses on the problem of how to intervene in a concrete
reality in order to bring about a certain aim.[8] The modern Prince is
not Utopian, according to Gramsci, for it is the organism which links
political initiative with the objective situation in order to change it. It
is this realism, this founding of politics in experience which further
links the two thinkers, and provides a common factor in Gramsci's
interest in both Machiavelli and the Jacobins.[9]

The element which Gramsci emphasises above all else is 'the real
effectiveness of the party, its determining force, positive and negative,
in having contributed to bringing certain events about and in having prevented other events from taking place.' (*SPN*, p. 151.) This ability to
intervene in the concrete situation and to modify it is the background
to any discussion of the form of the party in Gramsci's works. The
organisational form is always a *political* question and is always relative
to the stage of development of the class struggle.

We shall discuss this further, but first let us consider the question,
how in Gramscian terms does a party represent a class? We know from
his discussion of the intellectuals that the class background of the individual members is only one factor which is of only relative importance

because of the functioning of all members of the party as intellectuals. In fact, in Gramsci the word party has a variety of meanings. On the one hand he writes:

> In the modern world, a party is such—integrally, and not, as happens, a fraction of a larger party—when it is conceived, organised and led in ways and in forms such that it will develop integrally into a State (an integral State, and not into a government technically understood) and into a conception of the world. *SPN*, p. 267.

In this sense, the party of the working class is that party which successfully wages the political struggle on the whole range of fronts so that a new State and a new historical bloc is formed under the hegemony of the working class. Yet, he also notes the fact that fractions of parties appear in a variety of guises so that 'fundamental and organic parties' or the capacity of a class to build a State and conduct political activity in the wide sense are not necessarily contained within a single organisation. He maintains, for example, that a newspaper or journals can also have the function of serving as a faction of a party, mentioning the *Times* and the *Corriere della sere.* [10] Here Gramsci's concept of the intellectuals as the organisers of ideas intersects with his view of what can be called a party or has the function of a party.

It is necessary to bear this complex picture in mind in order to understand what Gramsci means when he writes, 'every party is only the nomenclature for a class'. (*SPN*, p. 152.) He specifies, in fact, that even if this is so, 'it is also true that parties are not simply a mechanical and passive expression of the classes themselves, but they act energetically upon them to develop, unite, and universalize them'. (*Q*, p. 387.) He is interested in the relationship and interaction between parties and classes, and the way in which parties do or do not enable a class to fulfill its historic potential.

While he writes, 'every party is the party of a single class' (*Q*, p. 772) he also describes a multitude of parties performing various tasks for a class. This might be understood by maintaining that the policies of a single party at any moment *objectively* represent the interests of a single class. At the same time, this does not mean that each party need represent an entire class. Rather it may well represent only a fraction of a class. Here we must make a distinction, which Gramsci often makes, between the role of a party in the State apparatus in the narrow sense, and the ability of a fundamental class, like the bourgeoisie as a whole, with its many fractions (e.g. industrial bourgeoisie, financial bourgeoisie) to organise its hegemony. This ability to form intellectuals and organise an historical bloc may be fulfilled for the bourgeoisie in a partial way by different parties which reflect the different factions, or it may take place partly even outside any parties because of the ability of the bourgeoisie to use the State apparatus and a number of cultural institutions.[11] There may also be moments when the government function may be undertaken by a party ostensibly serving different class interests[12] or no particular class interests.[13] In this last case the very political function may seem to disappear when there is only one party.[14]

With regards to the working class the situation is different in that Gramsci argues, as we have seen, that it is only through its party that the proletariat can create its organic intellectuals and build its hegemony. Yet does this mean that the party of the working class is totalitarian to the extent that it absorbs the most important activities of this class in the political class struggle because the class is unable to achieve its aims in a partial way through organisms outside the party, such as non-party newspapers or cultural institutions? It is true that the working class is never in the same position to develop autonomously as was the bourgeoisie under feudalism so that the party always remains its chief instrument.[15] We shall consider the position after the achievement of State power later, but we must anticipate our argument slightly. The party of the working class according to Gramsci has the potential to expand enormously so that in the *integral* sense, organised to realise a new hegemony and a new conception of the world, it must unite a whole spectrum of the population having different organisational forms. This unity must be of a particular quality based on a new concept of democracy and going beyond corporative demands to forge a new collective will. The party in its widest sense *assumes* the existence of diversity. At the same time, in creating the organic intellectuals of the working class, it *changes* the relationship between intellectuals and masses so that in entering the terrain of pre-existing cultural and political institutions, it cannot simply use them, as a bourgeois party or parties would, nor can they serve as 'parties' of the working class in a similar way, because the institutions themselves must change if they are to express a new relationship to the mass of the population. In our discussion of the passive revolution and in our conclusion, we will see how the nature of the unity created by the working class in realising its project for a new society and its particular relationship to pre-existing institutions must be qualitatively different from that established in bourgeois society.

But how do we comprehend the variety of ostensibly working class but non-revolutionary parties? Are they fractions of the organic party of the working class? To answer this we must go beyond their claims to speak for the working class. Methodological indications are furnished by Gramsci's analysis of the fascist party in which he distinguishes between the claims of the party, the class base of its membership and those supporting it, and the objective effects of its policies. All of these factors were to be taken into account in order to avoid a simplistic analysis, but the emphasis is definitely on the last. A party is defined as the organic, integral party of a class when it is organised in such a way as to have the capacity to found an integral State and transform the world view of the mass of the population.[16] The fact that Gramsci does not place the Italian Socialist Party in this category needs no re-iteration. But if 'every party is only the nomenclature of a class'.[17] what class or classes do social democratic parties represent? Or indeed other parties which enjoy a mass popular base? The nature of the representation of class interests by a party is an extremely complicated question, not simply for socialist or social democratic parties but also for ostensibly bourgeois parties.

Perhaps the question is better phrased, what is the concrete significance in class terms of a given party at any moment in the class struggle? This is the aspect which is most important to the strategy and tactics of a revolutionary party. The concrete consequences for the various classes and fractions of classes of the activities of a given party in a given conjuncture indicate the way in which a party is to be understood as representing a class or a fraction of a class. The accent must be put above all on the effectiveness of a party. Therefore depending on the role of their activities in a given conjuncture various parties have different concrete meanings for the different classes. In terms of the revolutionary claims of a party, it can be argued that the justification of such claims depends not on abstract rhetoric but on the correctness and effectiveness of a party's strategy and tactics in any concrete situation, with regard to a shift of the balance of forces toward the progressive forces.

But the nature of the membership of a party and the social forces supporting it are also important. In his analysis of fascism and the fascist party, Gramsci takes very seriously the ideological beliefs of the mass base of the party, who act *as if* the party is serving their interests, as well as the objective function of the policies of the party. The answer, therefore, to the question about the way in which a party represents a class is always related to the concrete situation.

The class nature of a party must be seen in dynamic terms. Gramsci argues that in times of crisis a party can both lose its base and die an historical death when the class interests it used to represent come to be represented by another organisation or organisations or when the class itself disappears. A revolutionary party whose practice is incorrect also faces the possibility of losing its class base. Furthermore, when a fundamental change takes place, a revolutionary change, the transition to another social formation, class divisions themselves may begin to disappear.

With regards specifically to a social democratic party, it can be argued that depending on its policies, it may promote the immediate interests, for example, of a fraction of the capitalist class, say manufacturing capital, at the same time as it represents the *corporative* class interests of the working class on the political rather than on the economic terrain. It will not represent the organic, long-term political interests of the working class, to the extent that it does not promote the hegemony of that class in the Gramscian sense, and is unable to intervene politically according to a strategy and tactics correctly designed to transform society, in order to provide the conditions for the eventual elimination of wage slavery. A party represents the political interests of the working class only if it succeeds in promoting a new type of politics, a new type of state based on the protagonism of the masses. The concept of State implicit in the politics of a party is a key measure of a party's ability to lead the working class as it transforms society. A party which merely reproduces a traditional relationship between the State and the mass of the population, even if in different forms, undertakes what Gramsci calls a passive revolution, which we discuss below.

At the same time the revolutionary party can justify its claim to this title and to the representation of the long-term political interests of the working class *only* if its strategy coincides with the interests of other social forces.[18] In other words, its political practice must include the representation of other interests if this is part of a strategy which tends towards the creation of an alternative historical bloc under the hegemony of the working class. It must take account of the national-popular dimension of any revolutionary struggle. The ability of the working class to establish its hegemony is indeed defined in terms of its ability to represent more than its own corporative interests in promoting a universal interest. Yet this implies that the other social forces in this historical bloc unite in such a way that they too are able to go beyond merely corporative demands. This relates to the qualitatively different type of unity established by the working class.

Returning to Gramsci's description of a party as the nomenclature of a class, to what extent does this adequately describe the way in which a party represents a class? We would argue that the phrase itself is not a particularly happy one because it too easily can lead to a reductive notion of the relationship between parties and social forces. While Gramsci's writings in general do not lead to this reduction, it is possible that his lack of experience of the great variety of forms of mass parties which have since developed explains his use of the phrase even though the very development of his ideas carries his ideas beyond it.

Gramsci's discussion of party organisation is thus firmly planted in its role in any particular conjuncture. When he discusses specific aspects of organisation, he has in mind a certain moment in the development of class forces, a moment of harsh struggle under fascist repression when the mere existence of the party required enormous efforts.[19] In a note entitled 'Machiavelli. When one can say a party is formed and cannot be destroyed by normal means',[20] he writes:

> a party is never complete and fully-formed, in the sense that every development creates new tasks and functions, and in the sense that for certain parties the paradox is true that they are complete and fully-formed only when they no longer exist—i.e. when their existence has become historically redundant. Thus, since every party is only the nomenclature for a class, it is obvious that the party which proposes to put an end to class divisions will only achieve complete self-fulfilment when it ceases to exist because classes, and therefore their expressions, no longer exist. *SPN*, pp. 151-2.

Gramsci is specifically concerned with the communist party whose aim it is to create a society in which there are eventually no class divisions and therefore no need for *any* parties, including a communist party. He goes on to say that he wants to examine a particular moment when there are the objective historical conditions but not necessarily the subjective ones for the existence of this party. This moment is defined as, 'When the conditions for its "triumph", for its inevitable progress to State power, are at least in the process of formation.' (*SPN*, p. 152.) Here again we are clearly presented with the State as the object of the existence of the party. But given these material conditions, Gramsci is interested in the structure of the subjective elements which gives the party a permanence such that it cannot be destroyed by 'normal means'. Here he intends anything short of the imprisonment or physical destruction of all leaders of a party.[21]

A party can be said to exist, he writes, when three elements come together. The first is:

> A mass element, composed of ordinary, average men, whose participation takes the form of discipline and loyalty, rather than any creative spirit or organisational ability. Without these the party would not exist, it is true, but it is also true that neither could it exist with these alone. They are a force in so far as there is somebody to centralise, organise and discipline them. In the absence of this cohesive force, they would scatter into an impotent diaspora and vanish into nothing. *Mach*, pp. 23-4.

The rank and file of the party are a necessary but not sufficient element. The disciplinary basis of the activity of these members of the party would seem to contradict Gramsci's other statement that all members of a party are intellectuals.[22] He makes the distinction, however, of different grades of intellectual activities and says that the exact number of different intellectuals is not important. It is rather the fact that in the party all members are agents of the directing and organisational function of the party as a whole. As we shall see, this description of the rank and file is a dynamic one, because Gramsci views the mass of the membership in terms of their potential to develop. Yet we should be clear that the rank and file are not viewed as cadres in the Leninist sense.

> The principal cohesive element, which centralises nationally and renders effective and powerful a complex of forces which left to themselves would count for little or nothing. This element is endowed with great cohesive, centralising and disciplinary powers . . . It is also true that neither could this element form the party alone; however, it could do so more than could the first element considered. One speaks of generals without an army, but in reality it is easier to form an army than to form generals. So much is this true that an already existing army is destroyed if it loses its generals, while the existence of a united group of generals who agree among themselves and have common aims soon creates an army even where none exists. *SPN*, pp. 52-3.

In circumstances in which a communist party is under severe attack and is forced into clandestinity, a unified leadership element is of crucial importance.

Between these two elements is a third one 'an intermediate element, which articulates the first element with the second'. (*SPN*, p. 153.) These are the trained cadres of the party. These cadres, Gramsci suggests, perform not only an organisational function in a narrow sense by 'physically' connecting the leadership with the rank and file, but they also have a specific political role in providing intermediary moral and intellectual leadership.

Gramsci argues that the necessary condition for the prevention of the destruction of the party is the existence of the second element, the leadership, given certain concrete conditions. Gramsci specifies this so that we can be quite clear about his position. He is not talking about a voluntarist leadership unconnected to the material conditions which allow for the real possibility of the creation of a party, that is, the possibility of the establishment of a new State. If this leadership exists, has the correct concept of the State and politics and is rooted in the potential of concrete reality, then a party can be founded.

Gramsci expresses the numerical relationship between these elements in terms of a metaphor drawn from chemistry, 'the theorem of definite proportions'.[23] He cautions that the application of this law to human organisations must not be mechanical because the qualitative element (or that of the technical and intellectual capacity of the individual components) is predominant . . .' (*SPN*, p. 190.) None the less if used metaphorically this law can be used to understand

> how a 'movement' or current of opinion becomes a party—i.e. a political force which is effective from the point of view of the exercise of governmental power: precisely to the extent to which it possesses (has developed within itself) cadres at the various levels, and to the extent to which the latter have acquired certain capabilities. *SPN*, p. 191.

There is a clear emphasis on the leadership element, not just in the sense of preventing the destruction of the party or recreating it once attacked, but in terms of its very ability to intervene effectively in any given situation. Yet the proportion between different elements depends precisely on the 'qualitative' level of the individual components.

> The theorem can be seen in application politically in parties, trade unions or factories. It is also possible to see how each social group has its own law of fixed proportions, which varies according to the level of its culture, independence of mind, spirit of initiative and sense of responsibility, and according to the degree of discipline of its most backward and peripheral members. *SPN*, p. 191.

There are thus no abstract rules of organisation because organisation must always be seen in terms of the concrete situation, in all its complexity, with regards to its potential development. And very importantly, the level of preparation of all the members of the party is given the weight of a material factor within the concrete.

Indeed the efficacy of the second, leadership, element in preventing the destruction of the party is related specifically to its ability to develop cadres in the lower ranks who can become leaders themselves if the existing leadership is destroyed.[24] Gramsci argues that leaders should be judged both by their ongoing political work and by their preparation of their successors. This is completely counterposed to Bordiga's emphasis on the leadership as the depository of orthodoxy against all threats of contamination from a hostile world. Gramsci emphasises above all else the importance of the effectiveness of the party's politics and the development of cadres.

Yet the picture is undeniably one in which Gramsci puts overwhelming importance on the party leadership within the context of his grave concern over the mere survival of the party under fascism. His struggle of will to survive in prison, in a period in which the PCd'I has reached one of its lowest ebbs, must not be ignored.[25] By his own definition his description of the organisational pattern of the party must reflect only one moment of its development. His discussion of the law of definite proportions simply implies that there is a correct ratio between the different elements for every situation.

One thing is clear. Gramsci is not talking about a cadre party. Party cadres mediate between the leadership and the rank and file membership, who are not yet cadres. This leads us to the question of whether Gramsci had in mind a mass party at some moment in history. The only answer we can give is that there is no explicit evidence that he did, but that on the other hand his way of relating his discussion to the development of the situation and the fact that his is not a cadre party makes its development into a mass party conceivable. He thus *allows* for but does not specify a mass party. In fact, the party has the potential to include a very large proportion of society, at least the whole of the class it represents. It has the potential to include 'a whole social group, which itself is conceived of as tending to unify the whole of humanity'. (*Q*, p. 750.)[26] This leaves open the question of the precise boundaries of the party and whether they are so extensive as to leave the definition of the party equivocal.

We therefore cannot arrive at a general theory of party organisation by a reading of Gramsci. This is all the more evident when we turn to his views on the relationship between the three elements inside the party.

9. Democratic Centralism versus Bureaucratic Centralism

The fact that organisational questions must be resolved in terms of a concrete political reality is emphasised by Gramsci's discussion of democratic as opposed to what he calls bureaucratic or organic centralism. This discussion, in fact, tells us very little about the internal organisation of the party in any detail, but a great deal about his concept of the party in general. What is particularly significant are the themes which Gramsci considers to be within the bounds of this discussion. For him the internal functioning of the party is directly connected with a non-mechanical view of history and with an ability by the party to relate constantly to an ever-changing reality. From this comes the possibility of concrete political intervention. This is also the basis for the role which Gramsci portrays for the rank and file of the party and their relationship to the leadership. The reference point for his discussion in prison of this topic is the polemic with Bordiga, and many of the phrases he uses echo very closely the terms of that earlier debate. In Gramsci's experience a mistaken concept of the party could be of tragic consequence for a class, and the failures of the PCd'I in the twenties are his most immed iate terms of reference. Yet, as we know, he was not isolated in his years in prison from developments in the international communist movement. The effects of Stalin's methods on the various communist parties, particularly with regard to the implementation of the Third Period policies, could not help but make Gramsci think that the dogmatism and sectarianism so evident in Bordiga's leadership, a dogmatism and sectarianism rooted in a mechanical and ultimately economistic view of the revolutionary process, were being reproduced on a world-wide scale. Thus, although we do not have enough direct evidence to prove that Stalinisation was the direct object of Gramsci's critique, the fact that he was familiar with changes taking place through discussions with party cadres newly arrived in prison suggests that the appropriateness of these notes for developing such a critique was not accidental.

Democratic centralism, which would normally refer rather narrowly to the internal organisation of the party and the relationship of the rank and file to the leadership, does so in Gramsci's writings only in so far as the whole question of organisation is placed within a vastly wider framework. Gramsci defines democratic centralism as:

> a 'centralism' in movement—i.e. a continual adaptation of the organisation to the real movement, a matching of thrusts from below with orders from above, a continuous insertion of elements thrown up

from the depths of the rank and file into the solid framework of the leadership apparatus which ensures continuity and the regular accumulation of experience. Democratic centralism is 'organic' because on the one hand it takes account of movement, which is the organic mode in which historical reality reveals itself, and does not solidify mechanically into bureaucracy. *SPN*, pp. 188-9.

The dialectical relationship between the moment of spontaneity and the moment of leadership, the emphasis on the need to root the activities of the party deeply within the mass movement go back to Gramsci's experiences at the *Ordine Nuovo*. The fear that the party may become detached from the mass movement was a crucial feature of his debate with Bordiga. The separation between communist parties and the masses they hoped to influence was of course one of the main defects of the Third Period policies. The leadership function of the party is expressed by Gramsci in terms of its ability to create a strategy and tactics which is based on an organic relationship with the mass movement. This organic relationship between party and masses was probably the most problematical aspect of building socialism in the USSR, a problem already considered by Gramsci in his letters of 1926. What we observe, then, is that a discussion of a principle of internal organisation is immediately related to the general political tasks of the party. This is re-emphasised in the following passage.

> Democratic centralism offers an elastic formula, which can be embodied in many diverse forms; it comes alive in so far as it is interpreted and continually adapted to necessity. It consists in the critical pursuit of what is identical in seeming diversity of form and on the other hand of what is distinct and even opposed in apparent uniformity, in order to organise and interconnect closely that which is similar, but in such a way that the organising and the interconnecting appear to be a practical and 'inductive' necessity, experimental, and *not the result of a rationalistic, deductive, abstract process* – i.e. one typical of pure intellectuals (or pure asses). This continuous effort to separate out the 'international' and 'unitary' element in national and local reality is true concrete political action, the sole activity productive of historical progress. *SPN*, pp. 189-90. [My emphasis.]

We will consider the method for determining a strategy and tactics later, but here we should note that it was precisely Bordiga's rationalistic, deductive approach to the application of Marxist theory and his lack of understanding of the correct relationship between the national and international moments of the struggle which were attacked by Gramsci. What is significant is that Gramsci expressed the principle of democratic centralism in these terms. It has nothing to do with an abstract schema of organisation unconnected with the ability of the party to analyse the conjuncture and create 'an organic unity between theory and practice, between intellectual strata and popular masses, between rulers and ruled' (*SPN*, p. 190) or a new relationship between the State and the mass of the population. Counterposed to this view, a dogmatic and schematic interpretation of Lenin's writings on the party became the hallmark of the Stalinist interpretation.

The dangers of the lack of democratic centralism in this wide sense in a particular moment of the class struggle are the object of Gramsci's analysis in a note where he considers the ability of a party to react to a threat of a Bonapartist or fascist solution to a political crisis.[1] He writes that one of the most important questions with regard to the political party has to do with the

> party's capacity to react against force of habit, against the tendency to become mummified and anachronistic. Parties come into existence, and constitute themselves as organisations, in order to influence the situation at moments which are historically vital for their class; but they are not always capable of adapting themselves to new tasks and to new epochs, nor of evolving *pari passu* with the overall relations of force (and hence the relative position of their class) in the country in question, or in the international field. In analysing the development of parties, it is necessary to distinguish: their social group; their mass membership; their bureaucracy and General Staff. The bureaucracy is the most dangerously hidebound and conservative force; if it ends up by constituting a compact body, which stands on its own and feels itself independent of the mass of members, the party ends up by being anachronistic and at moments of acute crisis it is voided of its social content and left as though suspended in mid-air. *SPN*, p. 211.

It was precisely the fact that the PCd'I under Bordiga was detached from reality that made it incapable of maintaining its links with the masses during severe repression by the fascists. It was this separation of the party from the masses which presented the greatest potential danger in the struggle to protect and extend socialism in the Soviet Union. The ability of parties to continue to perform the function for which they exist, 'to influence the situation at moments which are historically vital for their class' (*SPN*, p. 211), depends on their internal organisation, on their democratic centralism in Gramsci's terms. This series of reflections must be related to Gramsci's emphasis in other notes on the leadership element and more specifically on the unity of political will of that element. While this is a primary condition, it is not a sufficient one for the survival of the party as a political force. The leadership element will be successful only in so far as it is able to organise a party along democratic centralist lines.

Gramsci's position with regards to organisational questions becomes even clearer when we consider the way in which he criticises bureaucratic or organic centralism.[2] This type of organisation is based ultimately on a mistaken, mechanical view of historical development,[3] and consequently an incorrect conception of the role of the party. This in turn affects its internal organisation and the content of its politics.[4] The leader of the party is considered to hold a body of dogma which can be applied mechanically to the historical process.[5] The party itself becomes a rigid construct. The application of Gramsci's criticisms to the Stalinist party becomes obvious.

The consequences of Bordiga's view of the party were a rigid centralisation in which individual members applied a dogmatic political line in a mechanical way. Gramsci describes this type of centralism in this way:

> If the constitutive element of an organism is posed in a rigorously and rigidly formulated doctrinaire system, there is a caste-like, priest-like type of leadership. But does 'the guarantee' of immutability still exist? It does not exist. Formula will be recited from memory without changing a single syllable or comma but real activity will be something else. Ideology, doctrine must not be conceived of as something artificial, imposed from above . . . but historically as an incessant struggle. Organic centralism imagines it can create an organism, already objectively perfect, once for all time. An illusion which can be disastrous. *Q*, p. 337.

In what is an ironic comment on Bordiga's ideas but also on Stalin's, Gramsci argues that organic or bureaucratic centralism is more appropriate to the organisation of a church than a revolutionary party. Gramsci often contrasts the two, especially with regards to internal organisation and to the relationship between the organisation and the masses.[6] The Church, Gramsci writes, encourages the idea that as an organisation it transcends its individual members. Applied to a political party, this 'fetishistic' attitude to organisation has a very real political result. The organisation falls into passivity as the activity of individual members is paralysed, partly because it seems as if the organisation exists despite the individual, and partly because there is a great fear that the organisation will crumble if there is democratic discussion and debate with it.[7]

The fact that the party cannot be conceived in terms of some type of objective perfection and that indeed 'a party is never complete and fully formed, in the sense that 'every development creates new tasks and functions' (*SPN*, p. 151) means that in Gramsci's conception the only principle of organisation is the ability of the party to relate to the on-going historical process. This in turn implies an ability to analyse the concrete situation, to create a strategy and tactics demanded by that analysis, and to develop continually rank-and-file members to enable them to apply this strategy and tactics creatively in every new situation, that is, to create a new relationship between the individual and reality. In order for the party to be organised along the correct lines, a proper relationship between theory and practice must replace a dogmatic conception of Marxism. Only in this way will the party be able to intervene successfully in history. Gramsci's conception of the party is an attempt to overcome the voluntarist-mechanistic problematic that constituted the basis of the Second International view of the role of the party, an object of his work since his earliest political activities and now a task all the more urgent because of the reproduction of the errors stemming from this problematic by the Comintern.

All of this has very real implications for the internal relations of the party. Gramsci's writing on organisation becomes the basis of a *method* of politics both in terms of the relationship between the party and the rest of society and in terms of the ethos within the party itself. We arrive at a theoretical argument for the need for an active preparation of all members as 'intellectuals' which can serve to prevent the party from becoming rigid, anachronistic, unable to fulfil its function. This function is to help the working class to construct a new type of State based on an intellectual and moral reform, a reform implying the transformation of politics itself. This reform must begin within the party itself. This is the basis for constructing an organisation which is democratic in what he considers the fullest sense of the word,[8] in which all members are able to take an active part in discussion and carry out policy creatively because this activity is seen to be *intrinsically* necessary to the role of the party. The active, direct participation and consent of individual party members is absolutely vital, and it can only come after full discussion in which differences and disagreements must be brought into

the open to be resolved.[19] Gramsci's discussion of internal party organisation is rooted in his attempt to suggest a new relationship between
leaders and led in society at large.

The preparation and education of party members cannot itself be
schematic within Gramsci's logic because there are no rigid organisational or doctrinal formulae. It is an incessant struggle to prevent 'dop-
piezza',[10] or the coexistence of a political line of the party, which is
not fully understood by the rank and file, with rank and file activities
which bear no resemblance to this line. Thus the very unity of the party
comes about by the active development and participation of all members
who do not merely apply mechanical orders but intervene creatively to
apply a strategy and tactics which they fully understand. At the same
time the strategy and tactics of the party and indeed the general political
line is also a result of an analysis of the experience of the rank and file.
It is the rank and file which provides the links with the mass movement
and with what is an ever-changing and contradictory reality. The cost of
not building the party on this democratic basis is its degeneration into
bureaucratic centralism with all that this implies. This kind of degeneration can take place, Gramsci writes, when there is a 'lack of initiative
and responsibility at the bottom, in other words, because of the political
immaturity of the peripheral forces'. (*SPN*, p. 189.) What is interesting
here is that while Gramsci is not arguing for a cadre party, he is at the
same time arguing against the situation in certain contemporary mass
parties in which the mass of members is connected to the leadership
through a generic loyalty, and these members are there simply to be
manoeuvred without a role of their own.[11]

The need for all members of the party to be intellectuals and for the
party to be organised with reference to his conception of democratic
centralism is the basis of Gramsci's argument against the veracity of
Michels 'iron law of oligarchy'. A democratic organisation of the party
is possible but only if it is conceived in certain ways:

> questions of democracy and oligarchy have a precise meaning which
> is derived from a class difference between leaders and followers: the
> question becomes *political*, that is, it acquires a real value and is no
> longer a matter of sociological schematism when there is a class divi-
> sion in the organization. This has happened in the trade unions and
> in the social democratic parties. If there is no class division, the question
> becomes purely *technical* (the orchestra does not think that its director
> is an oligarchic boss) *of division of labour and of education.* That is,
> centralization must take account of the fact that in popular parties

education and political 'apprenticeships' in very large part take place through *the participation of the followers in the intellectual life (discussions) and organization of the parties.* The solution of the problem, which is complicated precisely because of the fact that the intellectuals have such a large function in advanced parties, can be found in the formation of an intermediate stratum, as numerous as possible, between the leaders and followers, which can serve as a balance to prevent the leaders *from deviating in moments of radical crisis and to elevate continually the mass of members. Q*, pp. 236-7.[12] [My emphasis.]

The best way of understanding what Gramsci means here is to examine it within the context of this passage where he is arguing that oligarchy need not arise, if the division between the rank and file is considered a functional one, based on a division of labour rather than a fundamental and static division between two groups, who are considered intrinsically and innately different, as if the difference were between two classes. The question of an oligarchy arising is placed by Gramsci within a political rather than an abstract, schematic context. It depends on the method, the orientation, the correct theoretical understanding of the way in which the party should function. Thus the democratic nature of the party is intimately entwined with the fulfillment by the party of its historical function, a function which is defined by Gramsci in terms of founding a new type pf state in which those barriers between leaders and led which are not simply 'technical' but reflect class divisions are abolished. The party must create a new kind of network of relationships which go beyond those instituted between leaders and led in bourgeois society. To the extent that this was not done the intellectual and moral reform implicit in the building of socialism was not undertaken, and old forms of politics were merely reproduced. A criticism of the bourgeois mode of politics and of Bordiga's position intersect with a critique of Stalinism.

It can be argued that oligarchy in the party has the consequence in fact that the rank and file are less prepared to carry out active political initiatives because there is a split between the base and the leadership. This is the context within which the need for unity and discipline must be understood. Discussion and debate are necessary in very real political terms to prevent the rise of oligarchy and at the same time to provide the basis for a true unity of purpose, a true collective will.[13] It is significant that Gramsci suggests that the leadership is prevented from deviations, not by requiring them to hold a dogma, or by guarantees, but by the general functioning of the party. The argument for unity or stability in the party is bound up with Gramsci's view of the way in which the working class must struggle for its hegemony, and influence other classes in the process. This means that the revolutionary party must never lose its leadership role.

> In parties which represent socially subaltern classes, the element of stability is necessary to ensure that hegemony will be exercised not by privileged groups but by the progressive elements — organically progressive in relation to other forces which, though related and allied, are heterogeneous and wavering. *SPN*, p. 189.

Unity and discipline are also necessary for more practical reasons. Once a decision has been reached by the party it must be carried out, because disobedience would cause more damage than a decision which was in part mistaken.[14] Debate is absolutely vital to the party, but because the need for democracy is not a formalistic one, Gramsci also states clearly that it must not result in the unity of action being broken. It should be noted that even in this context he is by no means claiming that discussion and debate should stop. At the same time it must also be clearly recognised that he is not claiming an abstract freedom for members to do whatever they like. In a simile which he often uses[15] he points out that an orchestra needs a leader, and as we shall see below, Gramsci is quite adamant about the need for leaders. He is just as explicit, however, with regard to the importance of a clear understanding of the nature of discipline which if it is to be effective, must never be merely formal. The way in which he defines discipline is extremely significant in terms of his general concept of the party.

> How should discipline be understood if what is meant by this word is a continual and permanent relationship between rulers and ruled which realizes a collective will? Certainly not as a passive and servile acceptance of orders, as a mechanical execution of a command (which, however, will also be necessary on particular occasions, as for example in the middle of an action which has already been decided and begun), but as a conscious and lucid assimilation of the directive to be fulfilled. Discipline, therefore, does not annul the personality in the organic sense but only limits arbitrariness and irresponsible impulsiveness. *Q*, p. 1706.

The need for a continuous and permanent relationship between different levels of an organisation in order to achieve a particular end, a collective will, is the political basis for discipline which is connected to the role of the party. The fact of discipline is not considered in the abstract but is discussed by Gramsci in terms of the democratic functioning of the party. While arguing against an authoritarian imposition of orders on a passive object, he does so for concrete political reasons, and by the same token, unlike the anarchists, he does not attack discipline *per se* but focuses on the type of discipline and, importantly, on the nature of the source of discipline.

> Discipline therefore does not annul personality and freedom. The question of 'personality and freedom' has to do not with the fact of discipline but with the 'origin of the power which orders the discipline'. If this origin is 'democratic', that is, if authority is a specialized technical function and not a 'will' or an exterior and extrinsic attitude, discipline is a necessary element of democratic order, of freedom. *Q*, p. 1706.

The 'technical' nature of leadership is once again emphasised. If there are moments when there is a need for mechanical carrying out of orders, perhaps when the party is forced underground, this is related to the objective situation, and the objective difficulties of the party in carrying on a normal democratic life.

What results from this discussion is an argument against any mystification of the leadership function. It is technical, reflecting skill and expert knowledge. A correct understanding of the basis of leadership would help prevent the organisation itself from assuming a mystical or fetishistic appearance. Gramsci is once again carrying on a discussion on a variety of fronts, against the traditional Italian socialist attitudes to organisation, against Bordiga's rigid sectarian alternative, and against the Stalinist party. In a note entitled 'Dilettantism and Discipline', he addresses himself to these problems. Using particularly severe language, he writes:

> The necessity of a sincere and rigorous internal criticism, without conventionalities and half measures. There exists a tendency of historical materialism which solicits and favours all the bad traditions of middle Italian culture and seems to accept certain traits of the Italian character; improvisation, 'talentism', fatalistic laziness, mindless dilettantism, lack of intellectual discipline, irresponsibility and intellectual and moral disloyalty. *Q*, p. 749.

Reflecting earlier comments on the Italian socialist tradition, Gramsci goes on to argue that the solution was not provided by Bordiga, nor indeed by Stalin. In a harsh criticism of Bordiga's attitude, he writes that the vanguard party must not be considered an indistinct jumble of members,

> in which, by the grace of a mysterious holy spirit, or of another mysterious and metaphysical unknown deity, there struck the grace of intelligence, of capability, of education, of technical preparation, etc. . . . The collectivity must be understood as a product of an elaboration of will and collective thought achieved through individual concrete effort and not through a fatal process extraneous to the individuals, therefore through an external and mechanical duty. If there must be polemics and splits, one must not be afraid to confront them and overcome them. They are inevitable in these processes of development and avoiding them simply means postponing them until they are definitely dangerous or quite catastrophic, etc. *Q*, pp. 750-1.

What appears in this discussion of party organisation is a very particular argument for party democracy. Gramsci discusses organisation as dependent on and subordinate to the political tasks of the party. There are no absolute, abstract principles. These are the terms in which he argues for the concrete political need for discussion and debate. He is not putting forward the case for abstract democratic rights within the party. Democratic participation is placed firmly within the concrete needs of the party in order for it to fulfil its political role. It cannot function successfully without internal democracy which means active consent and active participation, so that the party must conduct itself in such a way that all members are encouraged to be active, and so that means are provided to raise their political and cultural level continuously. In this sense Gramsci's argument goes beyond each member having merely abstract democratic rights. If these rights are not put into concrete practice, the party is not truly democratic. And, as we shall see below, the strategy and tactics of the party are not the result of the totalling up of the different views of individual party members but a result of a particular analysis of the concrete social formation and of the conjuncture. Differences within the party can only be resolved by a full discussion which produces a unity which takes account of but is not reduced to the different positions.

It is the party which must produce organic intellectuals of the class, and all members are such intellectuals. To create intellectuals who are organic with regard to the creation of a new social formation, that is, organic to the task of founding a new type of State by the proletariat, the mode of existence of these intellectuals must be fundamentally transformed. As the mode of existence is transformed within the party, their relationship to the masses is transformed, and the mode of existence of those intellectuals organic to the capitalist social formation, existing in a *traditional* relationship of separation from the masses, is increasingly challenged by a new pattern of relationships. The ethos must be created within the party in which a real democracy is possible. A style of politics, an atmosphere which considers discussion and debate intrinsic to the role of the party must be promoted. There are both manifold consequences for the day-to-day activities of the party from the way in which Gramsci conceives of the party in general and of its organisational principles in particular, and for a new concept of democracy for society as a whole. A new concept of politics begins within the party itself. It is in this sense that the party prefigures a new type of State.

10. The Party as a Vanguard: the Relationship with the Masses

One of the most controversial aspects of the discussion of the political party in the Marxist tradition has to do with its role as a vanguard, its relationship to the working class and to the mass movement in a broader sense. The question of the party 'substituting' the class is not just theoretical but a question which is historically given with the experience of the difficulties in building socialism in the Soviet Union. Thus when we consider this topic in Gramsci's thought it is important to make explicit his terms of reference and the way in which it fits into his whole problematic. It is necessary, in fact, to summarise some of our previous discussion in order to understand how it can be argued that Gramsci avoids both a 'spontaneist' and a 'voluntarist' problematic in confronting the problem of the relationship between subjective and objective forces.

Taking up themes from his earlier work Gramsci's discussion of internal organisation in the *Notebooks* continues his argument that it is the mass movement which is the protagonist of historical change.[1] As mentioned above, the terms of reference for his writing on organisational questions are predominantly the debate with Bordiga. When he discusses the party as a vanguard organisation, he counterposes it to a *sect* and defines vanguard in terms of a vast network of links to the mass movement. A 'normal association' as opposed to a sect,

> conceives of itself as a vanguard, that is conceives of itself as tied by millions of threads to a given social group and through it to the whole of humanity. Therefore this association does not pose itself as something definitive and rigid, but as tending to enlarge itself to a whole social group, which is also conceived of as tending to unify the whole of humanity. *Q*, p. 750.

Thus his very definition of the vanguard nature of the party is founded on the need to relate to the mass movement. The form of the party must be flexible because it must envisage the possibility of expanding to include a whole class. As we have tried to suggest, Gramsci criticises both an instrumental view of the masses[2] and a spontaneist view of the development of human history. In order to understand the party as a vanguard, we shall have to examine his ideas on the relationship of spontaneity to conscious leadership and of the relationship of leaders and led in terms of the revolutionary party.

In a note entitled 'Spontaneity and Conscious Leadership', Gramsci denies that pure spontaneity can exist.[3] This position rests on two arguments which are based on his general view of the world. The first is that 'pure' spontaneity would coincide with 'pure' mechanical necessity. Indeed a full discussion of this topic would imply an examination of Gramsci's concept of the social totality and the relationship between freedom and necessity in his thought.[4] It is important to note that since Gramsci denies the inevitable development of historical necessity, he also denies that classes act spontaneously without any conscious direction, because this would imply that material conditions 'automatically' produce historical movement. What may seem to occur spontaneously will simply be the result of influences which are undocumented.[5]

This leads us to the second argument which he uses to deny the possibility of pure spontaneity. He maintains that when there seems to be no homogeneous, explicit set of ideas directing a mass movement, it simply means that this movement is in fact influenced by the various ideas contained within what Gramsci calls 'common sense' or a 'traditional conception of the world'.[6] 'Spontaneous' movements are those which

> are not the result of any systematic educational activity on the part of an already conscious leading group, but have been formed through everyday experience illuminated by 'common sense', i.e. by the trad-

itional popular conception of the world—what is unimaginatively called 'instinct', although it too is in fact a primitive and elementary historical acquisition. *SPN*, pp. 198-9.

Ideas therefore do not develop spontaneously,[7] and the complex set of ideas prevalent in the masses at any one moment is the result of an historical process in which the present and potential historical blocs conduct the battle for a dominant hegemony.[8] So the question is never one of spontaneity of the masses as opposed to the conscious leadership of the party, but rather it concerns the way in which the party can relate to the present ideological positions of the various groups in society, in order to influence these groups by the hegemony of the working class, thus decreasing the influence of the dominant classes.

The experience of the post-First World War period is very much in Gramsci's mind when he warns:

> Neglecting, or worse still despising, so-called 'spontaneous' movements, i.e. failing to give them a conscious leadership or to raise them to a higher plane by inserting them into politics, may often have extremely serious consequences. It is almost always the case that a 'spontaneous' movement of the subaltern classes is accompanied by a reactionary movement of the right-wing of the dominant class, for concomitant reasons. An economic crisis, for instance, engenders on the one hand discontent among the subaltern classes and spontaneous mass movements, and on the other conspiracies among the reactionary groups, who take advantage of the objective weakening of the government in order to attempt *coups d'état*. Among the effective causes of the *coups* must be included the failure of the responsible groups to give any conscious leadership to the spontaneous revolts or to make them into a *positive* political factor. *SPN*, p. 199.[9] [My emphasis.]

The inability of the left in Italy to maintain its leadership over the mass movement in 1919-20 allowed the situation to be dominated by reactionary forces. Left to themselves the spontaneous movements could not develop into a 'positive political factor', but remained on a negative terrain. The revolutionary process of construction-destruction could not come to fruition, and into the political void stepped the most reactionary elements.

In contrast to the dominant attitude in the PSI, Gramsci cites the example of the *Ordine Nuovo* movement to suggest the way in which the party should relate to the mass movement. Noting ironically that the Turin movement had been accused simultaneously of being 'spontaneist' and 'voluntarist', he maintained that it in fact provided the correct type of leadership because it understood the so-called spontaneity of the mass movement.

> This leadership was not 'abstract'; it neither consisted in mechanically repeating scientific or theoretical formulae, nor did it confuse politics, real action, with theoretical disquisition. It applied itself to real men, formed in specific historical relations, with specific feelings, outlooks, fragmentary conceptions of the world, etc., which were the result of 'spontaneous' combinations of a given situation of material production with the 'fortuitous' agglomeration within it of disparate social elements. This element of 'spontaneity' was not neglected and even less despised. It was *educated*, directed, purged of extraneous contaminations; the aim was to bring it into line with modern theory — but in a living and historically effective manner. *SPN*, p. 198.

Because the potential within the mass movement was appreciated, because the historical and material basis for this movement was understood, the *Ordine Nuovo* group could intervene to 'educate' this spontaneity so that it was no longer confined within the limits of the hegemony of the dominant classes but could form the basis of an alternative, autonomous hegemony. Convinced that there was an historical basis for the potential development of the movement, the *Ordine Nuovo* leadership, 'gave the masses a "theoretical" consciousness of being creators of *historical* and institutional *values*, of being founders of a State'. (*SPN*, p. 198.) Incipient in the activity of the *Ordine Nuovo* had indeed been the conception of the dialectic construction-destruction within the capitalist system. The ultimate political goal of the foundation of a new State, of a new moral and social order was in an intimate relationship to the day-to-day struggle of the mass movement. 'This unity between "spontaneity" and "conscious leadership" or "discipline" is precisely the real political action of the subaltern classes, in so far as this is mass politics and not merely an adventure by groups claiming to represent the masses.' (*SPN*, p. 214.)

The discussion of the relationship between the party and the spontaneous movement was directed against Bordiga, who, Gramsci argued, had tended to ignore or not to appreciate the potential of this spontaneity. Moreover, the nature of the 'education' of spontaneity had to be a democratic, not an authoritarian one.[10] Gramsci discusses the kind of relationship which must exist between intellectuals and masses, or between the party and the mass movement:

The popular element 'feels' but does not always know or understand; the intellectual element 'knows' but does not always understand and in particular does not always feel. . . . The intellectual's error consists in believing that one can know without understanding and even more without feeling and being impassioned . . . in other words that the intellectual can be an intellectual (and not a pure pedant) if distinct and separate from the people-nation, that is, without feeling the elementary passions of the people, understanding them and therefore explaining and justifying them in the particular historical situation and connecting them dialectically to the laws of history and to a superior conception of the world, scientifically and coherently elaborated—i.e. knowledge. *One cannot make politics-history without this passion, without this sentimental connection between intellectuals and people-nation.* In the absence of such a nexus the relations between the intellectual and the people-nation are, or are reduced to, relationships of a purely *bureaucratic* and *formal* order; the intellectuals become a caste, or a priesthood (so-called organic centralism). *SPN*, p. 418. [My emphasis.]

If it is not to be distorted, the argument which Gramsci puts forward for the party as a vanguard or leader of the class must be understood within the context of his general problematic. To summarise, the fact that historical development is not automatic is precisely the concrete basis for the political intervention by the party. Indeed, the full potential of objective material conditions can only be realised, according to Gramsci, if subjective conditions do not arise spontaneously but are the result of a conscious struggle, the ability of the working class and its allies to become an effective political force depends on the activities of the revolutionary party. The party is the means by which a new alternative hegemony can be formulated and organic intellectuals of the working class can be developed. It is in this sense that the party must produce leaders for the working class. The development of leaders by the working class through its political party is also related to what Gramsci considers the fundamental premise of politics, the division of the world into rulers and ruled.[11] This is historically determined, based on class divisions, and is one of the concrete facts which the party must take into consideration in undertaking its role. Given this split between leaders and led,

it will have to be considered how one can lead most effectively (given certain ends); hence how the leaders may best be prepared (and it is more precisely in this that the first stage of the art and science of politics consists); and how, on the other hand, one can know the lines of least resistance, or the most rational lines along which to proceed if one wishes to secure the obedience of the led or ruled. In the formation of leaders, one premiss is fundamental; is it the intention that there should always be rulers and ruled, or is the objective to create the conditions in which this division is no longer necessary? *SPN*, p. 144.

The division between rulers and ruled cannot be ignored, nor can it be done away with so long as the objective conditions for such divisions exist. If the question is not to be posed in a Utopian way, the real nature of this division must be analysed to create the basis of a new type of relationship between leaders and led.

The task of the revolutionary party in producing leaders, in this sense in being a vanguard of organisation, is again discussed by Gramsci in terms of 'technical' necessity. Just as he argued against Michels that divisions within the party must be based on a technical division of labour, the vanguard nature of the party in relation to the mass movement is based on the specific need of the working class in establishing its hegemony.

Critical self-consciousness means, historically and politically, the creation of an *élite* of intellectuals. A human mass does not 'distinguish' itself, does not become independent in its own right without, in the widest sense, organising itself; and there is no organisation without intellectuals, that is without organisers and leaders, in other words, without the theoretical aspect of the theory-practice nexus being distinguished concretely by the existence of a group of people 'specialised' in conceptual and philosophical elaboration of ideas. *SPN*, p. 334.

The party represents the way in which the skills which the working class needs in its historical struggle can be acquired.

Another aspect of the party providing political leadership for the class has to do with the tenuous nature of the collective will organised by the party. It does not develop spontaneously, and in any defeat it can break down very rapidly. The party in its leadership capacity must be aware of this danger and understand the consequences of the stratification of political leadership. With the experience of fascism in mind, Gramsci writes, in every political situation the active part is a minority . . . if this minority, when it is followed by the multitudes, does not organize this following in a lasting way, and it becomes dispersed through whatever circumstances which is propitious to the adverse minority, the whole apparatus will break up and a new one will be formed in which the old multitudes no longer count and can no longer move or have any effect. What is called 'mass' has been pulverized in many atoms without will and orientation. *Q*, p. 1789.

The role, therefore, of this active minority is of the utmost importance in the political struggle. Thinking of the situation of the PCd'I under fascism, when its own ranks, but also independent working-class and peasant organisations in general, had been destroyed so that masses were in the situation described above, Gramsci goes on to write, 'the political realist, who knows the difficulty of organizing a collective will, does not come to believe easily that it is restored mechanically after it is broken up.' (*Q*, p. 1789.) The task of the party is to work actively to maintain this collective will. Thus Gramsci is quite explicit about the importance of the leadership role of the party. He does not hold a 'fetishistic' view of the 'people'[12] because, he argues, it is only by conscious political intervention in the concrete situation that the political party can forge a collective will based on the hegemony of the working class, around which an ever increasing mass can unite in order to transform the society. It is in this sense that the party must relate to the spontaneous mass movement. To ignore it is to leave it under the hegemony of the dominant classes. By the same measure, to fail to lead it is to succumb to the most backward positions, themselves a product of the subaltern nature of the masses, with the result that a new, autonomous hegemony will not be built and the present dominant classes will not be challenged.

The guarantee, on the other hand, that a party has a proper relationship with the masses and not simply an instrumental one can only come from its day-to-day work, based on a particular perspective on the nature of revolutionary change.[13] Just as internal democracy is the only guarantee against oligarchy, the political work of the party is the real basis on which a fetishistic attitude to the party or its leader can be prevented. The possibility of something like a personality cult or the situation of a party like his own in danger of losing its leaders is perhaps in Gramsci's mind when he writes that if the attitude of a leader or of a party towards the masses is the correct one, then the party will be able to construct a strategy of what he calls a 'higher demagogy' or of a 'great ambition', that is, with a goal which is greater than small personal ends. Most likely thinking of Mussolini's appeals to the masses, Gramsci writes:

> if the leader does not consider the human masses as a servile instru-
> ment, good for achieving his own aims and thus to be cast aside, but
> tends to achieve organic political ends for which these masses are the
> necessary historical protagonist . . . then there is a 'higher demagogy';
> the masses cannot be helped to raise themselves through raising
> single individuals or entire 'cultural' strata . . . The political leader of
> great ambition . . . tends to create an intermediate stratum between
> himself and the masses . . . *to raise the level of ability of the masses,*
> *to create elements which can substitute him in the function of leader.*
> He thinks according to the interests of the masses and they do not
> want the apparatus of conquest and domination to break down because
> of the death or incapacity of the individual leader, plunging the masses
> once again into chaos and primitive impotence. *Q*, p. 68. [My
> emphasis.]

The concrete political importance of the correct relationship to the
masses is underlined by this passage.[14] The danger that the masses are
plunged into 'chaos and impotence' can only be prevented by undertaking political work to raise the cultural level of increasing numbers of
people around a new alternative hegemony[15] and by building a party,
composed of organic intellectuals, who can undertake the leadership
function and become the links with the masses. This kind of organic, of
democratic relationship is necessary for the creation of a new type of
State, and it is on this that the endurance and the strength of the party
lies. The continuous process of education and development is based on
full discussion and democracy within the party. There is also a democratic relationship with the masses in the sense that political work is undertaken in an attempt to elicit ever greater participation by increasingly
politically and culturally prepared elements from the masses. This is the
concrete basis on which to prevent the party from instrumentalising the
struggle of the working class and its allies. As we have argued above, democracy and discussion in the party are intrinsic to its being able to fulfill
its role, in terms of being able to relate to the ongoing struggle in the
real world. In the same way, a correct understanding of the 'spontaneous'
mass movement and a concept of politics based on the fight for hegemony
which implies a cultural struggle as well as a more strictly political one
is the very foundation of the forging of a collective will, of the founding
of a new State, of the transformation of society. The building of organic
links between the party and the mass movement is intrinsic to Gramsci's

view of revolutionary change. An instrumental view of the masses is totally alien to it.

11. The Analysis of the Conjuncture and the Argument Against Economism

The whole thrust of Gramsci's work in prison is to unmask the complexity of the concrete situation which is the basis for the activity of the party and to delineate the terrain of political struggle. The ability of the party to relate to the concrete situation depends on its having accurate knowledge of the historical moment in which it is working. The very object of political science, according to Gramsci, consists in

> The study of how 'situations' should be analysed, in other words how to establish the various levels of the relations of force, (which) offers an opportunity for an elementary exposition of the science and art of politics—understood as a body of practical rules for research and of detailed observations useful for awakening an interest in effective reality and for stimulating more rigorous and more vigorous political insights. This should be accompanied by the explanation of what is meant in politics by strategy and tactics, by strategic 'plan', by propaganda and agitation, by command structure or science of political organisation and administration. *SPN*, pp. 175-6.

Fundamental to Gramsci's view of the world is an emphasis on the complexity of any moment, a complexity which makes impossible any simple cause and effect relationship between the economic and the other levels of the social totality.

> A certain social-historical moment is never homogenous. On the contrary, it is rich with contradictions. It acquires 'personality', it is a 'moment' of development because a certain fundamental activity of life predominates over the others, represents an historical 'peak'. But this presupposes a hierarchy, a contrast, a struggle. *Q*, p. 2187.

It is into this complex moment that the party must intervene, and there are several points which must be borne in mind in analysing the concrete situation in order to create a strategy and tactics. The very existence or not of the party or the subjective factor is one element in the situation. Therefore any analysis which is made to attempt to forecast or predict the possible development of a situation which leaves out the 'predictor', and the *fact* of his knowledge of the prediction itself will lead to false conclusions. Gramsci is attempting to suggest a solution to the fundamental philosophical problem of the split between the subjective and the objective when he writes:

> It is certain that prediction only means seeing the present and the past clearly as movement. Seeing them clearly: in other words, accurately identifying the fundamental and permanent elements of the process. But it is absurd to think of a purely 'objective' prediction. Anybody who makes a prediction has in fact a 'programme' for whose victory he is working, and his prediction is precisely an element contributing to that victory. . . . Indeed one might say that only to the extent to which the objective aspect of prediction is linked to a programme does it acquire its objectivity . . . because reality is a product of the application of human will to the society of things . . . therefore if one excludes all voluntarist elements, or if it is only other people's wills whose intervention one reckons as an objective element in the general interplay of forces, one mutilates reality itself. *SPN*, pp. 170-1.

At the same time the fact that the analysis is being used by the party in order to intervene in the reality confronting it gives the analysis a concrete meaning. Implicit here is the argument that the analysis of society depends on tools which are quite different from the tools used in the natural sciences.[1] In a new context Gramsci continues the struggle of his youth against a positivistic interpretation of Marxism.

The relationship between viewer and object, between the party and the concrete situation, becomes an integral part of the very comprehension of the objective reality.

> One bases oneself on effective reality, but what is this effective reality? Is it something static and immobile, or is it not rather a relation of forces in continuous motion and shift of equilibrium? If one applies one's will to the creation of a new equilibrium among the forces which really exist and are operative—basing oneself on the particular force which one believes to be progressive and strengthening it to help it to victory—one still moves on the terrain of effective reality, but does so in order to dominate and transcend it (or to contribute to this). *SPN*, p. 172.

In order to be able to intervene effectively in a given reality to change it, the existing relationship of forces must be understood clearly, both in terms of the subjective factor of the party and in terms of the adversary. Knowledge of the class opponent is fundamental if the working class is to assume an autonomous political role and to win over to its hegemony sectors of society at present under the hegemony of the enemy.[2] State and non-State apparatuses, cultural and ideological organisations and activities, all aspects of the dominance of the ruling class are within the proper object of the party's analysis, and much of the *Notebooks* is devoted precisely to this. An understanding of these aspects of the social totality will allow the party both to understand where the strengths and weaknesses of the enemy lie and how to counterpose its own activities on the same wide front.

By developing this complex view, Gramsci delineates a particular task for the party. Both by the example of his work in prison and by his very approach, he indicated that simplifications and easy assumptions about the terrain in which the party had to work could only be misleading and at worst disastrous. In tackling the problem of the relationship between the structure and the superstructure from the point of view of the creation of a strategy of a party he attempted to suggest the basis for overcoming a distortion which he considered particularly dangerous, an economistic interpretation of historical development. The notes on the party, on the analysis of the relationship of the base and superstructure on the strategic level, and his notes on economism significantly are all situated together in the *Notebooks*.[3] The task of the party, according to Gramsci, is to undertake the work necessary to understand the dynamic of the situation based on a correct theory of the relationship of the different levels of the social totality and of the different dynamics within each. The consequence of the type of analysis which he suggests is to revalue the moment of the political in terms of its influence on the actual outcome of any struggle. Since the party intervenes in the terrain of the political, its very existence and the type of activities it undertakes become crucial. He places the discussion within the context of the problem of the nature of the relationship between base and superstructure. With regards to the strategy and tactics of the party, this problem becomes one of distinguishing, 'organic movements (relatively permanent) from movements which may be termed "conjunctural" (and which appear as occasional, immediate, almost accidental)'. (*SPN*, p. 177.)[4] A crisis of long duration, Gramsci writes, will mean that there are irresolvable contradictions in the structure which are organic. The attempts by the various political forces to preserve the present economic structure by overcoming these contradictions

> form the terrain of the 'conjunctural', and it is upon this terrain that
> the forces of opposition organise. These forces seek to demonstrate
> that the necessary and sufficient conditions already exist to make
> possible, and hence imperative, the accomplishment of certain histor-
> ical tasks (imperative, because any falling short before an historical
> duty increases the necessary disorder, and prepares more serious cata-
> strophes). *SPN*, p. 178.

The political struggle, then, takes place on the *terrain* of the occasional
and finds expression in a series of political, ideological, religious and
philosophical polemics. Understanding that this is the *mode* of the
struggle at the level of the occasional in the realm of politics and ideology is vital. Realising that there is a dialectical if uneven relationship
between organic contradictions at the base, and the playing out of the
political and ideological struggle in the superstructure is crucial to a
correct understanding of the relationship between base and superstructure. Only in this way can the status of the political be delineated
correctly.

An organic crisis is a 'given' from the point of view of a single moment
of the class struggle but at the same time it is a 'product' of the long-
term class struggle. For Gramsci the organic crisis refers both to the
whole historical period when the revolution is *actual*, that is, has a real
basis in the period of imperialism, and to the determinant moment. This
latter is on the terrain of the political. Unless the relationship between
these two dimensions is understood, the space within which the party
operates cannot be comprehended.

The historical tasks of the party stem from the fact that the material
conditions already exist for a transformation of society. These material
conditions are formed by the development of the organic contradictions
of the structure. Since these contradictions cannot be resolved unless
society is transformed, the inability of the revolutionary forces to provide a solution through the struggle at the level of the occasional or the
political, both increases the chaos, which for Gramsci is not at all necessarily auspicious, and most importantly, leaves that terrain open to
attempts by the conservative forces to arrive at an outcome favourable
to them. The catastrophic nature of such an outcome, according to
Gramsci, stems from the fact that those forces able to renew society are
defeated while the old forces which are incapable of resolving the organic
contradictions are triumphant.

Thus the *appearance* of the organic contradiction at the level of the occasional has its own reality and its own specificity. It cannot simply be reduced to the economic moment. Yet neither is it completely autonomous. According to Gramsci there is a dialectical relationship between the two which must be understood properly. If not,

> This leads to presenting causes as immediately operative which in fact only operate indirectly, or to asserting that the immediate causes are the only effective ones. In the first case there is an excess of 'economism', or doctrinaire pedantry; in the second, an excess of 'ideologism'. In the first case there is an overestimation of mechanical causes, in the second an exaggeration of the voluntarist and individual element. *SPN*, p. 178.

Gramsci describes the two deviations which are two expressions of the same theoretical mistake.[5]

We shall return to Gramsci's criticism of economism below. Here we may note that the excess of emphasis on one type of cause or another can only mislead the working-class movement and therefore the correct analysis of causal relationships is one of the crucial points of contact between the theory of the working-class movement and its practice. Gramsci seems to suggest that there exists something like a structural causality.

> Often the necessary distinctions are not made in the study of different 'degrees' or 'moments' of political or military situations between the 'efficient cause' which prepares the political or historic event . . . and the 'determinant cause', which immediately produces the event and is the general and concrete result of the efficient cause, the concrete 'precipitation' of the elements which are really active and necessary from the efficient cause in order to produce the determination. *Q*, pp. 1945-6.

All these distinctions are crucial in the creation of a strategy and tactics. In further trying to elucidate the complexity of the concrete situation, Gramsci draws up a schema as a guide for analysis. In the relationship of forces he indicates three different levels or moments of analysis. It is important to emphasise that these three levels are separate only in a methodological sense since they are aspects of a single phenomenon at a single moment of time. The first has to do with the objective material conditions of any situation, which he describes as,

A relation which is closely linked to the structure, objective, independent of human will . . . The level of development of the material forces of production provides a basis for the emergence of the various social classes, each one of which represents a function and has a specific position within production itself . . . By studying these fundamental data it is possible to discover whether in a particular society there exist the necessary and sufficient conditions for its transformation. *SPN*, pp. 180-1.

This first moment is at the level of the structure where organic contradictions occur.

A second or successive moment of the analysis[6] is the moment of the relationship between political forces, 'that is, an evaluation of the degree of homogeneity, self-awareness, and organization attained by the various social classes'. (*SPN*, p. 181.) This is the moment of the subjective conditions, and it is at this level of analysis that the formation of a collective will or collective political consciousness can be studied. This political moment is the most complex in Gramsci's exposition which reflects a concept of uneven development.

For a given relationship of structural forces, a variety of political relationships can exist since each force in the field can vary in its own political development whatever its structural features. It is here that the ability of a political force to establish its hegemony can be measured. It is only when the force has become hegemonic that it has a truly political existence. It should be noted once again that Gramsci has a particular use of the word political which parallels his view of the State. In the full sense it has to do with the potential of a class to found a new *integral* State, that is, a State based on a deeply-rooted and widely extended hegemony. Short of this, as we noted above, a class may take part in politics, such as participation by its party in Parliament, but if the *content* of this participation is not such as to tend to make the class hegemonic, then this politics is not autonomous and is not the politics of founding a new State, and the class has not achieved full political development in Gramsci's sense.

This dimension of analysis is itself complex because it takes account of the fact that a social force does not necessarily have a political existence at all. In measuring the degree of political development there are three sub-levels. To summarise an earlier discussion, the first concerns the achievement of a sectional consciousness when all those within a skill or trade are aware of common interests, but there is no general class-consciousness, even of an economic nature. A second moment comes when this class-consciousness exists. At this stage the class may even address the problem of the State but only in an economic-corporative mode, not in a political or hegemonic one. Only the third moment is really political, and it is when a class reaches this level of development that it can be said to have a political existence.

> A third moment is that in which one becomes aware that one's own corporate interests, in their present and furture development, transcend the corporate limits of the purely economic class, and can and must become the interests of other subordinate groups too. This is the most purely *political* phase, and marks *the decisive passage from the structure to the sphere of the complex superstructures*; it is the phase in which previously germinated ideologies become 'party', come into confrontation and conflict, until only one of them, or at least a single combination of them, tends to prevail, to gain the upper hand, to propagate itself throughout society — bringing about not only a unison of economic and political aims, but also intellectual and moral unity, posing all the questions around which the struggle rages not on a corporate but on *a 'universal' plane, and thus creating the hegemony of a fundamental social group* over a series of subordinate groups. *SPN*, pp. 181-2. [My emphasis.]

It is at this stage that the subjective forces can have full play for it is only now that the class goes beyond its structural existence and exists fully at the level of the superstructure. When this happens, the realm of necessity or constraint by material conditions recedes and the realm of freedom or of subjective forces emerges.[7] The party must understand at what stage of political development the working class finds itself and strive to bring it to a hegemonic and therefore fully political position. At the same time its analysis of the political development of other contending forces will form part of its concrete understanding of the situation.

The third dimension measures the relationship between military forces which, according to Gramsci, is decisive in the most immediate sense. Yet, even here there is an interrelationship between force and consent because the military capacity of a social force, except in the narrowest technical sense, is always in relation to its political cohesion. A people can be oppressed, Gramsci argues, not just because it is subjected to a military power by the oppressor but because its own lack of military preparation reflects its relative inability to wage a political struggle, both for its own cohesiveness and in order to weaken the enemy.

Thus while material structural conditions are given, as a product of the past, of an earlier stage of the class struggle, and while in decisive moments the element of physical force or 'military' preparedness is vital, the subjective political dimension is the most crucial because it forms the terrain upon which ultimately the element of force depends.[8] Thus while the moment of force or violence is not ignored in the relationship of forces and in the question of a transformation of society, the dialectic between force and consent, the 'dual perspective', is always present in Gramsci's thought. To the extent that a revolutionary force is hegemonic, the need for it to depend on physical force is diminished. The military potential of the enemy is also lessened as the enemy's own hegemony has been undermined. By the same token, the real ability of a class to transform society can never depend solely on violence or force. The party cannot ignore this dimension because it can be decisive, but it must be aware of its connection with the hegemonic or political dimension.[9]

In drawing up this schema to analyse the different levels of the relationship of forces in order to allow the party to act Gramsci has a particular object, practical political activity.[10] The party must intervene on the basis of an understanding of the structural or objective features of a situation related to the potential of the subjective factors. According to Gramsci, there is one particular theoretical error above all else which hinders the ability of the party to maximise its political initiative—economism. On the theoretical level, the discussion concerns the nature of the relationship between the structure and the various areas of the superstructure. On a political and historical level it concerns the nature of the dynamic of a conjuncture and of historical development.[11] Gramsci argues that although an economic crisis, itself a product of the class struggle, opens up the possibility for a political and ideological struggle, which can ultimately affect the State, if, however, the subjective, political factor does not intervene successfully, an economic crisis will not automatically result in the transformation of society.[12] A revolutionary change can only be brought about by a class struggle which goes beyond the economic and envelops the realm of the State in the full sense, challenging the hegemony of the dominant class.[13]

The fact that this is a crisis of hegemony, related to but not necessarily determined in the first instance by an economic crisis, opens up and extends a particular field of struggle for the party which the economistic deformation cannot comprehend. This field is that of ideology and politics. The comprehension of the full extent of this terrain is crucial. Otherwise any analysis based on the economistic deformation reduces the role of the party since the possibility of the subjective factor actually having any potential for political initiative within an economistic framework is practically nil.

It is important here to make clear that Gramsci's discussion is of a slightly different nature than Lenin's. While Lenin put forth the argument for the need for a revolutionary party *per se* against certain tendencies which either minimised the need for a party (e.g. the Economists) or thought that the party could be fundamentally the same as a bourgeois party (the Mensheviks), Gramsci assumes in the early 1930s the acceptance by at least substantial sections of the working-class movement of the idea of the revolutionary party. His argument is directed against those who, while accepting this idea in principle, are prevented from in fact realising the potential of the party because they are hindered by economism.[14]

Even though a party may claim to have a different view of the world, it may well be trapped within an economistic problematic. The most crucial evidence of this is an inability to undertake effective political initiatives. When Gramsci links phenomena such as Bordiga's abstentionism, the type of intransigence of the PSI during the First World War, and the concept held by sections of the PSI of 'the worse it gets, the better it will be' under the label of economism,[15] he is arguing that what they have in common is a view that events will mature in favour of the working class without the active, conscious intervention of that class led by its party. The party is thereby consigned to passivity to await the automatic evolution of the situation. It could be argued that this 'wait and see' position, at times accompanied by a militant rhetoric, is a hallmark of the limits of the Second International problematic in both its Kautskyian and Bernsteinian forms, and to the extent that any party falls into this type of approach, whatever the point in time, it remains within this problematic. Implicit in Gramsci's discussion is a criticism of Bordiga and the argument that the theoretical mistake which was the basis of Bordiga's incorrect view of the party was economism.

The area for political initiative is reduced by economism since on the one hand economism limits the field of battle because it underestimates the concrete importance of the terrain of ideology and on the other, and intimately connected, it does not understand the State because it does not possess the concept of hegemony. An important Marxist proposition which is often forgotten, Gramsci writes, is

that 'popular beliefs' and similar ideas are themselves material forces .... It is therefore necessary to combat economism not only in the theory of historiography, but also and especially in the theory and practice of politics. In this field, the struggle can and must be carried on by developing *the concept of hegemony* — as has been done in practice in the development of the theory of the political party and in the actual history of certain political parties. *SPN*, p. 165.[16] [My emphasis.]

The realm of ideology cannot simply be reduced to an immediate reflection of the structure.[17] It has its own complexity and a certain degree of autonomy. By diminishing this field of battle, economism prevents a subordinate class from creating its own hegemony, and thus the hegemony of the dominant class remains unchallenged. The terrain of ideology and any area of social reality not connected directly to a very narrowly defined interest of the working class is left in the hands of the enemy.

Economism prevents the revolutionary party from fulfilling its role in another way. It makes it impossible for the party to relate to concrete reality because since it reduces the causal relationship in the political arena to the most immediate economic, corporative interest of the various social forces, it cannot see the complexity of the dynamic of any social formation.[18] It is incapable of an analysis which takes into account this complexity because the question it asks, who is immediately served by a particular initiative,[19] cannot have as its *object* a complex causality. An example which Gramsci gives of a phenomenon which could not be understood by this approach is a fascist or a Bonapartist solution to a crisis.[20] The aspects of such a phenomenon are multifold and complex and a differentiated analysis of the social base of the movement as well as the nature of the leadership and the significance of such a movement in a particular conjuncture cannot be explained by any immediate interest of the participants.[21]

In general by reducing every single political activity to an immediate change or need in the structure a whole range of phenomena are misunderstood. At the level of government, for example,

a particular political act may have been an error of calculation on the part of the leaders [*dirigenti*] of the dominant classes, an error which historical development, through the parliamentary and governmental 'crises' of the directive [*dirigenti*] classes, then corrects and goes beyond. Mechanical historical materialism does not allow for the possibility of error, but assumes that every political act is determined, immediately, by the structure, and therefore as a real and permanent (in the sense of achieved) modification of the structure. The principle of 'error' is a complex one: one may be dealing with an individual impulse based on mistaken calculations or equally it may be a manifestation of the attempts of specific groups or sects to take over hegemony within the directive grouping, attempts which may well be unsuccessful. *SPN*, p. 408.

If this kind of process is not understood, a general confusion can arise whereby the 'occasional' movement is mistaken for an 'organic' change, and the specificity and relative autonomy of the contradictions of the political level is missed. Consequently the ability of the party to intervene effectively in such a situation is lost. This has consequences both for an analysis of the positions of various parties and individuals in bourgeois society and for the kinds of debates and mistakes which arise in a society undertaking the construction of socialism. As an argument against class reductionism in the interpretation of mistakes, it is a strong condemnation of Stalin's treatment of a generation of Soviet politicians. Stalin's logic was that every mistake had a class basis, that the perpetrator of the mistake was objectively the agent of an enemy class, and that this agent must be physically destroyed. At the level of the dynamic of political organisations, Gramsci argues:

> It is not sufficiently borne in mind that many political acts are due to internal necessities of an organisational character, that is they are tied to the need to give coherence to a party, a group, a society. This is made clear for example in the history of the Catholic Church. If, for every ideological struggle within the Church one wanted to find an immediate primary explanation in the structure one would really be caught napping: all sorts of politico-economic romances have been written for this reason. It is evident on the contrary that the majority of these discussions are connected with sectarian and organisational necessities. *SPN*, p. 408.

If the party operates within an economistic problematic, it will have a false picture of the significance of the multitude of ever-changing elements in an extremely complex conjuncture, and its ability to intervene most effectively will be sharply hindered even in those areas where it is aware that it should intervene. Thus not only is the terrain for political struggle reduced severely by an economistic problematic, but the potential of the party to relate to *any* terrain is fundamentally weakened.

One of the aspects of the Italian working-class movement which

Gramsci had always criticised was empty revolutionary posturing unrelated to an effective revolutionary strategy and tactics.[22] This had often resulted in a dogmatism which had as one of its consequences an objection to any kind of compromise on principle.[23] This kind of intransigence in fact resulted in passivity and was related, Gramsci argued, to an economistic position which assumed that since history unfolded with the regularity of natural laws, intervention by the subjective factor could necessarily produce little of any value.[24] Gramsci goes on to argue that the only task assigned to the subjective factor within this schema is force of arms to destroy the old order, once history, conceived of mechanically, has created a crisis. The possibility of positive political intervention to destroy the present social system by creating an alternative hegemony and an alternative historical bloc is inconceivable within this intransigent framework which maintains that 'the intervention of will is useful for destruction but not for reconstruction. . . . Destruction is conceived of mechanically, not as destruction/reconstruction'. (*SPN*, p. 168.)

On the question of compromise we can see how Gramsci's criticism of economism and the way in which his concept of the historical bloc, his revaluation of the specificity of the ideological and political struggle through the concept of hegemony, and his concept of revolutionary change as the couple destruction-construction all intersect. All of these aspects of his thought are bound up with the view that not only is history not determined in any immediate sense by a development of the productive forces, and that the superstructure is not a mere reflection of the economic base, but that the political and ideological realms are *behind* in their development compared to the economic. It must be understood, he writes,

> that mass ideological factors always lag behind mass economic phenomena, and that therefore, at certain moments, the automatic thrust due to the economic factor is slowed down, obstructed or even momentarily broken by traditional ideological elements —hence that there must be a conscious, planned struggle to ensure that the exigencies of the economic position of the masses, which may conflict with the traditional leadership's policies, are understood. *SPN*, p. 68.[25]

This is based on a particular view of the contradiction between the forces of production and the relations of production. To the extent that the superstructure represents the need of the relations of production to reproduce themselves, the realm of politics and ideology will suit, in a general sense, a particular social formation whose economic base already contains the objective, material factors whose full development would require a *new* social formation, and *new* relations of production. It is this contradiction, Gramsci argues, which opens up the terrain for an ideological and political struggle, and is also the basis for compromises.

> An appropriate political initiative is always necessary to liberate the economic thrust from the dead weight of traditional policies—i.e. to change the political direction of certain forces which have been absorbed if *a new, homogeneous politico-economic historical bloc, without internal contradictions, is to be successfully formed.* And, since two 'similar' forces can only be welded into a new organism either through a series of compromises or by force of arms, either by binding them to each other as allies or by forcibly subordinating one to the other, the question is whether one has the necessary force, and whether it is 'productive' to use it. If the union of two forces is necessary in order to defeat a third, a recourse to arms and coercion ... can be nothing more than a methodological hypothesis; *the only concrete possibility is compromise.* Force can be employed against enemies, but not against a part of one's own side which one wishes rapidly to assimilate, and whose 'good will' and enthusiasm one needs. *SPN*, p. 168. [My emphasis.]

This is an example of the relationship between Gramsci's general theory of society and of historical change, his theory of the party, and the theoretical basis for strategy and tactics. Translation of these principles into daily practice cannot be indicated by Gramsci. The actual practice of the party, the type of compromises it enters into can only be judged in terms of a particular strategy and a particular conjuncture. What Gramsci is suggesting is that because the party must be able to form an alternative historical bloc, and thus intervene at the political and ideological level to promote a development of the superstructure in keeping with the potential for development in the economic base — a completely different proposition from waiting for the superstructural development to take place automatically be it before or after the seizure of State power—the ability to know the type of compromises necessary to form such a bloc under the hegemony of the proletariat is fundamentally necessary in its fulfilling its task. Far from a dogmatic refusal to enter into such compromises being a guarantee of the revolutionary nature of the party, this refusal on principle is one more aspect of resigning the party to passivity.[26] At the same time Gramsci attempts to establish an analytical yardstick to determine the nature and the limits of these compromises related to his theory of hegemony. This yardstick is the notion of passive revolution which we discuss below.

12. The War of Position: the Development of a Concept

The question of the context of a strategy and even more so that of tactics cannot be answered at the level of theory since it depends ultimately on a particular analysis of a specific concrete social formation. It is with regards to the theoretical tools which are needed in order to be able to analyse the conjuncture correctly that Gramsci's whole theoretical work is of direct interest to the party. In terms of the practice of the party, probably the most important single area of theoretical knowledge, which itself implies a whole problematic, has to do with a theory of the State and consequently in Gramsci's terms, the concept of hegemony.

It is the concept of hegemony which is the basis of Gramsci's attack on economism, and hegemony is the link between this discussion and the notes on strategy, in particular what he metaphorically calls the war of position, or a kind of trench warfare, as opposed to the war of movement, or frontal attack.[1] On the strategic level the war of position is Gramsci's answer to the theoretical mistake of economism, in particular that aspect of economism which is a miscomprehension of the full meaning of the State and therefore of the political terrain of the party.[2]

In the case of this topic a real development within the *Notebooks* can be observed.[3] By tracing this development it will become clear that Gramsci's discussion of the war of movement and the war of position are not merely contingent on reflections on the defensive nature of the struggle in Western Europe in the 1930s.[4] We shall see that it is a false dichotomy to identify the war of movement with an offensive struggle and the war of position with a defensive one. At the same time, by examining the theoretical basis of the discussion, we shall see how Gramsci transcended his own definition of the problem concerning the differences between the experience of Russia and that of the West. When considered at the theoretical level, there are many implications not only for the way in which State power can be achieved, but also for the building of socialism after the achievement of State power. Because it brings together so many of Gramsci's ideas and because it is absolutely central to the practice of the party in what he calls an advanced country, it is worth considering the development of Gramsci's discussion of the war of position in some depth, reconstructing the development of the notion in the *Notebooks*.

In a very early note Gramsci first directly compares the art of politics with that of military science in the context of a discussion of the difficulties which the working class faced in Italy in combatting the tactics of the fascists.[5] Warning that the military metaphor must be used cautiously,[6] he compares these tactics to those of the 'arditi' or commando units, which he says have a particular role within the war of position as exemplified by the war of 1914-18. He defines these commando tactics of the fascists in an extremely significant way:

> In the current struggles this phenomenon often occurs. A weakened State structure is like a flagging army; the commandos — i.e. the *private* armed organisations — enter the field, and they have two tasks: to make use of illegal means, while the State appears to remain within legality, and thus *to reorganise the State itself. SPN*, p. 232. [My emphasis.]

It is in terms of private, or non-State organisations in the restricted sense, that in certain circumstances the State itself is reorganised and strengthened.[7] What is primarily a discussion of the *tactical* level in this early note is based on a theoretical view which has much wider application and which becomes the basis of Gramsci's discussion later in the *Notebooks* at the *strategic* level.[8]

Here we can see how a lack of understanding the relationship of these private organisations to the State can result in a crucial mistake for the working class. In an example of the link between theory and practice, in terms of its *tactics*, the proletariat must understand the importance of hegemony and the terrain of civil society or the *non-State* arena with regards to the maintenance of *State* power by the dominant class. Gramsci identifies the choice between a war of movement or a war of position predominantly with a tactical decision depending on the constraints of the structural position of a class.[9] The discussion is not completely unambiguous, but he tries to avoid any pitfalls in his analogy. It is foolish, he writes, to be fixated by a military model since 'politics, here too must have priority over its military aspect . . . *only politics creates the possibility for manoeuvre and movement.*' (*SPN*, p. 232.) [My emphasis.] This is the proposition which emerges immediately and which is the foundation of his discussion of the strategic principle of the war of position.

The fact that it is the realm of politics which creates the possibility of a frontal attack is crucial in his discussion of strategy. Politics includes the realm of civil society when Gramsci identifies it with the State in the widest sense. This is the specific terrain of the party, and just as it prepares the military moment of a relation of forces, it also is the crucial factor in terms of even the possibility of a war of movement.

Gramsci reinforces this point when in the note which follows immediately he writes that compared to military war,

> Political struggle is enormously more complex: in a certain sense, it can be compared to colonial wars or to old wars of conquest — in which the victorious army occupies, or proposes to occupy, permanently all or a part of the conquered territory. Then the defeated army is disarmed and dispersed, but the struggle continues on the terrain of politics and of military 'preparation'. *SPN*, p. 229.

The military moment can be successful but the struggle is then transposed once more onto the terrain of the *political.* The political and the military or the war of position and the war of movement are not two separate moments but part of a single, dialectical process. They form two poles of what Gramsci calls the 'dual perspective'. What begins to disappear in Gramsci's problematic is the question of whether a moment or period is 'revolutionary' or not. It is rather a question of which pole of the dialectic is nearer at hand. Neither pole is wholly revolutionary or not revolutionary on its own. Rather it is the unity of the whole and the relation of the elements within it which must be analysed.

Gramsci's first full articulation of the difference between the war of movement and the war of position comes in a note written slightly later, entitled 'The Transition from the War of Manoeuvre (Frontal Attack) to the War of Position — in the Political Field as Well'.

> This seems to me to be the most important question of political theory that the post-war period has posed, and the most difficult to solve correctly. It is related to the problems raised by Bronstein [Trotsky], who in one way or another can be considered the political theorist of frontal attack in a period in which it only leads to defeats. *SPN*, p. 238.

We shall return to the various aspects of Trotsky's position which Gramsci is criticising. What begins to become clear in this note is that the *period* in which a frontal attack can only cause defeat, while it seems to concern a relatively short-term change in tactics, in fact extends to the whole period of the development of the modern State and is therefore not simply connected with a temporary downturn in the revolutionary fortunes of the working-class movement, nor merely the debate with Trotsky.

There are several different elements in Gramsci's argument here. On one level in this note Gramsci is interested in the link albeit indirect between the actual military war of position between states and the type of political organisation it imposes upon the State. He is also thinking of the difficulties of building socialism in the Soviet Union.

> The war of position demands enormous sacrifices by infinite masses of people. So an unprecedented concentration of hegemony is necessary, and hence a more 'interventionist' government, which will take the offensive more openly against the oppositionists and organise permanently the 'impossibility' of internal disintegration—with controls of every kind, political, administrative, etc., reinforcement of the hegemonic 'positions' of the dominant group, etc. *SPN*, pp. 238-9.

He is at the same time considering the class struggle within any State when the war of position forces the State to attempt to preserve its hegemony by intervening more directly in the realm of civil society. The crucial nature of this struggle shows that it is posing the question completely wrongly to reduce the war of movement-war of position relationship to the difference between an offensive and a defensive struggle. Gramsci continues:

> All this indicates that we have entered a culminating phase in the political-historical situation, since *in politics the 'war of position', once won, is decisive definitively.* In politics, in other words, the war of manoeuvre subsists *so long as it is a question of winning positions which are not decisive*, so that all the resources of the State's hegemony cannot be mobilised. But when, for one reason or another, these positions have lost their value and only the decisive positions are at stake, then one passes over to siege warfare; this is concentrated, difficult, and requires exceptional qualities of patience and inventiveness. *SPN*, p. 239. [My emphasis.]

The key phrase is Gramsci's specification that once the war of position is won, it is won definitively. Or in other terms, only when the working class has won the battle of hegemony will it have triumphed definitively. This triumph cannot be reduced to the seizure of State power in the frontal attack. The war of position is the culmination of of the historical process.[10] Once again we find the organic relationship of the two moments of the revolutionary struggle, of the moment of consent and the moment of force. In this passage the moment of force or the war of movement is consigned to a relatively subordinate place. At most it is able to win within a terrain which is not decisive. The basis of this argument becomes clearer in later notes. Here Gramsci is quite explicit that the war of position is the decisive struggle and that the difficulty of this kind of struggle, far from being merely defensive or passive, necessitates the political initiative of the party.[11]

The fact that the party and the working class are potentially able to affect the outcome of the revolutionary struggle in this kind of battle, and not simply in terms of a frontal attack, is made absolutely clear in the last sentence in the note 'In politics, the siege is reciprocal, despite all appearances, and the mere fact that the ruler has to muster all his resources demonstrates how seriously he takes his adversary.' (*SPN*, p. 239.) Even though the dominant class may *appear* to be superior because it has the State apparatuses on its side, it is forced to use all its political and ideological resources to maintain its hegemony and ultimately State power. Its dominance therefore is conditional far more than may seem to be the case on its ability to maintain itself on this terrain. To the extent that the working class and its allies through its political party is able to challenge it on this terrain, it is weakened. In this sense the siege is mutual. The political activities of the dominant class must always be understood as, in part, a response to the activities or lack thereof of the subaltern classes which are thus not simply viewed as an object of history but a subject which can help to define the terrain of struggle whatever the situation.

The party can only undertake an effective political struggle, however, if it has a correct understanding of the enemy it faces. Gramsci attributes a mistaken view of the kind of struggle facing the working class to 'an inaccurate understanding of what the State (in its integral meaning: dictatorship and hegemony) really is', which in turn 'leads to an underestimation of the adversary and his fighting organisation'. (*SPN*, p. 239.) If a party undertakes the war of movement as a strategic option, far from in any real sense undertaking the most 'militant' or offensive type of struggle, it does not comprehend the nature of the enemy and thus underestimates him, remaining on a terrain which is not decisive. Without the concept of hegemony and the consequences that it has for the class struggle, the working class cannot fight a winning battle. In a note written at more or less the same time, Gramsci says cryptically, 'the war of position in politics, *is* the concept of hegemony.'[12]

Bearing in mind that these are the terms of Gramsci's development of the concept of war of position, we can go on to a note in which he addresses directly the problem of the differences between the reality facing the Bolsheviks in 1917, and that facing revolutionaries in the West. The *raison d'être* of the war of position is rooted in the different reality of State power.[13]

> In the East the State was everything, civil society was primordial and gelatinous; in the West, there was a proper relation between the State and civil society, and when the State trembled a sturdy structure of civil society was at once revealed. The State was only an outer ditch, behind which there stood a powerful system of fortresses and earthworks. *SPN*, p. 238.

The difference is posed in terms of geographical position, but in fact Gramsci is talking about two different types of States. In an advanced Western State, the State apparatuses depend on civil society and are only the most obvious 'appearances' of the power of the dominant class. Gramsci specifically says that the question of the transition from the war of movement to the war of position 'is posed for the modern States, not for backward countries'. (*SPN*, p. 243.) The fact that the Tsarist State was not rooted in a fully developed civil society meant that in certain respects it resembled rather that feudal State which Gramsci described in the following way:

> In the ancient and mediaeval State alike, centralisation, whether political-territorial or social . . . was minimal. The State was, in a certain sense, a mechanical bloc of social groups . . . The modern State substitutes for the mechanical bloc of social groups their subordination to the active hegemony of the directive and dominant group. *SPN*, p. 54.

In certain circumstances then, the war of movement on its own, without a preceding war of position, may be able to achieve the seizure of state power. But if we connect this line of discussion with another, we shall see that in this case, the war of position, which is the 'only definitive one' must still be waged *after* the revolutionary class has achieved State power because in the modern period this class must in every case establish its hegemony in order to establish a new State in a full, integral, modern sense.[14] Furthermore, according to Gramsci, the development of new superstructures, the development of hegemony and civil society, will not happen spontaneously. Thus, by bringing together the various strands of Gramsci's thought, we begin to have some theoretical criteria useful for analysing the transition to socialism not only in Western Europe but in the socialist countries as well.

Gramsci's identification of the war of position with the particular needs of the struggle in a modern advanced State becomes quite clear in his later notes. These are worth detailed consideration because the topic is one of the most controversial and, it could be argued, the most misunderstood in Gramsci's work. In these notes he traces the genesis of the war of position from the type of society which developed in Europe after 1870.[15] Up until then a type of 'permanent revolution' was appropriate.[16] It is important to examine what he considers to have changed in the period after 1870:

> In the period after 1870, with the colonial expansion of Europe . . . the internal and international organisational relations of the State become more complex and massive, and the Forty-Eightist formula of the 'Permanent Revolution' is expanded and transcended in political science by the formula of 'civil hegemony'. *SPN*, p. 243.

This, then, is the period of the expansion of the apparatuses of hegemony internal to the State and the expansion of imperialism in terms of the relations between States. Ensuing from these changes is a change in the mode of the political class struggle.

> The massive structures of the modern democracies, both as State organisations, and as complexes of associations in civil society, constitute for the art of politics as it were the 'trenches' and the permanent fortifications of the front in the war of position: *they render merely 'partial' the element of movement which before used to be 'the whole' of war, etc. SPN*, p. 243. [My emphasis.]

The war of movement becomes a tactical instance within the general strategy of a war of position.[17] Victory comes to the extent that the various forces prepare for the decisive moment, which will only in the most immediate sense be the military one of the moment of force. Indeed, to the extent that the hegemony of the revolutionary class has already been established on a wide basis, 'in time of peace' the moment of force recedes in importance.

It is in the first version of this note that Gramsci wrote, *'the war of position in politics is the concept of hegemony which can only come into being after the advent of certain premises.* That is, the modern type of large, popular organizations which correspond to the trenches and permanent fortifications of the war of position.' (*Q*, p. 973). (My emphasis.) In the second version cited above, he goes on to specify that the question of the war of position is posed only for modern States. His argument for the need to change the mode of the struggle is based on the change in the reality of State power.

The period when the war of position is appropriate in Western Europe thus encompasses the period immediately after the First World War.[18] It is still appropriate today if Gramsci's problematic is applicable unless the fundamental premises upon which this problematic is based no longer exist. Although the perspective of a frontal attack may at certain points in time have been closer, it could only have led to victory if within the overall strategic context of a war of position. The mode of struggle depends on objective, organic factors, not subjective or occasional ones. Only in exceptional circumstances can the choice of the mode of struggle be determined by the working class and its party. In general it must fight on the terrain which exists objectively as the chief bulwark of the dominance of another class. The terrain of struggle is widened to include civil society and the war of position is a fundamental principle, not merely a contingent, tactical necessity.[19]

Its relationship to Gramsci's critique of economism, and a further demonstration that he considers the war of position a fundamental strategic principle, is found in the last note in which the concept is mentioned. Originally entitled 'Structure and Superstructure',[20] it was written very soon after his notes on economism and in fact shows how the two orders of discussion are intimately connected. Arguing against what he considers Luxemburg's overestimation of the consequences of an economic crisis,[21] he now articulates the transformation of the war of movement to a tactical instance in terms of the system of defences of a State which protect the dominance of a class during an economic crisis. This change of strategy is implied:

> at least in the case of the most advanced States, where 'civil society' has become a very complex structure and one which is resistant to the catastrophic 'incursions' of the immediate economic element (crises, depressions, etc.). The superstructures of civil society are like the trench-systems of modern warfare. In war it would sometimes happen that a fierce artillery attack seemed to have destroyed the enemy's entire defensive system, whereas in fact it had only destroyed the outer perimeter; and at the moment of their advance and attack the assailants would find themselves confronted by a line

of defence which was still effective. The same thing happens in politics, during the great economic crises. *SPN*, p. 235.

One consequence of this, he further argues, is that the organised subjective element, the party, will not necessarily develop speedily nor spontaneously during an economic crisis. And in terms of the resolution of a conflict, a rapid development of the struggle is determinant only in the most immediate sense. The perspective, while still 'dual', is predominantly one of a lengthy struggle on the terrain of civil society and hegemony which 'requires exceptional qualities of patience and inventiveness'. (*SPN*, p. 239.) The party must build its organisation as it fights the war of position realising that the struggle will be successful in so far as it is prepared 'minutely and technically in peace time'. (*SPN*, p. 243.) The war of position, far from being the moment of passive defence, is the moment during which victory or defeat is assured. It is the strategic answer to economism in that it allows the full potential of the subjective factor to be made a real or concrete element in the class struggle.

In this last discussion in the *Notebooks* of the war of movement and the war of position, Gramsci also states quite clearly that the last example of a war of movement, 'was the events of 1917'. (*SPN*, p. 235.) In the early 1920s, the fact that Western Europe would have to contemplate a different strategy and tactics than those which had proved successful in Russia was widely discussed in the Comintern. What was not generally understood, however, was the *theoretical* basis for the need for a different strategy.[22]

Gramsci's development of theory in this area places particular emphasis on the national dimension.[23] The prime task of the party is to study '"in depth" which elements of civil society correspond to the defensive systems in a war of position'. (*SPN*, p. 235.)[24] Articulated in this way, this task can only be fulfilled if the party has made its point of departure a detailed analysis of the *national* context.[25] This is the basis of his argument against Trotsky.[26] The lack of the concept of hegemony reflects an economistic deviation[27] and a miscomprehension of the State. Without a precise understanding of the national context there cannot in fact be an accurate analysis of the international setting which Gramsci argues is indeed important. What is important is the relationship between the two at any one moment, not the dominance of one over the other in the abstract. In a passage written in the period 1932-5, which echoes very closely an argument of Gramsci's against Bordiga many years earlier, he writes:

To be sure, the line of development is towards internationalism, but the point of departure is 'national' — and it is from this point of departure that one must begin. Yet the perspective is international and cannot be otherwise. Consequently, it is necessary to study accurately the combination of national forces which the international class [the proletariat] will have to lead and develop, in accordance with the international perspective and directives [i.e. those of the Comintern]. The leading class is in fact only such if it accurately interprets this combination — of which it is itself a component and precisely as such is able to give the movement a certain direction, within certain perspectives. *SPN*, p. 240.[28]

It is through the concept of hegemony that a class in fact provides the basis for a national unity. What is of particular importance is that the thrust of Gramsci's argument has to do with the ability of the party to undertake political initiatives. The war of position, the concept of hegemony, and the national context as a point of departure from which it is then possible to purge as the Bolsheviks did, 'internationalism of every vague and purely ideological . . . element to give it a realistic political content' (*SPN*, p. 241) are all necessary if the party is not to be relegated to passivity. Trotsky's position, then, according to Gramsci, is rooted in a mechanistic or economistic problematic which robs the party, or the subjective factor, of any concrete possibility to intervene in history.[29]

To summarise, what Gramsci has asserted thus far is that in any concrete social formation where there is a modern State, a revolutionary strategy must be based on a war of position within which there can be a tactical moment when the war of movement is appropriate. Now this has very wide implications which have not always been understood. As we mentioned above, the war of position has very often been seen as an *alternative* to the war of movement, forced upon the working class in a defensive period. Specifically it has come to be identified with a change in tactics in the 1920s when after a period of frontal attack, the stabilisation of capitalism made necessary the establishment of the united front policy.[30] On the basis of one or two isolated passages, it can be construed that this is Gramsci's position.[31] The fact that there is an ambiguity in Gramsci's own mind may be the symptom, we would suggest, of a certain difficulty in making a thorough-going criticism of the strategic confusion of the socialist and then communist movement in the post-First World War period based on his own theoretical discussion in the *Notebooks*. This criticism is none the less implicit. The State which the working-class movement was facing in the various countries of Western Europe was a modern, integral State which at all times enjoyed a degree of hegemony and a level of organisation in the realm of civil society, whatever economic or political crises it underwent. Only by mistaking the 'occasional' for the 'organic' could it be suggested that the war of movement, unconnected with a war of position, was the correct strategy for the Western working-class movement until the relative stabilisation of capitalism in the early 1920s. Based on Gramsci's own analysis, faced with a modern State, the war of movement is never more than a tactical instance. This does not at all necessarily contradict the idea that the period of imperialism is a revolutionary period, in the sense of there being an objective basis for revolution, but rather changes the way this is understood in terms of the mode of the struggle.[32]

Further, although space will not allow us to develop this argument fully, implicit in Gramsci's approach is a criticism of the 'third period' strategy, not simply because it was based on an inaccurate analysis of the conjuncture but because it is based on an undialectical and economistic view of the different moments of the struggle.[33] By defining the period as one of frontal attack,[34] the perspective of the war of position disappeared entirely. Using Gramsci's theoretical tools, such as the concept of hegemony and the war of position, a criticism could be made that despite the seemingly very different turns of the Comintern, to the extent that the strategy was not based on a theoretical understanding of the full meaning of the State and of the way in which the dominance of a particular class is assured, the Communist movement was still trapped within an economistic problematic.[35] Gramsci's originality here is not so much his interest in the concept of hegemony but rather the way in which he developed it and its implications for the strategy of the working class movement.[36] He did not, perhaps, realise its full implications for a self-criticism and a criticism of the communist movement.

With regard to the political party, the war of position delineates the whole range of its practice. By organising its activities in terms of the dual perspective, in terms of a strategy of a war of position, the party is able to confront the dominant class on the whole terrain which guarantees its dominance. In so doing, the party both widens the range of its activities considerably and brings into focus the specific national context of the particular set of defences of any one State. This is the basis on which it is able to relate to the international reality. But most importantly of all, by basing its practices on a dialectical concept of revolutionary change, it no longer arbitrarily splits defensive from offensive struggles, it no longer divides the revolutionary process into revolutionary and non-revolutionary moments. It is thus enabled to maximise any potential for political intervention in whatever concrete situation faces it. It is able to maximise the potential of the subjective forces in the historical process. The crucial result is to minimise the possibility that the party falls into passivity.

13. Passive Revolution: a Strategy for the Bourgeoisie in the War of Position

The relative passivity of the party does not necessarily consist in the absence of activity as such but in the absence of an intervention by the subjective forces so as to represent the fullest expression of the potential of the working class at any single moment of the relation of forces. Gramsci is concerned about this kind of intervention by the party in the most immediate sense because of the difficulties faced by the party under fascism. Yet fascism represents, in his opinion, only the most recent in a series of attempts in Italian history to eliminate the threat to the dominant classes represented by the insertion in political life of the the mass of the population. In order to take account of the phenomenon whereby a dominant class maintains its power more because of a weakness on the part of the adversary, promoted by the form of politics of the dominant class itself, than because of its own positive hegemony, Gramsci develops the concept of passive revolution. It is rooted in Gramsci's earlier writings where he analysed the crisis of the Liberal State stemming from the changed relationship between the State and the economy. The passive revolution is an attempt to explain the fact that

> a social form 'always has marginal possibilities for further development and organisational improvement, and in particular can count on the relative weakness of the rival progressive force as a result of its specific character and way of life. It is necessary for the dominant social form to preserve this weakness. *SPN*, p. 222.

Inspired by an idea of Cuoco,[1] which is, however 'completely modified and enriched' (*SPN*, p. 108), it is one of the most complex as well as one of the more obscure of Gramsci's ideas, not the least because it must be related to a whole series of notes in which it is only indirectly the subject of analysis. Moreover, it is a concept which represents an integral asymmetry between the type of strategy which the bourgeoisie can undertake in establishing and maintaining its State and that which is appropriate for the proletariat. Gramsci insists on the fact that while the passive revolution, (or, in another formulation, revolution-restoration after Quintet),[2] that is, an attempt to promote change which is not based on a positive, concrete hegemony, can be a technique or a programme for the bourgeoisie, it can only be a 'criterion of interpretation' for the working-class movement.[3] One of the least explicit of his ideas, it is, we would argue, at the same time one of the most important to enable the revolutionary party to understand its task because it is a further explanation of the margin for political survival which the bourgeoisie enjoys despite political and economic crises, and because it indicates the *novel* nature of the building of a new state by the working class.

This concept functions at two levels as do so many others in the *Notebooks*—as a discussion of some aspects of historical events and as an expression of a theoretical problem. The historical analysis is only of interest here in so far as it clarifies the way in which Gramsci is putting forth a theoretical argument. In addition, a certain methodology of reading Gramsci may be indicated, without entering the argument whether this is a proper way of reading of history, in Gramsci's own statement that 'Interpretations of the past, when one seeks the deficiencies and the errors (of certain parties or currents) from the past itself, are not "history" but present-day politics *in nuce*'. (*Q*, p. 1815.) Although the mode of his discussion is historical, it is possible to derive key aspects of Gramsci's political theory from the way in which he reads history.

Gramsci describes the Risorgimento and in fact a whole series of other historical phenomena in nineteenth-century Europe as the product of a passive revolution. Contrasted with the way the French Revolution established a bourgeois state on the basis of popular support and its concomitant elimination of the old feudal classes both economically and politically, the institution of political forms to suit the expansion of the capitalist mode of production in the rest of Europe took place in a different manner, as

the 'passive' aspect of the great revolution which started in France in 1789 and which spilled over into the rest of Europe with the republican and Napoleonic armies—giving the old régimes a powerful shove, and resulting not in their immediate collapse as in France but in the 're-formist' corrosion of them which lasted up to 1870 . . . the demands which in France found a Jacobin-Napoleonic expression were satisfied by small doses, legally, in a reformist manner—in such a way that it was possible to preserve the political and economic position of the old feudal classes, to avoid agrarian reform, and, especially, to avoid the popular masses going through a period of political experience such as occurred in France in the years of Jacobinism. *SPN*, p. 119.

While Gramsci uses the French Revolution as a model of a bourgeois revolution, he is careful to avoid schematisms. He warns:

The conception of the State according to the productive function of the social classes cannot be applied mechanically to the interpretation of Italian and European history from the French Revolution throughout the nineteenth century. Although it is certain that for the fundamental productive classes (capitalist bourgeoisie and modern proletariat) the State is only conceivable as the concrete form of a specific economic world, of a specific system of production, this does not mean that the relationship of means to end can be easily determined or takes the form of a simple schema, apparent at first sight. *SPN*, p. 116.

It is precisely because the form of the State may represent a disjuncture between the economic and political levels of a social formation that the exact form of political rule with all its peculiarities must be studied in order to avoid oversimplifications.

In this passive revolution or revolution-restoration the old feudal classes maintained a political role, gradually being transformed from an economically and politically dominant class into a governing group serving the dominance of another class, the bourgeoisie. Gramsci explains:

restoration becomes the *political form* whereby social struggles find sufficiently elastic frameworks to allow the bourgeoisie to gain power without dramatic upheavals, without the French machinery of terror. The old feudal classes are demoted from their *dominant position to a 'governing' one*, but are not eliminated, nor is there any attempt to liquidate them as an organic whole; *instead of a class they become a 'caste'* with specific cultural and psychological characteristics *but no longer with predominant economic functions. SPN*, p. 115. [My emphasis.]

At the same time this type of revolution, in the sense of changing the political superstructure to take account of the needs of a new mode of production, occurred without the prerequisite for massive popular support, an agrarian reform which would have meant the destruction of the old feudal classes. In terms of the Italian Risorgimento this method of political change is represented by the success of Cavour and the moderates over the Partito d'Azione, the name Gramsci uses to indicate the groupings around Garibaldi, Mazzini and other 'radicals'. The new Italian state is somewhat of a 'bastard'[4] according to Gramsci because it is founded with an extremely restricted hegemonic base, the product of the compromise between agrarian and industrial interests. Rather than the hegemony of a whole class over the rest of society, the moderates based in Piedmont represented the hegemony of only a *part* of a class over the rest of that class.[5] A weak political unity is both a result and a cause of a weak economic transformation of society.[6]

The new State which is made in the first instance by part of the bourgeoisie against feudal conditions, (the lack of a nation-State in Italy representing the survival of feudal cosmopolitanism which does not, however, eliminate but gradually transforms the old feudal classes in building a new historical bloc, survives using the same strategy but now against a new adversary, the popular classes. The 'passive' aspect consists in preventing the development of a revolutionary adversary by 'decapitating' its revolutionary potential. In Italy the form of this is transformism whereby the leadership of opposing parties, first individuals of the radical bourgeoisie, and after 1900, whole groups, such as sectors of the working-class movement, are transformed into politically harmless elements not threatening the fundamental social relations by absorption into more traditional political organisations.[7] The European-wide dimension of this technique is reformism, according to Gramsci.[8] The acceptance of certain demands from below at the same time encouraging the working class to restrict its struggle to the economic-corporative terrain is part of this attempt to prevent the hegemony of the dominant class from being challenged at the same time as changes in the world of production are accommodated within the current social formation.

The passive revolution is in fact a technique which the bourgeoisie attempts to adopt when its hegemony is weakened in any way. Its hegemony may be weakened for a variety of reasons. The bourgeois State may never have enjoyed a strong hegemony, as in Italy. A previously strong hegemony, such as in France, might be weakened because the dominance of the bourgeoisie and the capitalist mode of production no longer corresponds to the expansion of the productive forces as Gramsci would argue is the case in the epoch of imperialism.[9] In this case the concrete basis for bourgeois hegemony, the fact that the bourgeoisie at a certain stage of history represents the advancement of the whole of society, no longer holds. As masses of people become organised economically and politically, as capitalism reorganises itself in the period of imperialism, there is the potential for the first time in history of masses becoming the protagonists of a social transformation. Therefore the foundation of bourgeois rule changes and reforms which provide a concrete basis for the consent of the majority must be part of an attempt by the bourgeoisie to prevent its adversary, the working class, from developing an alternative hegemony. Further weakening of bourgeois hegemony can occur as a result of a great upheaval such as the First World War when the old apparatuses of hegemony (such as the traditional parties) are themselves thrown into a crisis.[10] Moreover, the gap between the changes necessitated by a development of the economic base in the period of the dominance of monopoly capital, and the ability of the traditional political structures to accommodate these changes represents an organic contradiction which can only be overcome without destroying the dominance of the traditional forces, the traditional relations of production, through a passive revolution which can have a variety of forms. Thus it is a strategy which allows the bourgeoisie to reorganise its dominance politically and economically, a concomitant of the extension of the State as 'force plus consent'.

In the 1930s the reorganisation of capitalism took a variety of political forms from the New Deal to Fascism in which State intervention in the economy and society increased dramatically and some element of planning was attempted to overcome the effects of anarchy in market relations. The form of passive revolution in Italy in this period was fascism.[11]

> there is a passive revolution involved in the fact that—through the legislative intervention of the State, and by means of the corporative organisation—relatively far-reaching modifications are being introduced into the country's economic structure in order to accentuate the 'plan of production' element; in other words, that socialisation and co-operation in the sphere of production are being increased, without however touching (or at least not going beyond the regulation and control of) individual and group appropriation of profit. In the concrete framework of Italian social relations, this could be the only solution whereby to develop the productive forces of industry under the direction of the traditional ruling classes, in competition with the more advanced industrial formations of countries which monopolise raw materials and have accumulated massive capital sums. *SPN*, pp. 119-120.[12]

This attempt to provide for the expansion of the forces of production has as its political concomitant the strengthening of the historical bloc of social forces underpinning the State by an expansion of the relatively weak hegemony of the dominant class to include new popular elements. Fascism did not simply restore a *status quo* but it changed the way in which masses of people related to the State, a State which had never enjoyed a mass base.

> Whether or not such a schema could be put into practice, and to what extent, is only of relative importance. What is important from the political and ideological point of view is that this schema of fascism is capable of creating—and indeed does create—a period of expectation and hope, especially in certain Italian social groups such as the great mass of urban and rural petit bourgeoisie. It thus reinforces the hegemonic system and the forces of military and civil coercion at the disposal of the traditional ruling classes. *SPN*, p. 120.

Gramsci's discussion of fascism in these terms is the key to the importance of the concept with regards to the revolutionary party and to a series of theoretical problems. Faced with the dilemma of the resilience of the variety of political forms of capitalism, a resilience which exists despite the fundamental contradiction at a stage in history between the forces of production and the relations of production, Gramsci produces a concept at the political level to take account of this disjuncture between the superstructure and the structure. That this disjuncture is a central problem for Gramsci is evident from his notes on the different moments in the relations of forces and on economism. Both in these notes and the ones on the passive revolution he refers to a passage from Marx's Preface to a *A Contribution to the Critique of Political Economy* which he paraphrases:

> The concept of 'passive revolution' must be rigorously derived from the two fundamental principles of political science: 1. that no social formation disappears as long as the productive forces which have developed within it still find room for further forward movement; 2. that a society does not set itself tasks for whose solution the necessary conditions have not already been incubated, etc. It goes without saying that these principles must first be developed critically in all their implications, and purged of every residue of mechanism and fatalism. They must therefore be referred back to the description of the three fundamental moments into which a 'situation' or an equilibrium of forces can be distinguished, with the greatest possible stress

on the second moment (equilibrium of political forces), and especially on the third moment (politico-military equilibrium). *SPN*, pp. 106-7.[13]

The crucial phrase is 'still find room' because the ability of the bourgeoisie to manoeuvre in terms of the passive revolution depends on its adversary. This is amplified when Gramsci writes, as we noted above:

> a social form 'always' has marginal possibilities for further development and organisational improvement, and in particular can count on the relative weakness of the rival progressive force as a result of its specific character and way of life. It is necessary for the dominant social form to preserve this weakness. *SPN*, p. 222.

The failure of the proletariat to exert its alternative hegemony allows the bourgeoisie to continue its rule despite the weakening of its own hegemony. The bourgeoisie may be able to undertake the strategy of the passive revolution, using the tools of the war of position, the various ideological apparatuses, the trenches of civil society, to whatever extent possible to *pre-empt* the creation of an hegemony by the working class. The passive revolution has different forms, 'decapitating' the working-class movement through reformism whereby these leaders remain on a non-hegemonic terrain, or by, for example, fascism whereby the leadership and the organisational autonomy of the working class is eliminated.[14] This is certainly not done in a 'passive' way. Here passive refers rather to the nature of the attempt at 'revolution' or development of the productive forces through a degree of State intervention and the inclusion of new social groups under the hegemony of the political order without any expansion of real political control by the mass of the population over politics.

To summarise, when the bourgeoisie is ascendant, the 'passive' aspect of its political revolution has to do with the molecular transformation of the old traditional classes and any relatively more progressive ones.[15] The revolution consists in the establishment of a new State, or a political superstructure generally suited to the eventual dominance of the capitalist mode of production. Gramsci argues that in the Italian case this State was the precondition for the development of an economic base which was very backward.[16] Once this State is established, whatever the nature of its foundation, the bourgeoisie will attempt a strategy of a passive revolution whenever its hegemony is weakened *or* whenever its political superstructure in the integral sense (force plus hegemony) cannot cope with the need to expand the forces of production. If *allowed* to do so, the dominant class may find new forms of political domination.

Yet, as Gramsci points out, any situation is a product of all the forces in the field, not just the dominant forces. He writes the following passage about the Risorgimento, but it could as well apply to any historical development.

> The Risorgimento is a complex and contradictory historical development, which is made an integral whole by all its antithetical elements, by its protagonists and its antagonists, by their struggles, by the reciprocal modifications which these very struggles determine and also by the function of passive and latent forces like the great agricultural masses, as well as, naturally, the function stemming from international relations. *Q*, p. 961.

Indeed the form of the outcome of a clash of forces is dependent on the activity of all the antagonists. It is in this connection that the development of the concept of passive revolution is of vital importance to the revolutionary party. If we go back to Gramsci's discussion of the Risorgimento, a discussion which he says is more of political than historical interest,[17] he argues that the backward base of the outcome is not simply because of the attributes of Cavour and the moderates but also, dialectically, because of the deficiencies of Mazzini and the Partito d'Azione.

> the absence among the radical-popular forces of any awareness of the role of the other side prevented them from being fully aware of their own role either; hence from weighing in the final balance of forces in proportion to their effective power of intervention; and hence from determining a more advanced result, on more progressive and modern lines. *SPN*, p. 113.

Cavour knew his own task, building an historical bloc based on an alliance between a section of the bourgeoisie and the old feudal classes, Gramsci writes, using a metaphor, because he understood the task of his 'dialectical' opponent, Mazzini, and therefore could pre-empt him from being effective. Mazzini would have needed a programme of agrarian reform to create a popular base and to eliminate the economic and political power of the old feudal classes in order to build an alternative historical bloc. Cavour was faced, however, by an adversary who represented a weak 'antithesis' because Mazzini would have been able to understand the nature of his own task in building an historical bloc only if he had understood that of Cavour.[18] In other words, the need for an alternative rooted in the popular masses, an historical bloc based on an agrarian reform, the content of a concrete political line, which would have prevented the formation of the historical bloc built by Cavour, could only have been understood, according to Gramsci, as the dialectical opposite of the historical bloc being established by the moderates.[19]

Gramsci repeatedly criticises the Partito d'Azione for lack of realism and lack of a concrete political programme.[20] The religious question was an example of how an abstract stance actually prevented the solution of a problem. Gramsci argues that an abstract anticlerical position merely prevented the creation of alliances with the peasantry which would have provided for a concrete solution to the problem of the social and economic influence of the Vatican and indirectly put the question of religion in a framework where its political consequence was greatly lessened.[21] Only a concrete analysis of the specific array of forces confronting each other could produce the basis for an adequate political line.

The lesson for the revolutionary party is clear. Its analysis must be centred on the specific configuration of class forces confronting it in order to be able to know the nature of the alternative historical bloc which it must build. It can only provide this kind of analysis by a nonschematic application of Marxist theory to the specific national context, not by 'intellectual and rational schemas'. (*Q*, p. 1362.) This is a further argument for the national perspective to be the point of departure. When only one of the opponents in the field 'knows' its task, there is, according to Gramsci, a kind of asymmetry at the theoretical level, a misconception of the dialectic whereby one element attempts to assert itself not by a dialectical overcoming of the adversary but by an absorption of certain elements of the antithesis.[22] The result is not as advanced as it would have been had the antithesis been fully asserted. Thus by posing the question in this way, the result of a clash of different forces, of a conflict which is not simply one dramatic instance but the ongoing class struggle, is presented as a resultant of the political ability of the different forces in the field rather than as a simple victory or defeat. The question is always present for the revolutionary party whether its strategy is producing the optimal results, and difficulties it faces or achievements by the enemy are seen to be in part a result of its own efforts or rather failures.

The lesson for the working class is that the strategy of passive revolution will be attempted by the bourgeoisie. In order to counteract this, to prevent this kind of margin for political survival developing, the working class must exert its hegemony in the war of position. It is by exerting itself fully in this sense that it can push each moment of historical development forward so that it will be relatively more to the advantage of the working class than otherwise. A failure by the proletariat will allow the result of a clash of forces to be more to the advantage of the adversary. Moreover, an effective intervention by the proletariat depends on a precise comprehension of the political strategy of its enemy.

Gramsci's discussion of the dialectic thus has to do with the difference between reformist and revolutionary politics. Arguing that from the point of view of the dominant class, reformism is a version of passive revolution, he notes that one aspect of the strategy is to break up the struggle into finite moments. It is based on an ideology which 'tends to weaken the antithesis, to break it up into a series of moments, that is, to reduce the dialectic to a process of reformist evolution, of "revolution-restoration", in which only the second term is valid'.[23] On the theoretical level, Bernstein argued that a qualitative change would come about through a series of small, partial changes which, one added to the other, would result in a qualitative change.[24] Gramsci affirms that in the real world the dialectic presents itself, or appears, as separate moments, or, we would suggest, in more concrete terms as a struggle for reforms, but the relation between these reforms and a qualitative change has to do with the way in which they reflect a shift in the balance of forces as part of a concrete political strategy, as the result of political intervention in a particular concrete reality. As Gramsci writes, 'knowing how to find each time the point of progressive equilibrium (in the sense of one's own programme) is the art of the politician, not of the golden mean, but really of the politician who has a very precise line with a wide perspective of the future.' (*Q*, p. 1825.)[25] Outside of this context, if these partial moments are elevated to a theoretical principle of historical change, reforms can become a question of 'empirical opportunism'.[26]

Reformism or any other version of the passive revolution cannot be a suitable strategy for the proletariat. In a note entitled significantly, 'First Epilogue', Gramsci summarises the main points which he wants to make in his writings on the passive revolution. It is not, he writes, a *'theory of the "passive revolution"* . . . as a programme, as it was for the Italian liberals of the Risorgimento, but as a criterion of interpretation'.[27] When Gramsci writes that it must not be a programme for the working-class movement, an argument which must be related to his general critique of reformism as not going beyond an economic-corporative struggle, his reasoning is based on an idea of a fundamental asymmetry between the revolution made by the working class and that of the bourgeoisie. Since the bourgeoisie could transform the old feudal classes into political allies, converting traditional intellectuals to perform an organic function serving the new bourgeois dominance as they take over the existing State machinery, they can found a new state on the basis of the passive revolution, doing without a massive popular consent in a positive sense as long as they can continue a passive revolution in one form or another against any new adversaries. Thus the bourgeoisie could simply adapt the existing State to its own use maintaining a certain split between politics and society without transforming the mode of existence of the intellectuals, their relationship to the masses.

The proletariat cannot found a State on the same basis for several reasons. First of all, the proletariat is founding a State to do away with all exploitation in the Marxist sense, whereas the bourgeoisie were replacing one form of exploitation with another. It has as its historical project the creation of a new *type* of State, in which the very concept of politics is transformed, as the masses intervene and control politics and economics.[28] The proletariat cannot, therefore, simply instrumentalise cadres of the bourgeoisie to their own ends through a passive revolution. Furthermore, Gramsci argues throughout his work that an integral State can only be founded if a class enjoys hegemony before it achieves State power and in terms of the struggle in an advanced capitalist country, if the war of position has been waged successfully. All of this implies widespread popular consent. This is also demonstrated if we reverse the argument. Since the proletariat cannot bring about its transformation of society through the passive revolution, it can only do so on the basis of a concrete programme which engenders widespread consent and a system of alliances under its hegemony. This hegemony is based on compromises and on a struggle to achieve reforms, but reforms of a qualitatively different nature than those conceded by the bourgeoisie in the passive revolution, for if the proletariat is to weld together an alternative historical bloc, it must promote changes which go beyond the corporative interests of the groups concerned and challenge the traditional mode of political control. Its historical project involves the overcoming of the split between politics and society and the establishment of a new relationship between leaders and led. It thus cannot simply take over the existing State and a pre-existing mode of intellectual activity in which all the old divisions are maintained but must transform the State and its relationship with the mass of the population, and the very nature of the consent it maintains must be quantitatively different.

The usefulness of the concept of the passive revolution as an interpretative device for the revolutionary party thus consists in measuring the adequacy of its own strategy and in the way it helps to explain the durability of bourgeois rule despite economic and political crises. Yet, there is nothing fatal about its application if the party develops a correct strategy.[29] Gramsci insists that even when a party is restricted by events to existing as a small and possibly clandestine organisation, it must avoid sectarianism by conceiving of itself as the nucleus of a much larger party, viewing its very existence as the subjective 'symptom' of an objective potential which is prevented from developing only because of a temporary relation of forces. Even in the most difficult circumstances the party must view its function in terms of a mass movement even if the passive revolution has temporarily destroyed this movement.[30] It must always aim for a mass base, insisting on the fact that 'in order to create *lasting* history, it is not enough to have the "best". The largest and most numerous national-popular energies are necessary.' (*Q*, p. 1999.) To base party organisation on a restricted group of 'the best' is really a symptom of passivity, Gramsci argues.[31]

Gramsci is referring specifically to the situation under fascism, and his interpretation of fascism as a passive revolution has a very precise object. The party must avoid any unilateral interpretation of fascism as a reaction or as a restoration. When Gramsci writes that there are never restorations *in toto* in a note on Caesarism where the parallel with fascism is quite clear,[32] he is suggesting that the full significance of the phenomenon of fascism or any other form of passive revolution will never be comprehended unless that aspect which represents the 'revolution' side of the binomial is analysed. The 'progressive' element, or the fundamental change, which the passive revolution effects in the reorganisation of bourgeois rule must not be ignored. Thus in analysing fascism, its real political support among sections of the population which considered fascism to be able to provide the solutions to their problems, in particular sections of the urban and rural petty bourgeoisie, must be given full weight in understanding how this kind of passive revolution could serve to maintain the State, both as a hegemonic system and in terms of the instruments of coercion, which provided the conditions for the dominance of the 'traditional' social forces and the capitalist mode of production.

In this regard it had also to be recognised that fascism attempted to provide the conditions for the expansion of the productive forces in a period in which some kind of planning was necessary because of the dominance of monopoly capital.[33] Indeed, in his notes on

Americanism and Fordism and in those on the concept of the falling rate of profit Gramsci studies the way in which State intervention in the economy in the period of 'organised capitalism' represented an attempt to overcome the tendency for profits to fall and to reorganise the masses both economically and politically. Because of the increasing contradictions in the period of imperialism, a new form of State, is both required by and provides for a development of the economic base. Gramsci once more indicates the extremely complex nature of the relationship between base and superstructure, at the same time insisting on the multitude of essential features of any political phenomenon. Fascism may represent a form of bourgeois rule, but it or any other type of State cannot be reduced to a single feature without failing to understand its real significance. Moreover, the dynamic of the historical process during a passive revolution is something which cannot be controlled to suit the wishes of those who promote this form of political rule, and the contradictory consequences of the reorganisation of capitalism in its different forms must be fully appreciated by the party. Indeed, in developing the concept of the passive revolution, Gramsci is in fact reconsidering Marx's argument that capitalism is forced to revolutionise itself, and he is trying to purge it of the mechanistic interpretation of the Second International which considered the development of the forces of production as leading in a unilinear manner to the downfall of capitalism. By insisting that capitalism must reorganise itself, Gramsci emphasises that the changes introduced always represent a challenge to the working-class movement which must be able to intervene in a qualitatively different situation. Its politics must represent an 'anti-passive revolution'[34] in which the changes taking place within capitalism are developed as the basis for creating new social and political relations which overcome divisions between individuals and between groups and between individuals and the realms of politics and economics. Any given development must be viewed in its contradictions as having the potential to serve as the basis of an advance toward a new organisation of society and human relations or as an aspect of the reorganisation of capitalism.[35]

The is one last aspect of the conditions under which a passive revolution may take place which is of importance. In several passages Gramsci relates it to the relative economic backwardness of the progressive forces.[36] He is very clear, however, that the level of economic development is only one factor in the possibility of a class establishing a State. The success of a class may be more related to a particular international conjuncture, for example, than to its innate strength as an internal, subjective force.[37] In what is a description of uneven development, he suggests a particular danger which exists when a State is founded, in a situation where the concrete conditions for a new social formation do exist but more as potential than as reality.

One can see how, when the impetus of progress is not tightly linked to a vast local economic development which is artificially limited and repressed, but is instead the reflection of international developments which transmit their ideological currents to the periphery — currents born on the basis of the productive development of the more advanced countries — then the group which is the bearer of the new ideas is not the economic group but the intellectual stratum, and the conception of the State advocated by them changes aspect; it is conceived of as something in itself, as a rational absolute. The problem can be formulated as follows: since the State is the concrete form of a productive world and since the intellectuals are the social element from which the governing personnel is drawn, the intellectual who is not firmly anchored to a strong economic group will tend to present the State as an absolute; in this way the function of the intellectuals is itself conceived of as absolute and pre-eminent, and their historical existence and dignity are abstractly rationalised. *SPN*, pp. 216-17.

In this passage he is specifically referring to the attitude to the State held by intellectuals of the modern idealist school, such as Croce, but we would argue that it is also suggestive of the type of pitfall which a socialist revolution might face if it is not made and continued on the basis of a widespread consent, if it does not create a new relationship between the masses and politics. Gramsci certainly is not maintaining that a political revolution must wait upon the development of economic factors, but rather he is insisting on the importance of the *form* of the revolution given the existence, at least in potential, of certain concrete conditions. We thus arrive at the possibility of a socialist State maintaining itself through a passive revolution and thus remaining the expression of an economic-corporative change in which the development of an extended hegemony is stunted, and the working class is unable to represent the universal interests of the whole of society. Gramsci in fact offers a powerful tool of analysis with which to examine the first concrete example of the establishment of a workers' State. To the extent that a separation is preserved between the realm of politics and the mass of the population and a traditional mode of existence of the intellectuals is reproduced, the historical task of the proletariat has still to be accomplished.

14. The Party as the Decisive Element

The object of Gramsci's development of theoretical concepts to analyse the historical process is to enable the practice of the party to fulfill its potential at every moment in the struggle. Given a certain level of development of the objective or material elements, themselves a product of the class struggle, the subjective element is always decisive even when it is absent because its very absence becomes an element in the outcome of any situation. Objective conditions are made *real*, they are realised, to the extent that the subjective elements are developed.[1] The lack of a socialist revolution in the West despite the great economic and political crises of the bourgeois social formation can be explained, according to Gramsci, by the gap or margin between on the one hand the objective contradictions existing at a certain stage of history between the forces and the relations of production, and on the other, the ability of the subjective forces, bourgeois and proletarian, either to prolong or to shorten the life of the present social formation. The prolongation of the organic crisis or the crisis of hegemony, the crisis of the State in an integral sense is the terrain on which the subjective forces contend.

Given these premises, Gramsci's argument that the subjective forces are always the decisive element[2] can be understood without mistaking it for an idealist position. Nor does this subjective force arise spontaneously. Its organisation and the development of its capabilities must be the result of a long-term preparation. The party is decisive to the extent that it comprehends the nature of the organic crisis and consequently avoids the trap of a voluntarist-economistic problematic. Within this general theoretical framework, and only within this framework, can Gramsci's insistence on the party be placed within the kind of unity of structure and superstructure described by the concept of historic bloc.

If it is clearly understood that it is on the basis of this disjuncture between the objective and subjective conditions[3] that the party is decisive, then we can understand and 'translate' Gramsci's notes on the role of the Jacobins in the French Revolution into terms applicable to the modern revolutionary party. These notes in some senses provide us with a summary of the way in which the party can represent the most vigorous assertion of the intervention of the subjective forces in an organic crisis:

> the Jacobins won their function of 'leading' [*dirigente*] party by a struggle to the death; they literally 'imposed' themselves on the French bourgeoisie, leading it into a far more advanced position than the

originally strongest bourgeois nuclei would have spontaneously wished to take up, and even far more advanced than that which the historical premises should have permitted —hence the various forms of
backlash and the function of Napoleon I. This feature, characteristic
of Jacobinism (but before that, also of Cromwell and the 'Round-
heads') and hence of the entire French Revolution, which consists in
(apparently) forcing the situation, in creating irreversible *faits
accomplis*, and in a group of extremely energetic and determined men
driving the bourgeois forward with kicks in the backside. *SPN*, p. 77.

While the Jacobins may have *appeared* to force the objective situation,
this situation, according to Gramsci, was only *apparently* or superficially
lagging behind its real potential. Pushing the bourgeois revolution towards its ultimate conclusion, and as Gramsci suggests, to some extent
beyond what seemed to be the concrete historical premises, was an
'imposition' only in terms of what would have been the economic-corporative results if the process had been left to a spontaneous development.[4]
Gramsci is arguing that it is only through the leadership of the party
that the real and not merely the 'apparent' potential of a concrete situation can be realised.

Yet, he makes a distinction between what he considers the proper
meaning of Jacobin and what was a mistaken view. Jacobinism in the
proper sense, he maintains, is inevitably concerned with the establishment of hegemony over the mass of the population based on a *concrete*
political programme derived from a *realistic* assessment of the potential
of a given situation.[5] The term Jacobinism, in a 'lesser' sense,[6] represents
a voluntaristic, rhetorical position, which is not based on the concrete
possibilities of building a hegemony including the great majority of the
population. This type of abstract, arbitrary, unrealistic stance, in the
sense of not corresponding to a concrete analysis of the real potential
of any situation, is repeatedly the object of Gramsci's criticism of the
inadequacies of the Action Party,[7] a criticism which may be applied to
the Italian socialist tradition and at times to the modern revolutionary
party.[8] Gramsci's reference to Bordiga is quite clear when he writes that
this meaning of Jacobinism is marked by the prevelance of

the destructive elements derived from hatred of rivals and enemies,
more than the constructive one derived from having made the demands of the popular masses one's own; the sectarian element of the
clique, of the small group, of unrestrained individualism, more than
the national political element. *SPN*, p. 66.

But he is also making a parallel with the failings of the PSI when he writes,

> The representatives of the Third Estate initially posed those questions which interested the actual physical members of the social group, their immediate 'corporate' interests (corporate in the traditional sense, of the immediate and narrowly selfish interests of a particular category). The precursors of the Revolution were in fact moderate reformers, who *shouted very loud but actually demanded very little*. Gradually a new élite was selected out which did not concern itself solely with 'corporate' reforms, but tended to conceive of the bourgeoisie as the hegemonic group of all the popular forces. *SPN*, p. 77. [My emphasis.]

Rhetorical statements according to Gramsci in fact hide a backward, corporativist position. A constructive, hegemonic position must be related to the real needs of as great a part of the population as is possible, given the concrete historical conditions. This is why Gramsci writes that the Jacobins

> were the only party of the revolution in progress, in as much as they not only represented the immediate needs and aspirations of the actual physical individuals who constituted the French bourgeoisie, but they also represented the revolutionary movement as a whole, as an integral historical development. For they represented future needs as well, and, once again, not only the needs of those particular physical individuals, but also of all the national groups which had to be assimilated to the existing fundamental group. *SPN*, p. 78.

The present and future needs of the mass of the population were 'represented' by the Jacobins in two, related ways, in terms of their political ideology and in terms of their concrete programme. The effectiveness of the Jacobins as a subjective force fulfilling the potential of an objective situation depended on the coexistence and interrelationship of these two aspects which provided the conditions for the success of the revolution. In terms of political ideology,

> They were convinced of the absolute truth of their slogans about equality, fraternity and liberty, and, what is more important, the great popular masses whom the Jacobins stirred up and drew into the struggle were also convinced of their truth. The Jacobins' language,

their ideology, their methods of action reflected perfectly the exigencies of the epoch, . . . *SPN*, p. 78.

The relationship between the ideology of the Jacobins, their concrete programme, and their victory is clarified when we consider the way in which Gramsci explains the strategic requirements of the situation.

The first necessity was to annihilate the enemy forces, or at least to reduce them to impotence in order to make a counter-revolution impossible. The second was to enlarge the cadres of the bourgeoisie as such, and to place the latter at the head of all the national forces; this meant identifying the interests and the requirements common to all the national forces, in order to set these forces in motion and lead them into the struggle, obtaining two results: (*a*) that of opposing a wider target to the blows of the enemy, i.e. of creating a politico-military relation favourable to the revolution; (*b*) that of depriving the enemy of every zone of passivity in which it would be possible to enrol Vendée-type armies. *SPN*, pp. 77-8.

The way in which these strategic objectives were accomplished indicates the fundamental importance of a concrete programme based on a correct understanding of the task of building a concrete historical bloc.[9]

Thus a revolution can be made and defended only through the creation of widespread popular consent, as a result both of an ideological struggle and a concrete programme of reforms. A new collective will is created around a new historical project. The very success of the revolutionary party is intrinsically bound up with its ability to organise this consent which far from being contingent is absolutely fundamental. In a new strategic context, during the war of position, the modalities of the struggle may be different, but the real needs of increasing the strength of the revolutionary forces and weakening the adversary can only be met by waging a *hegemonic* struggle, in which the working class goes beyond an economic-corporate vision of its task and unites a new historic bloc.

In a different situation, and with a *new* vision of politics and of the State, the task of the proletariat parallels that of the Jacobins.

If it is true that the Jacobins 'forced' its hand, it is also true that this always occurred in the direction of real historical development. For *not only did they organise a bourgeois government*, i.e. make the bourgeoisie the dominant class—they did more. *They created the bourgeois State, made the bourgeoisie into the leading, hegemonic class of the nation*, in other words gave the new State *a permanent basis* and created the compact modern French nation. *SPN*, p. 79. [My emphasis.]

It is the struggle for hegemony which in the modern period would take the form of the war of position, which ensures that the historical potential of a class is fulfilled at its highest level, crowned by the building of an integral State, and which at the same time provides the safeguard for the revolution. Yet the proletariat has an object which is historically novel: to transform politics and to overcome the division between leaders and led.

15. Conclusion: The Party, the State and Democracy

In discussing the parallels between the revolution made by the Jacobins and that of the proletariat, one thing must be obvious. The experience of a socialist revolution to which Gramsci could refer had run a different course. While there were moments in which the October Revolution represented a very widespread popular support won by the Bolsheviks in the period following the February Revolution, and while Lenin indeed argued that the revolution had to be made by the mass of the population,[1] the course of events caused the maintenance of such support to be problematic in the extreme. In his notes on the differences between the struggle in a backward State such as that of tsarist Russia and advanced States in the West, Gramsci had centred his analysis on the conditions of civil society. The revolution had been made in a country where civil society was 'primordial and gelatinous' (*SPN*, p. 239) and it was necessary, according to Gramsci, to construct a modern, integral State, to build a terrain on which the hegemony of the working class could be expanded so that a permanent hegemonic base could be provided for the State.

Gramsci seemed to be thinking of some of the problems facing a socialist revolution in a country like the Soviet Union when he wrote about the different attitudes of various classes in different historical periods to their States. One attitude is an acceptance of the State in the narrow sense as merely political society or the instruments of coercion.

For some social groups, which before their ascent to autonomous State life have not had a long independent period of cultural and moral development on their own (as was made possible in mediaeval society and under the absolute régimes by the juridical existence of the privileged Estates or orders), a period of statolatry is necessary and indeed opportune. This 'statolatry' is nothing other than the normal form of 'State life', or at least of initiation to autonomous State life and to the creation of a 'civil society' which it was not historically possible to create before the ascent to independent State life. *However, this kind of 'statolatry' must not be abandoned to itself, must not, especially, become theoretical fanaticism or be conceived of as 'perpetual'.* It must be criticised, precisely in order to develop and produce new forms of State life, in which the initiative of individuals and groups will have a 'State' character, even if it is not due to the 'government of the functionaries' (make State life become 'spontaneous'). *SPN*, pp. 268-9. [My emphasis.]

The task of building an integral State for the working class, unlike previous ruling classes, becomes a question of expanding the area of hegemony until the area of coercion eventually disappears.[2] Even an early period of 'statolatry' is acceptable only in so far as it enables a class to build civil society and widen the area of hegemonic support given to the State by ever increasing numbers of people. But even more importantly, the very activity of politics, of State activity in the widest sense is no longer separated from society but becomes an aspect of the lives of the whole of the population.[3]

Thus the building of hegemony, the gaining of widespread consent, and a democratisation of the practice of politics is an integral part of the socialist revolution in Gramsci's conception. He therefore provides an argument which can help to serve as a basis on which to develop the concept of the link between democracy and socialism. Furthermore, while Gramsci gives us very little idea of the precise nature of the relationship between the State and the party after the revolution, given the fundamental themes of his work in prison, this relationship must be conceived of in terms of the overall task of founding a State based on hegemony and creating a society in which the element of force is made unnecessary. In so doing, the very form of the party will of necessity change as the tasks before it change.

In the modern world, a party is such—integrally, and not, as happens, a fraction of a larger party—when it is conceived, organised and led in ways and in forms such that it will develop integrally into a State (an integral State, and not into a government technically understood) and into a conception of the world. The development of the party into a State reacts upon the party and requires of it *a continuous reorganisation and development*, just as the development of the party and State into a conception of the world, i.e. into a total and molecular (individual) transformation of ways of thinking and acting, reacts upon the State and the party, compelling them to reorganise continually and confronting them with new and original problems to solve. *SPN*, p. 267. [My emphasis.]

The party develops into the State; but both conceived of in the broad sense, the party as tending to encompass a very wide area of society and the State understood as an integral State. Gramsci gives the party an immense task,[4] which seems to leave little room for autonomous organisation, let alone provide the basis for any argument for pluralism after the socialist revolution.

We can, however, exclude from Gramsci's conception any identification of a narrowly conceived party with the governmental apparatus. Relevant in this context is his criticism of the 'totalitarianism' of the fascist régime in which the party not only come to be identified with the government, but the régime tried to encompass civil society while exalting an abstract concept of the State.[5] The concentration in the hands of the State of all political and cultural activities and the merger between State and party is for Gramsci a symptom of a restricted hegemony in which the political function of the party becomes increasingly one of 'propaganda and public order, and moral and cultural influence.' (*SPN*, p. 149.) Politics defined as hegemonic activity cementing an historical bloc around the universalistic vocation of the dominant class degenerates into a version of the passive revolution in which the economic-corporative interests of sections of society, in the case of fascism, for example, those of monopoly or finance capital and of sections of the petty bourgeoisie, are articulated. In a very contradictory manner, that State and that party which claims moral, ethical leadership in the absence of a pluralism of political and cultural forces, remains on the terrain of coercion and economic-corporativism.

Notes written in the first instance about fascism provide the basis for a criticism of Stalin's theory of the 'reinforcement' of the State and the elimination of pluralism in the Soviet Union. Indeed, it is the oppposite of this attempt to absorb civil society into political society, that is, it is the expansion of civil society and the absorption by civil society of the political realm, in which State and society become reunited, which is precisely the measure by which a new socialist State had to be judged.

Gramsci writes, for example, that the democratic rather than oligarchic nature of the State as educator is possible

> only in societies in which the historical unity of civil society and political society is understood dialectically . . . and the State is conceived of as potentially surpassed (superabile) by 'regulated society'. In this society the dominant party is not organically meshed with the government, but it is an instrument for the transition from civil-political society to regulated society. *Q*, p. 734.

This tendency of overcoming the division between political and civil society as progress is made towards the establishment of a 'regulated society' or communism is also the only basis on which the party may be accepted as the 'Head of State'.

> In certain States, the 'Head of State' . . . is precisely the 'political party'. With the difference, however, that in terms of traditional constitutional law it juridically neither rules nor governs. It has '*de facto* power', and exercises the hegemonic function and hence that of holding the balance between various interests in 'civil society'; the latter, however, is in fact entwined with political society to such an extent that all the citizens feel that the party both rules and governs. It is not possible to create a constitutional law of the traditional type on the basis of this reality, which is in continuous movement; it is only possible to create a system of principles asserting that the State's goal is its own end, its own disappearance, in other words the reabsorption of political society into civil society. *SPN*, p. 253.

It seems to be the intrinsically original task of *certain* States, i.e. of the socialist State, which makes acceptable a certain relationship between party and State. Yet this relationship is not enshrined in a constitution, but depends on the ability of the party to balance different interests, to fulfill the hegemonic function of the working class. Indeed, the new relationship between State and society cannot be fixed by a set of legal rules but has to be rooted in a new concept of politics based on a changing reality in which the whole of the citizenry comes to participate in a full sense in political activity.

Moreover, since the building of a socialist State entails the creation of positive support on the widest possible basis, the logic of Gramsci's argument, while not providing us with any specific suggestions with regard to the modes of building that hegemony, points towards full discussion and debate.[6] Unlike the bourgeois State which might achieve a balance between hegemony and coercion but never eliminates the element of force, the socialist State exists for a unique purpose – to develop civil society, to increase the area of hegemony until the coercive apparatuses are no longer necessary. That party and that State which exists for the elimination of class differences,[7] for the transformation of the mode of production, and for an intellectual and moral reform, a change in the superstructure which will not follow spontaneously upon changes in the economic sphere, must consciously provide the conditions under which all this can come to fruition.

Yet, while it can be argued that such an intellectual and moral reform necessitates full and free discussion in which disagreements are brought into the open and resolved politically and not administratively, and while a certain climate of debate necessitates real, legal-political guarantees of structures, such as autonomous political organisations, Gramsci does not explicitly provide us with this argument. The role of the party, which, as we have argued above, implies both internal democracy and a democratic relationship with the working class and its allies, remains for Gramsci an all-embracing one. Its relations with non-party organisations and indeed with other political parties remain unspecified while the extremely important question of the relationship between State and party during the transition to socialism does not consider the possibility of the kind of *de facto* identification between the two, which would, at the very least, make problematical the kind of full discussion necessary for an intellectual and moral reform, for the building of a widely extended hegemony. This is an area which is neglected by Gramsci and is a limit to his work, albeit an area which has assumed in the experiences of 'really existing socialism', it can be argued, its most obvious importance only after his death.

At the same time, we would suggest that Gramsci is in fact able to provide indications which go far beyond his particular experiences and furnish important elements for an extended notion of democracy. The qualitatively new aspects of the socialist State are not simply rooted in the revolutionary vocation of the leading party, as might seem from some passages in his work, nor in a written constitution, but in a fundamentally new concept of politics and political participation issuing from the whole of his work. We would suggest that recent attacks on Gramsci as providing the basis for a totalitarian domination by party and State are not only mistaken but in fact ignore a highly original contribution to a discussion on democracy.[8] This contribution is bound to be overlooked unless a primary question is posed: is the survival and extension of democracy in fact insured by a system of guarantees of formal rules and formal structures, that is, in the realm of constitutional practice narrowly conceived, or does the maintenance and expansion of democracy necessitate a consideration of the conditions and institutions of civil society which, as Gramsci writes, can no longer be thought of separately from political society?

The fact that Gramsci's contribution to a debate on democracy has to a large extent been neglected is explained in part because he gives us little indication of the precise *form* of the new State, which he would have considered a utopian exercise, and because his direct discussion of democracy is on the whole limited to on the one hand an examination of the crisis of the liberal State in the age of imperialism, of monopoly capitalism and of State intervention in the economy, and on the other of the limits of an 'abstract', 'formal' concept of democracy. Indeed, we would argue that one of the richest sources of indications for studying the problems involved in the creation of a full democracy has never been studied in depth: his writings on democratic centralism and party organisation.[9]

We must, however, be quite clear about our argument: Gramsci is very explicit that the party does *not* provide the *form* of the new State which can only develop from the experience of the mass movement and which has no previous model. Moreover, for Gramsci organisations as such are always related to their function and to the nature of society. Therefore, while there is a discussion in his writings about the internal relations of the party which constitutes an important contribution to the debate on the development of democracy, there is no one-to-one relationship of precise forms of organisation. The organisation of the State is not reducible to the organisation of the party. The two have similar but not identical tasks. What *is* present in his work on the party is a discussion of a process of politics which has parallels for the process of politics in the State and society as a whole.

As we have written earlier, Gramsci defines the Modern Prince in terms of its task: to found an integral State based on a fully extended hegemony, deriving from a collective will and reflecting an intellectual and moral reform. Gramsci's silence on the precise forms of organisation is significant. The lack of specific indications about both party and State organisational rules must be read in terms of a specific notion of politics, that notion which Gramsci maintains is adequate to the historical potential of the modern epoch, when the mass of the population becomes organised in a variety of forms and therefore acquires the potential to intervene in politics for the first time, to become protagonists in history.

Gramsci writes that parties are 'schools of State life' whose internal life reveals their view of the State and of society.[10] From the time of the *Ordine Nuovo* he argues that, in the period of the transition to socialism, in which the problems of building a new State with a new project (the political realisation of what can be termed the protagonism of the masses) becomes real and concrete, that party whose aim is to create a new *type* of State must itself be a new type of party. The internal organisation of this party must be appropriate to the way in which what Gramsci calls the fundamental problem of political science is posed: that there is a division between rulers and ruled—a fact which cannot be ignored—and that the questions which are now historically real are the following. How can this split be overcome? How can a democratic, a hegemonic relationship between leaders and led be established? How can a real, an organic social unity be forged in the period of the potential historical protagonism of the masses? These are the questions which must be reflected in the internal life of the revolutionary party.

Gramsci poses the question of the relationship between leaders and led and of the unity and cohesion of society in a particular context which he describes as demarcated by the organic, long-term crisis of capitalism and the transition to socialism—a context in which the very terms of the problem become transformed. When we read his notes on party organisation, we find in fact a constant redefinition of words which are related in a new way. This is an aspect of Gramsci's *rethinking* of certain organisational elements which is symptomatic of his attempt to rethink politics in general. First of all, democratic centralism is defined in terms of the creation of a true democracy as the only way for the organisation to be able to relate to an ever-changing reality. Secondly, centralism or the creation of unity, according to Gramsci, is only real and effective to the extent that the organisation is democratic. And democracy is possible in so far as there is a process of discussion and debate which ensures a constant raising of the intellectual and political level of the mass of members.

It is this preparation, this moral and intellectual reform which enables the individual to appropriate reality, to act as an autonomous subject in given material circumstances.[11] The necessary organisational condition for this to be accomplished, according to Gramsci, is the establishment of an intermediate stratum between the rank and file and the leadership which are thus linked through a mediated rather than a direct relationship, by a chain which is based on a division of labour, on what Gramsci calls technical differences, rather than 'class divisions',[12] implying that there is no innate difference between the different levels which cannot be overcome through a process of acquiring intellectual skills. Thus, all members of the party must be considered intellectuals. This in turn is related to Gramsci's redefinition of the nature of the skills of the intellectual. The term intellectual is redefined and broadened to enable it to comprehend the unity of theory and practice, of mental and physical labour so that the intellectual and moral reform of the masses can be conceptualised.

The very meaning of unity is expressed in a particular way by Gramsci. If it is not the result of positive consent and active participation, it is like 'a stagnant swamp', a situation in which the individuals relate to each other like a 'sack of potatoes'.[13] A true collective will in the party and in the nation as a whole, united around a new project for society cannot be established according to Gramsci through the imposition of a unity based on a passive relationship between leaders and led.

Yet for Gramsci this unity does not signify uniformity. His concept of hegemony implies the creation of a cohesion in society between different social forces based on compromises which go beyond the corporative demands of any single section, a necessary condition for avoiding a new version of the passive revolution. With regards to the party, unity takes account of the different opinions of the members of the party which relate to different interpretations of reality. Gramsci argues that discipline whose origin is not the result of a democratic exchange and debate in fact reproduces the political divisions of bourgeois society, because the attitude to the leaders becomes one of faith in which the individual feels extraneous to the outcome of any situation, or separated from reality, that is, what leaders do or the results of a party's policies are not understood as the product of the active intervention of *each* party member. Gramsci's redefinition of terms is made necessary by the very task of the party, to ensure an organic relationship between leaders and led, to realise the political protagonism of the masses. Without this democratic relationship within the party and between the party and the mass movement, the party is ineffective, it is unable to relate to reality, and its internal life does not reflect a new concept of politics.

There are various implications in this approach. First of all, for Gramsci a democratic relationship cannot be defined by a set of rules but only by a mode of conducting politics based on creating the conditions for active political intervention by the mass of the population and aimed at the abolition of the division between rulers and ruled. If this is to be accomplished, then links between individuals and the State or between leaders and led founded on a division of intellectual labour are necessary if the divisions which exist are in fact to be overcome. If the real problems of creating the possibility for the vast majority of people in society to appropriate reality and to participate in politics are not posed, then the appeal to the masses is pure demagogy, Gramsci writes, whether this appeal is by Mussolini or anyone else.[14] Consequently new problems of organisation are constantly raised related to the changing situation, both for the revolutionary party and for society at large.

Various objections to this comparison of Gramsci's discussion of the party and the creation of a fuller democracy may arise. We have noted that Gramsci attributes what could be described as a totalising function to the party. In fact, he maintains that the attempt to have a set of ideas gain acceptance by the majority of society is a feature of *any* party. In competition with other ideas any political force seeks the greatest support it can muster. We would argue that while a significant limitation in Gramsci's writings on the party is that he leaves little space for the autonomous activities of other parties and non-party organisations in a socialist society, and while it is true that he does not explicitly discuss pluralism, the logic of the fundamental concept of hegemony points to the necessity of a continuing plurality of political and social organisations. At the same time there is nothing which guarantees the longevity or success of a political force which is no longer able to represent the needs of an historical epoch or whose popular base ceases to give it support.

Gramsci's criticism of the PSI and of Bordiga's view of the party are relevant here. The PSI, wrote Gramsci, was an ineffective instrument for a fundamental change in society because it reproduced the bourgeois mode of politics, in particular the split between economics and politics, for example in the division of labour it established with the trade union movement. Its internal organisation provided for debate, but not a true democracy or unity of action. The lack of theoretical discussion prevented it from understanding concrete reality. A fundamental split between leaders and led remained in its ranks and no effort was made to go beyond a formal definition of citizens unrelated to their socio-economic position.

Attempting to overcome the limitations of the PSI, Bordiga's solution merely duplicated these features. His concept of rigid organisation in fact resulted in a lack of effective cohesion and reproduced the division between leaders and led and between human subjects and reality. Gramsci argued that a schematic concept of organisation in which a certain pattern is assumed as universally valid is related to a mechanical view of history in which the organisation itself is abstracted from the historical process, a philosophy of history which in fact cannot conceptualise the protagonism of the masses. Indeed this mechanical view of history was the common theoretical foundation underlying the organisation of the two parties, the PSI and the early PCI, a view shared with bourgeois thought. Organisations appear to exist and events seem to take place without the active intervention of human subjects, and the party, as the State, appears as a mystical creation separated from the activity of individual members.[15] Parties where the leadership has an instrumental relationship with their members, that is, which do not reflect in their internal life the problem of overcoming the division between rulers and ruled, in fact are an aspect of the passive revolution in that the traditional relationship between leaders and led is reproduced while at the same time providing for the organisation of large numbers of people on a new basis.

In this context, Gramsci was most concerned with analysing the fascist party. Yet, to the extent the relationship between leaders and led remains essentially that of bourgeois society, the party in question, with whatever ideology and in whatever society, cannot provide what Gramsci defines as real democracy or the organic exchange between rulers and ruled.[16] Thus Gramsci provides us with indications for an analysis of the lack of an effective democracy in a variety of parties, in capitalist or socialist societies, and indeed in non-party organisations as well.

He also provides us with an argument for pluralism. Gramsci writes that in one-party States, the party in fact loses its direct political function. 'The political function is indirect. For, even if no other legal parties exist, other parties always do exist and other tendencies which cannot be legally coerced.' (*SPN*, p. 149.) This elimination of pluralism reproduced what Gramsci calls bureaucratic centralism, in which it is impossible to achieve a collective will, a positive unity, a true democracy because 'political questions are disguised as cultural ones, and as such become insoluble'. (*SPN*, p. 149.) A critique of fascism, yes, but also of Stalinism.

At the same time, we would suggest that the mere existence of several parties is not itself a guarantee of pluralism and the further development of democracy. Dramatic examples would be South Africa or indeed several of the socialist countries, but in addition a wide range of literature, from a variety of theoretical positions, has also criticised the quality of pluralism and the limits of democracy in countries like Great Britain or the United States where the 'rules' are undoubtedly democratic in a formal sense.[17] In the transition to a new society, if the mass of the population becomes organised politically, a multitude of possible forms of pluralism may manifest themselves as the problems of liberal democracy are revealed and its limits are constantly being challenged. In this period, the work of Antonio Gramsci should prove increasingly useful.

Notes

2. The State as 'Hegemony Fortified by Coercion'

1. Any definition at this stage runs the risk of being at best partial and at worst misleading if not connected to a whole range of concepts, but a useful working definition is provided by Gwyn Williams: 'By "hegemony" Gramsci seems to mean a socio-political situation, in his terminology a "moment", in which the philosophy and practice of a society fuse or are in equilibrium; an order in which a certain way of life and thought is dominant, in which one concept of reality is diffused throughout society in all its institutional and private manifestations, informing with its spirit all taste, morality, customs, religious and political principles, and all social relations, particularly in their intellectual and moral connotation.' 'The Concept of "egemonia" in the Thought of Antonio Gramsci', in *Journal of the History of Ideas*, vol. 21, no. 4 (Oct.-Dec. 1960), p. 587. Without at all diminishing the importance of Gramsci's *development* of the concept of hegemony, Christine Buci-Glucksmann traces different versions of the idea to Lenin, Bukharin, and Stalin, *Gramsci and the State*, pp. 7-8. See also Perry Anderson, 'The Antinomies of Antonio Gramsci', for a discussion of the use of the term in the Russian working-class movement.

2. See Buci-Glucksmann for a parallel argument, *Gramsci and the State*, pp. 10ff.

3. For an extended discussion of the problems involved in translating into English the word *dirigere* and its various derivatives, *direzione, dirigente, diretto, direttivo*, etc. see the extended footnote in *Selections*, pp. 55-7.

4. For Gramsci political science is the science of the State and the State equals *all* activities preserving the dominance of the ruling class (*Q*, p. 1765). The centrality of hegemony to Gramsci's view of politics is demonstrated when he writes, 'In the phase of struggle for hegemony it is the science of politics which is developed.' *SPN*, p. 404.

5. For a discussion of the historical background to the usage of the term dual perspective in the Comintern see *SPN*, p. 169, footnote 70.

6. Nicola Auciello makes the point that the interchangeability between the two couples, force-consent and hegemony-dictatorship, reflects Gramsci's attempt to conceptualise the State both in terms of a reactionary involution of a bourgeoisie which sees its own basis of hegemony threatened and of the beginning of the development of a workers' State in a period of transition to socialism. It is 'this thematic of the *transition* which ends up emerging at the centre of the discussion on the relationship between hegemony and dictatorship'. *Socialismo ed egemonia in Gramsci e Togliatti* (De Donato, Bari, 1974), footnote, p. 33.

7. For a discussion of the Church as a hegemonic apparatus see Hughes Portelli, *Gramsci et la question religieuse* (Editions anthropos, Paris, 1974). Another example is Gramsci's discussion of the law which represents a relationship between a moment of coercion and one of custom and consent. The precise nature of the relationship depends on historical factors, i.e. the extensiveness of the hegemony of the State. See Gramsci, *SPN*, pp. 195-6 and Auciello, *Socialismo*, pp. 111-12.

8. Unless this is understood the relationship of hegemony to the coercive apparatuses remains obscured and the whole question of the State in Gramsci's problematic is diminished. J. Femia, 'Hegemony and Consciousness in the Thought of Antonio Gramsci', *Political Studies*, vol. 23, no. 1 (March 1975) and T.R. Bates, 'Gramsci and the Theory of Hegemony', *Journal of the History of Ideas*, vol. 36, no. 2 (April-June 1975) tend to make this mistake. Palmiro Togliatti made the point that the difference between dictatorship and hegemony was not organic but

methodological, 'Gramsci and Leninism', in P. Togliatti, *On Gramsci and Other Writings* (Lawrence and Wishart, London, 1979).

9. The new Italian edition makes this clear. As Perry Anderson points out there is in fact a third definition which presents the State as balancing between civil and political society. Anderson, *The Antinomies of Antonio Gramsci*, pp. 31-3. We discuss two because, we would suggest, Gramsci's extended concept, the State as hegemony plus coercion, encompasses this third definition, the State as balancing the two aspects of the domination of a class.

10. In addition to the definitions cited above, Gramsci defines the State as 'the entire complex of practical and theoretical activities with which the ruling class not only justifies and maintains its dominance, but manages to win the active consent of those over whom it rules'. *SPN*, p. 244. The State as such overlaps the boundaries of civil society and political society. The State, Gramsci says, 'presents itself in two forms in the language and culture of particular epochs, i.e. as civil society and as political society, as "self-government" and as "government by functionaries" . . . which is commonly understood as the entire State'. *Q*, p. 1020.

11. Gramsci also talks about 'civil hegemony' *SPN*, p. 243. In still another note Gramsci writes about the way in which a political activist has a contradictory consciousness which is resolved through 'a struggle of political "hegemonies"', *SPN*, p. 333, while in still another he describes hegemony as the 'organizer' of ideology which gives the most intimate cement to civil society, and therefore to the State'. *Q*, p. 1306. For a discussion of the relationship between the cultural and the political in Gramsci (as well as Togliatti), see Giuseppe Vacca, 'L'occasione "Politecnico" (Note su alcuni elementi della politica culturale di Togliatti)', *Lavoro critico*, vol. 5 (Jan-March 1976).

12. For example he argues against a contemporary identification of the individual and the State by Spirito by saying that on logical grounds the identification could not be reversed (the State is not identified with the individual) and that the error came from the 'absence of a clear enunciation of the concept of State, of the distinction in it between civil society and political society, between dictatorship and hegemony, etc.' *Q*, p. 1245.

13. In addition to differentiating himself from a tradition of Marxist thought which had maintained that the State consists in the instruments of coercion, developing a theme from his earlier writings Gramsci also criticises that aspect of liberalism which reduces the State to the government and maintains that there is a net separation between political and civil society, a critique of the State viewed as the 'night watchman'. *SPN*, p. 262. See also Buci-Glucksmann, *Gramsci and the State*, pp. 69-70, 97, 108.

14. In terms of the metaphor which Gramsci employs of hegemony as a system of fortifications, it should be noted that at times these are presented as a system of trenches in *front* of the fortress of the State (which is protected, for example, during economic crises) and at times as the trenches *behind* it implying that even when the State in the narrow sense is itself shaken, it is protected by civil society and implying that even if the State machinery itself is overturned, there are still obstacles to be overcome. See our discussion below about the definitive nature of the struggle for hegemony.

15. Thus Anderson's reading of this passage as merely contrasting two 'geopolitical theatre' would appear mistaken. 'The Antinomies of Antonio Gramsci', pp. 9-10.

16. The most complete articulation of this is to be found in N. Bobbio, 'Gramsci and the conception of civil society'. This has been criticised by Jacques Texier, 'Gramsci, theoretician of the superstructure and the concept of civil society'. Both are in Mouffe, *Gramsci and Marxist Theory*.

17. Several writers have begun to investigate the place of the economy in Gramsci's thought in relation to the remainder of his totality. See De Felice, *Serrati, Bordiga, Gramsci*, as well as 'Una chiave di lettura in "Americanismo e Fordismo"', in *Rinascita* (22 Oct. 1972). An interest in this aspect is one of the most important features of Nicola Badaloni's book, *Il marxismo di Gramsci*.

18. *SPN*, p. 262.

19. The fact is that this ethical function is very much rooted in the economic sphere. See Gramsci's notes on 'Americanism and Fordism', *SPN*, pp. 279-318, and the works of De Felice and Buci-Glucksmann cited above. This is a thematic rooted in the factory council period, and at the same time evidence of the way in which Gramsci, despite his isolation in prison, was in fact attempting to analyse the nature of the attempts by the various capitalist countries to overcome the great economic crisis of the 1930s. See Auciello, *Socialismo*, footnotes, pp. 110-11. See also our discussion of the passive revolution below. Anderson discusses these points but without reference to the thematic of the changed relationship between State and society.

20. See also the important note 'Question of "Collective Man"' and of 'Social Conformism' *Q*, pp. 1565-7.

21. *SPN*, p. 269.

22. This is the basis of the utopianism of the universalistic claims of the bourgeoisie and is the foundation of Gramsci's early description of the Jacobins as utopian. See *SG*, p. 312. As the bourgeoisie is revealed not to be able in fact to represent the universal needs of society, it enters into a period of crisis in its hegemony, which, however, is not an automatic process but depends in turn on the ability of the opposing forces to pose an alternative hegemony. This is discussed more fully below.

3. The Historical Bloc

1. In addition to Portelli's book, *Gramsci e il blocco storico* (Laterza, Bari, 1973), and Texier's article, 'Gramsci, theoretician', among the contributions are: Giorgio Napolitano, 'Roger Garaudy e il nuovo blocco storico', *Rinascita* (20 March 1970); Emilio Sereni, 'Blocco storico e iniziativa politica nell'elaborazione gramsciana e nella politica del PCI', *Critica marxista*, Quaderno 5 (1971), both of which enter into debate with the ideas of Garaudy as developed in his book *Le grand tournant du socialisme* and then in 'Révolution et bloc historique', *L'homme et la société*, no. 21 (July-August 1971). See also Umberto Cerroni, *Teoria politica e socialismo* (Editori Riuniti, Rome, 1973), Luciano Gruppi, *Il concetto di egemonia in Gramsci* (Editori Riuniti, Rome, 1972) and Nicola Badaloni 'Gramsci and the Problem of the Revolution', in Mouffe, *Gramsci and Marxist Theory*.

2. Including all versions of the various notes it is found only nine times. See index of the scholarly edition, *Q*, p. 3169.

3. Although attributed to Sorel, the concept of historical bloc is not found in so many words in Sorel's writings. Badaloni, however, argues that Gramsci took certain elements from Sorel and transformed them within his own problematic. *Il marxismo di Gramsci*.

4. Here he implies that there is a *connection* but not necessarily a causal relationship between structure and superstructure.

5. See note 3, section 2 above.

6. This is relevant to our discussion of the passive revolution. See below.

7. See Buci-Glucksmann for a discussion of the various other positions in the debate about the historical bloc. *Gramsci and the State*, pp. 317-20.

8. In Gramsci's terminology this refers to those classes fundamental to the dominant mode of production, i.e. where this is capitalism, the capitalist class and the proletariat.

9. See Buci-Glucksmann, *Gramsci and the State*, p. 323.

10. The one exception is when the area of hegemony is so extended as to make unnecessary the existence of the coercive apparatus at all. This leads to the question of the withering away of the State.

11. This is in fact Togliatti's phrase. It does not appear in so many words in Gramsci. See Togliatti, 'Il leninismo, etc.'

4. The Lessons of the Italian Bourgeois Revolution

1. Buci-Glucksmann is probably the scholar who does this in the most complete manner. *Gramsci and the State*. Guiseppe Fiori's biography of Gramsci was an earlier attempt to relate Gramsci in prison to the political debate of the period.

2. Gramsci is quite clear about the limit of the lessons to be learned from the bourgeoisie. See our discussion of the passive revolution. To argue that Gramsci's problematic remains trapped within bourgeois schema must be proved on the basis of the whole of his thought. It is not sufficient to criticise his drawing certain strategic conclusions from the bourgeois revolution as Anderson argues. 'The Antinomies of Antonio Gramsci', p. 46.

3. See for example, *PWI*, pp. 28-9 or *SG*, pp. 271-2.

4. See *PWI*, p. 29.

5. See *SG*, pp. 271-2 and *PWI*, pp. 46-55.

6. See *PWI*, p. 29.

7. See *SG*, p. 312.

8. Gramsci's definition of Jacobinism, his understanding of the differentiated nature of the bourgeois revolution and of the role of the party are *all* transformed so that Gramsci's changing attitude toward Jacobinism is symptomatic of change and development in his problematic as a whole in which the concepts of hegemony and of the party are crucial. The lessons Gramsci draws from Jacobinism are general ones going beyond a particular historical setting. We thus disagree with Portelli, 'Jacobinisme et anti-jacobinisme de Gramsci', *Dialectiques*. Giuseppe Galasso makes a point similar to ours. 'Gramsci e i problemi della storia italiana', *Gramsci e la cultura contemporanea*, p. 320.

9. For a summary of the debate see John Cammett, 'Gramsci and the Risorgimento', appendix in *Antonio Gramsci and the Origins of Italian Communism*.

10. See also *SPN*, pp. 57-9.

11. See for example the 'Theses of Lyon', *PWII*, pp. 340-75.

12. See *SPN*, p. 61.

13. See Lucio Magri, 'Problems of the Marxist Theory of the Revolutionary Party', in *New Left Review*, no. 60 (March-April 1970), p. 100.

5. The Conquest of Hegemony by a Subaltern Class

1. Implicit here is the argument that the hegemony of the current ruling class cannot be understood if it is considered simply from the point of view of legitimisation of the present social order, extracting it from a field of contending class forces. We would therefore disagree both with Ralph Miliband who depicts Gramsci's concept as a legitimisation mechanism in *The State in Capitalist Society* (Weidenfeld and Nicolson, London, 1969) and with Nicos Poulantzas who would reduce the concept to usage by the dominant classes, *Political Power and Social Classes* (New Left Books, London, 1973).

2. This type of 'State Worship' is undoubtedly in reference to the new Soviet State, but Gramsci probably also has the Italian Hegelian tradition in mind.

3. See *Q*, p. 1328.

4. This thematic has been considered by Badaloni, *Il marxismo di Gramsci*.

5. See *SPN*, p. 381.

6. According to Cesare Luporini Gramsci's designation of Marxism as the basis

for an intellectual and moral reform of the masses is perhaps the newest part of '
Gramsci's problematic. 'La metodologia filosofica del marxismo nel pensiero di
Gramsci', *Studi Gramsciani* (Editori Riuniti, Rome, 1958), pp. 39 and 41. To say
Marxism provides a *theoretical* basis for this reform does not necessarily give it an
exclusive role. While Gramsci does not *explicitly* provide for a plurality of ideologies, the tenor of his argument, we would suggest, envisages a complex process
in which a variety of systems of thought are considered each in competition with
the other.

7. See *Q*, p. 733.

8. See *SPN*, p. 404.

9. In a note rich in implications Gramsci discusses the way an intellectual and
moral reform and an expansion of freedom is related to the development of the
productive sphere. See 'Individual man and mass man', *Q*, pp. 861-3. See also
'Question of "Collective Man" and of "Social Conformism"', *Q*, pp. 1565-7, and
Nicola Badaloni, 'Libertà individuale e uomo collectivo in A. Gramsci', in Franco
Ferri (ed.), *Politica e storia in Gramsci*, vol. 1 (Editori Riuniti, Rome, 1977).

10. See *SPN*, p. 247.

6. The Organisers of Hegemony: the Intellectuals

1. In a letter from prison Gramsci suggests both the extension of the notion
of intellectual which he intends to use and the relationship between it and the
problem of the State. See *Lettere*, p. 481. See also Vacca, 'L'occasione "Politecnico"',
p. 105 and 'The "Political Question of the Intellectuals" and the Marxist Theory
of the State in Gramsci's Thought', in Anne Showstack Sassoon (ed.), *A Gramsci
Reader* (Writers and Readers Publishing Co-operative, London, forthcoming).
Bobbio situates Gramsci's own work in the same period as studies on the intellectuals
by Benda, Mannheim, Ortega y Gasset, and Croce. *Politica e cultura* (Einaudi, Turin,
1955), p. 126. Part of the immediate background to Gramsci's work in prison on
the intellectuals, was, of course, the support given by large numbers of Italian intellectuals to fascism.

2. The relationship between the study of the intellectuals and an understanding of the nature of the State is put forward when Gramsci writes that a serious
study of the cultural organisation of the ruling class would be important because
it would produce 'a more cautious and exact calculation' of the defences of the
bourgeoisie and provide the working-class movement with 'an exact knowledge of
the field to be emptied of its . . . human masses'. *Q*, p. 333. This type of study
thus becomes an essential part of the task of the party.

3. See Chantal Mouffe, 'Hegemony and Ideology', in Mouffe, *Gramsci and Marx-
ist Theory*, and Stuart Hall, Bob Lumley, and Gregor McLennan, 'Politics and Ideology:
Gramsci' in *Working Papers in Cultural Studies*, no. 10, *On Ideology* (Centre for
Contemporary Cultural Studies, Birmingham, 1977).

4. See *SPN*, p. 8.

5. According to Giuseppe Vacca, Gramsci places the question of the intellectuals within the context of considering the 'state of separation' of the various
classes and social groups in society, a state which is 'recomposed' during the period
of the transition to socialism which provides the basis of a new unity. 'L'occasione
Politecnico, etc.', p. 87. He relates Gramsci's discussion of the intellectuals to the
question of the middle classes and what he calls the 'protagonism of the masses',
ibid., p. 111.

6. In a later addition to the first version of his discussion of the categories of
organic and traditional intellectuals (which are discussed below) Gramsci warns
about being too schematic. See *Q*, p. 1515.

7. It should be noted that the homogeneity which intellectuals provide is not

uniformity but rather a coherence beneath a multitude of expressions.

8. Compare *Q*, p. 476 and *Q*, p. 1158.

9. I have changed the translation slightly to make it more faithful to the original.

10. Certain echoes of Marx's 'Theses on Feuerbach' can be noted here.

11. But here, too, Gramsci warns that the clergy's role was not monolithic and that a concrete study must be undertaken. *SPN*, p. 7.

12. See *SPN*, p. 8.

13. See *SPN*, pp. 7-8.

14. See *SPN*, p. 10.

15. Gramsci clearly considers this discussion of a lesser order of theoretical generalisation. See *SPN*, p. 15.

16. See *SPN*, pp. 11-12.

17. Gramsci includes in this category priests, lawyers, teachers, notaries, doctors, etc. *SPN*, p. 14.

18. See *PWII*, pp. 454-6.

19. Gramsci intends the bourgeoisie of the northern cities here.

20. This is of course an echo of one of the main themes of the *Ordine Nuovo* period.

21. See *SPN*, p. 6.

7. Intellectuals and the Political Party

1. Compare bottom *Q*, p. 477—top p. 478 with *Q*, p. 1522.

2. See Gramsci's footnote, *SPN*, p. 15.

3. Guiseppe Vacca observes that 'it is not a matter of substituting one intellectual group for another . . . but rather of creating the conditions so a new "social intelligentsia" is developed . . . from below, springing directly from production and from a different relationship of the producers with it', 'L'occasione "Politecnico"', p. 131.

4. See also *Q*, p. 863 where he writes, 'What is the point of reference for the new world in gestation? The world of production, labour.'

5. See *SPN*, p. 16, and Lucio Magri, 'Problems of the Marxist Theory', p. 114.

6. Vacca suggests how Gramsci's discussion of the intellectuals is related to the actuality of the transition to socialism, the process of forming a new type of state in which the old relationship between the mass of the population and knowledge is overturned. See 'L'occasione "Politecnico"', pp. 130-1.

8. The Modern Prince

1. See Alessandro Natta, 'Il partito politico nei Quaderni del carcere', in *Prassi rivoluzionaria e storicismo* in *Gramsci, Critica marxista*, Quaderno no. 3 (1967), p. 47.

2. For further discussion of Gramsci's interpretation of Machiavelli see Alistair Davidson, 'Gramsci and Reading Machiavelli', *Science and Society*, vol. 37, no. 1 (Spring 1973), and Luciano Gruppi, 'Machiavelli e Gramsci', in *Critica marxista*, vol. 7, no. 3 (May-June 1969).

3. See *Q*, pp. 1599-1600, *Q*, p. 1928, *SPN*, p. 172.

4. See *Q*, pp. 1690-1.

5. See also an early note, later amended, entitled 'Marx e Machiavelli', *Q*, p. 432.

6. *SPN*, pp. 129-30.

7. There has been a continual debate about whether Gramsci's concept of the party is totalitarian or not. Salvadori, for example, has suggested that the party is totalitarian to the extent that its objective, a moral and intellectual reform, is totalising but argues that at the same time this reform prevents the masses from

being instrumentalised. *Gramsci e il problema storico della democrazia*, pp. 44-5. In a more recent work in which he reduces Gramsci's view of the State to Lenin's, he is much more critical of Gramsci's position, he is quite critical of this aspect of Gramsci's thought. 'Gramsci e il PCI'. See L. Gruppi, 'Machiavelli e Gramsci', p. 90, where he suggests that there is an internal inconsistency. We shall return to this discussion in our conclusion.

8. It could be argued that there is a certain parallel between Machiavelli's concepts of *fortuna* and *virtù* and the more modern discussion of objectivity and subjectivity.

9. See *Q*, pp. 1690-1 and Cerroni, *Teoria politica e socialismo*, p. 183. Gramsci continues to criticise the utopian nature of the slogans of the Jacobins in so far as they remain limited by the bourgeois social formation whose class divisions prevent the full realisation of liberty, fraternity, and equality, but he thinks their politics was founded in a realistic analysis of the potential of the concrete situation. See my section on 'The Party as the Decisive Element'.

10. *SPN*, pp. 148-9.

11. Piotte points out that Gramsci distinguishes between an ideological party and a political party in the more usual sense. *La pensée politique de Gramsci*, p. 78.

12. With regards to an ostensibly 'agrarian' party in fact serving the interests of large industry, Gramsci discusses the British case. *SPN*, p. 156.

13. See *SPN*, p. 148 and the original version where he is even more explicit, *Q*, p. 432.

14. Gramsci is thinking of the Italian situation in the early 1930s when he writes: 'the functions of such a party are no longer directly political, but merely technical ones of propaganda and public order, and moral and cultural influence. The political function is indirect. For, even if no other legal parties exist, *other parties in fact always do exist* and other tendencies which cannot be legally coerced . . . In any case it is certain that in such parties cultural functions predominate, which means that political language becomes jargon. In other words, political questions are disguised as cultural ones, and as such become insoluble.' *SPN*, p. 149.

15. The bourgeoisie for example could dominate the economic sphere before dominating the political one, a situation which does not arise for the proletariat. Thus the need of the proletariat for a party is only in part connected to the need to avoid division within its ranks.

16. *SPN*, p. 267.

17. *SPN*, p. 152.

18. It can be argued against Magri, 'Problems of the Marxist Theory', p. 121, that 'the pressure towards opportunist political-organizational solutions' can only be avoided, if we follow Gramsci's reasoning, by a precise understanding of the hegemonic relationship between the working class and other classes in society on the basis of which to develop a line of political intervention, not simply by 'certain organisational choices' which themselves depend on this line. As Salvadori argues, it is only the content of the practice of the party and ultimately the capability of the mass movement developed through an intellectual and moral reform, which guarantees that the revolutionary party represents the historical needs of the proletariat. *Gramsci e il problema storico della democrazia*, p. 23.

19. See Ragionieri, 'Gramsci e il dibattito teorico', p. 141. There is therefore a certain danger in presenting this discussion as holding for all time, at least in its detail, as Piotte tends to do. *La pensée politique de Gramsci*.

20. See *Q*, p. 1732.

21. 'Abnormal' means would presumably include the various techniques of fascism. See Ragionieri, 'Gramsci e il dibattito teorico', p. 141.

22. See *SPN*, p. 16 and Buci-Glucksmann, *Gramsci and the State*, p. 33.

23. See Gramsci's quote from Maffeo Pantaleone, *Principi di economia pura*, *SPN*, p. 191.

24. See *SPN*, p. 153.

25. This discussion on organisation was written in the period 1933-5. We know that Gramsci was aware of the weakness of the party from the testimony of Athos Lisa. *Memoria*, ch. 5, 'L'analisi politica di Gramsci: il dissenso sulla "svolta"', pp. 81-103.

26. See also *SPN*, p. 114.

9. Democratic Centralism versus Bureaucratic Centralism

1. See *SPN*, pp. 210-11 where he refers specifically to Marx's *XVIII of Brumaire* and to Hitler's coming to power in Germany.

2. *SPN*, p. 188.

3. *Q*, p. 796 and *SPN*, p. 188.

4. For Gramsci the type of internal organisation of a party is an indication of its 'progressive' or 'regressive' nature. *SPN*, p. 155.

5. *SPN*, p. 187.

6. See for example *SPN*, pp. 331-3, 187; Portelli, *Gramsci et la question religeuse*, pp. 181-2.

7. Gramsci writes: 'The individual expects the organism to act, even if he does not do anything himself, and does not reflect that precisely because his attitude is very widespread, the organism is necessarily inoperative . . . since a deterministic and mechanical conception of history is very widespread (a common-sense conception which is related to the passivity of the great popular masses), each individual seeing that despite his non-intervention something still does happen, tends to think that there indeed exists, over and above individuals, a phantasmagorical being, the abstraction of the collective organism, a kind of autonomous divinity.' *SPN*, p. 187, footnote.

8. Gramsci distinguishes between an active democracy in the party and abstract democratic rights such as those asserted by bourgeois revolutions. See *SPN*, p. 187.

9. See *Q*, p. 1771.

10. This is a term which came into use with regards to the PCI in the period after the Second World War.

11. See also *SPN*, p. 150. While Gramsci seems to be talking most specifically about fascist parties, it can be argued that a largely passive membership can also be considered a hallmark of mass social democratic parties or indeed of a Bordighist party. To the extent that the Stalinist conception resembles that of Bordiga in several ways, it would presumably also be the object of a Gramscian critique.

12. With regard to the use of the term 'class division', we know that Gramsci is not arguing that all members of the party need come from the working class. He is arguing that the kind of division which is not based on a *technical* division of labour but reflecting class divisions is unacceptable.

13. Gramsci contrasts this unity to the kind established by the Church. For the party, he writes, it is vital to have an active, direct consent, rather than support which is passive and indirect, that is, individual participation, is essential 'even if this creates the appearance of splits and tumult'. *Q*, p. 1771.

14. See *Q*, p. 1707.

15. See for example *Q*, p. 236, *Q*, p. 1771.

16. Gramsci's argument is therefore different from that of a political philosopher like J.S. Mill for whom democratic participation is a 'good' in its own right.

10. The Party as a Vanguard: the Relationship with the Masses

1. See *Q*, p. 772.

2. See his criticism of other mass parties in which the mass is simply man-oeuvred. *SPN*, p. 150.

3. *SPN*, p. 196.

4. See Jacques Texier, 'Gramsci nécessité et créativité historique', *La Nouvelle Critique*, vol. 69 (1973); Badaloni, '"Direzione consapevole e spontaneità"', in Nicola Badaloni, *et al.*, *Ideologia e azione politica* (Editori Riuniti, Rome, 1972), p. 73 ff; Salvadori, 'Gramsci e il rapporto tra soggettività e oggettività nella prassi rivoluzionaria', *Gramsci e il problema storico della democrazia*.

5. *SPN*, pp. 196-7.

6. Ibid.

7. *SPN*, pp. 192-3.

8. According to Gramsci every member of society is always under the hege-mony of some group. 'In a particular society no one is disorganized and without a party, as long as organization and party are understood in a wide sense and not a formal one. In this multiplicity of particular societies ... one or more prevail rela-tively or absolutely, constituting the hegemony of a social group on the rest of the population (or civil society), the basis of the State strictly understood as a coercive-government apparatus.' *Q*, p. 800.

9. The phrase 'modern theory' is Gramsci's code for Lenin's thought. This is the context in which Gramsci says that Lenin's position is not in opposition to the 'spontaneous' sentiments of the masses. *Q*. pp. 57-8. See Badaloni, '"Direzione consapevole", e "spontaneità"', pp. 77-81 for the Gramsci-Lenin and Gramsci-Sorel relationship in this regard.

10. This has to do with the expansion of hegemony in such a way as to en-courage 'the molecular passage from groups which are ruled to the ruling group'. *Q*, p. 1056.

11. See *SPN*, p. 144.

12. *Q*, p. 1789.

13. See Salvadori, *Gramsci e il problema storico della democrazia*, p. 45.

14. Gramsci also discusses the importance of the correct relationship to the masses in a passage about the Risorgimento. See *SPN*, p. 97.

15. See how Gramsci contrasts the attitude of the Catholic Church which maintains a split between the 'simple' and the intellectuals to that of Marxism which undertakes an intellectual and moral reform. See *SPN*, p. 326ff, especially 322-3.

11. The Analysis of the Conjuncture and the Argument Against Economism

1. See *SPN*, pp. 171, 185. For a discussion of Gramsci's criticism of a pos-itivist view of the natural sciences, see Paolo Rossi, 'Antonio Gramsci sulla scienza moderna', *Critica marxista*, vol. 14, no. 2 (March-April 1976).

2. See *SPN*, p. 344 and *Q*, p. 333.

3. See *Q*, pp. 455-65 and *Q*, pp. 1578-97. Buci-Glucksmann points out that Gramsci's reflections in this area begin in 1929-30, the period of the greatest economic crisis and also of the 'third period' strategy of the Comintern.

4. Conjuncture here is used in its Italian sense of immediate, short-term phenomena. See footnote 1, *SPN*, p. 177, for a definition of conjuncture. There is a certain parallel with Della Volpe's distinction between *logico* and *storico*. See Donald Sassoon, 'An Introduction to Luporini', in *Economy and Society*, vol. 4, no. 2 (May 1975).

5. Gramsci draws a parallel between what he calls vulgar liberalism, which suggests that the true 'cause' of political events is limited to the activities of parties and syndicalism which attributes a causal effect to the economic sphere only. See note, *SPN*, p. 179. See also *SPN*, pp. 158-61. The basis of the parallel is Gramsci's argument that there is never a complete separation between economics and politics.

6. Gramsci writes 'a subsequent moment', *SPN*, p. 181, but it is subsequent only in a schematic sense. All three levels co-exist although it is true that they may have different historical times so that they have different dynamics within them and a disjuncted relationship between them.

7. See also *SPN*, pp. 366-7.

8. See *SPN*, p. 183.

9. As Gramsci writes, 'an analysis of the balance of forces – at all levels – can only culminate in the sphere of hegemony and ethico-political relations'. *SPN*, p. 167. Therefore it is not a question of either one moment or the other but the relationship between the two. Femia, *Hegemony and Consciousness*, Bates, *Gramsci and the Theory of Hegemony*, and Portelli, *Gramsci e il blocco storico*, all to some extent make the mistake of assuming that the two moments can be separated.

10. *SPN*, p. 185.

11. Gramsci's definition of economism will become clearer in the discussion which follows. Put simply, it attributes historical development to a crude understanding of the economic factor assuming some kind of automatic causal mechanism. See *SPN*, p. 163 for the main aspects of this crude view of the economic factor. See also *Q*, p. 1917.

12. *SPN*, p. 184. See *SPN*, p. 185 for the importance of the subjective element.

13. See *SPN*, pp. 210-11 for a description of this kind of crisis, which is what Gramsci calls an organic crisis. Gramsci criticises Rosa Luxemburg for precisely this type of mistake of confusing the two types of crises in her book on the general strike. See *SPN*, p. 233.

14. See *SPN*, p. 161.

15. Ibid.

16. Gramsci is suggesting in this passage that Lenin's contribution to revolutionary theory must be understood in these terms.

17. See the note 'Economy and Ideology', *SPN*, pp. 407-9.

18. *SPN*, pp. 165-6, *Q*, p. 1917.

19. *SPN*, p. 166.

20. *SPN*, pp. 166-7. He actually discusses a Boulangist type of movement but the discussion resembles very closely his analysis of fascism.

21. See *SPN*, p. 166.

22. See Togliatti, 'Gramsci and Leninism', with regards to the inability of the Italian socialist movement to find a precise objective and a perspective of the way to modify and overturn a relation of forces in order to break down the dominant historical bloc and to create a new one.

23. Bordiga is the most notable example, but the history of the Socialist Party was full of rhetorical and often dogmatic posturing. See De Felice, *Serrati, Bordiga, Gramsci.*

24. See *SPN*, pp. 167-8 for Gramsci's explanation of how an aversion on principle to compromises is rooted in economism.

25. I would suggest that a contemporary example is the way in which the image of women does not correspond to the reality: a steady and at times dramatic entrance into the work force. This means in Gramscian terms that a struggle must be undertaken to change the ideological views of men and women to take account of the changes taking place in the concrete economic position of millions of people.

26. See Franco Calamandrei, 'L'iniziativa politica del partito rivoluzionario da Lenin a Gramsci e Togliatti', in *Critica Marxista*, vol. 1, no. 4-5 (July-Oct. 1967), p. 48.

12. The War of Position: the Development of a Concept

1. It is misleading, we would argue, to reduce the war of movement to a mil-

itary or a violent struggle. It may, also, imply this kind of struggle, but the central feature is a conflict over the State machine in the narrow sense, as an instrument of coercion.

2. See Buci-Glucksmann, *Gramsci and the State*, pp. 244-50.

3. This, of course, is now possible because of the new edition.

4. This remains a tendency in interpreting the war of position. An example is Anderson, 'The Antinomies of Antonio Gramsci'. With a discussion of Gramsci's ideas which attempts to place them in a broader context, in such books as Piotte, *La pensée politique de Gramsci*, Portelli, *Gramsci e il blocco storico*, Macciocchi, *Per Gramsci*, and Buci-Glucksmann, *Gramsci and the State*, all of which argue from quite different standpoints that Gramsci's ideas provide the basis for a strategy in western Europe in a whole historical period, the war of position is no longer tied so closely to the theme of the restabilisation of capitalism in the 1920s. See my article 'Hegemony and Political Intervention' in Sally Hibbin (ed.), *Politics, Ideology and the State* (Lawrence and Wishart, London, 1978), for a discussion of some of Anderson's points.

5. *SPN*, p. 231. Note that my discussion follows the order in which the notes appeared in the original notebooks which is slightly different from the order in the translation.

6. See *SPN*, p. 231.

7. Gramsci specifies that this kind of warfare arises when the ordinary State organisation is weakened and demoralised. *SPN*, p. 233.

8. A general definition of the difference or relationship between strategy and tactics would require a long discussion. We would suggest that in the context of Gramsci's thought it is related to his differentiation between 'organic' and 'occasional' developments.

9. See *SPN*, p. 232.

10. In another context Gramsci argues that the highest development of a class coincides with the hegemonic moment of the State. *SPN*, pp. 181-2. This is another demonstration of the way in which the war of position is parallel to the concept of hegemony on the strategic level.

11. See Calamandrei, 'L'iniziativa politica'.

12. See *Q*, p. 973. This note which is the first version of the one which is modified later was written between 1931 and 1932. The emphasis is mine.

13. We would not agree with Salvadori when he reduces Gramsci's concept of the State to Lenin's arguing that the only difference is the relationship of the means to the ends. *Gramsci e il problema storico della democrazia*, p. 140. Both means and ends are different in Gramsci.

14. Interestingly enough Gramsci cites a speech by Trotsky which shows some awareness of this problem. See Trotsky, *The First Five Years of the Communist International*, vol. 2 (New York, 1953), pp. 221-2, as cited in *SPN*, p. 236. Gramsci comments: 'However, the question was outlined only in a brilliant, literary form, without directives of a practical character.' *SPN*, p. 236. See also *SPN*, pp. 84-5 footnote.

15. Thus we would tend to disagree with Auciello when he dates the period appropriate to the war of position from 1917, *Socialismo ed egemonia in Gramsci*, p. 68. The Russian Revolution does indeed represent a watershed but in the sense of changing the balance of forces and of *revealing* the actuality of the revolution in the period of imperialism, an actuality which, without attributing too much precision specifically to the year 1870, is rooted in the development of the world system in the latter part of the previous century, culminating in the First World War.

16. See *Q*, pp. 1636-8, and *SPN*, p. 80, footnote 49 for an explanation of Marx's use of the term.

17. See also the top of *SPN*, p. 235.

18. This is very significant because it logically contains the implication that any view that a revolutionary transformation of society could have successfully taken place in the immediate post-First World War period through a war of movement is incorrect and objectively constitutes a self-criticism by Gramsci. It also points to a certain tension in the *Notebooks* because at a certain point Gramsci identifies the period 1917-21 with a war of movement, in the West as well as the East. See for example *SPN*, p. 235 and our discussion below. Ragionieri suggests that the element of self-criticism is important and stems from an awareness of the serious defeat of the working-class movement in Europe, an awareness pre-dating the period in prison. 'Gramsci e il dibattito teorico', p. 202.

19. It depends on objective, organic factors, not subjective or occasional ones because 'The truth is that one cannot choose the form of war one wants, unless from the start one has a crushing superiority over the enemy'. *SPN*, p. 234. See also *SPN*, p. 237 where he says that the war of position 'was the only form possible in the West'.

20. See *Q*, p. 858.

21. He argues that the effects of an economic crisis are very complex and claims that Luxemburg's position betrays 'an iron economic determinism . . . an out and out historical mysticism'. *SPN*, p. 233.

22. Bordiga, for example, made this the foundation of his difference with the Comintern. With regards to Trotsky's position see note 14 above. Ragionieri discusses Lenin's awareness from as early as 1918 that the path to revolution would have to be different. 'Gramsci e il dibattito teorico', p. 118. Yet neither Bordiga nor Trotsky nor Lenin drew the implications which Gramsci did, and in terms of a theoretical elaboration as part of the development of an understanding of the State, it would be difficult to find anyone who did draw such implications besides Gramsci. For a discussion of the roots of the problem of the specificity of the socialist revolution in the West in Gramsci see Ragionieri, ibid., pp. 114-18.

23. Relevant to this in another context is Gramsci's discussion of the cosmopolitan nature of Italian intellectuals. He distinguishes cosmopolitanism from internationalism because the first is not founded in the necessary point of departure of a national consciousness. See, for example, *Q*, pp. 1358-62.

24. He continues, 'The use of the phrase "in depth" is intentional because these have been studied but only . . . from superficial and banal viewpoints', *SPN*, p. 235. (I have changed the translation somewhat because 'these' refers not to 1917 but to the elements of civil society.)

25. See *SPN*, p. 238.

26. See *SPN*, p. 240.

27. Gramsci clearly considers this to be the basis of Trotsky's inability to apply what were genial insights to actual political practice. He compares Trotsky's theory of the permanent revolution to the economistic, spontaneist positions of the French syndicalists and Rosa Luxemburg. *SPN*, p. 238.

28. He argues that the proletariat is an international class, but it can only fulfil its historical role if it comprehends the national reality. *SPN*, p. 241.

29. Rhetorical internationalism leads to passivity or to voluntarism. See *SPN*, p. 241. See Auciello, *Socialismo ed egemonia in Gramsci*, pp. 51-4, with regards to Gramsci's notion of internationalism.

30. For example, Anderson identifies the two. 'The Antinomies of Antonio Gramsci'. It should be noted with regard to the stabilisation of capitalism as seen by the Comintern that this stabilisation was not necessarily expressed simply in terms of an economic stabilisation. The argument which we shall put that none the less it did not manage to escape an economistic problematic rests on other grounds.

31. See for example *SPN*, pp. 237-8 or *SPN*, p. 120.

244 Gramsci's Concept of the Party and Politics

32. It could be argued that this is one of the reasons for Gramsci's insistence on the couplet from Marx's Preface to *A Contribution to a Critique of Political Economy*. See *SPN*, p. 177.

33. It is no accident that the criticism of economism and the full development of the discussion of the war of position coincides with a period in which Gramsci's distance from the policies of the Comintern are well documented. See for example Lisa, *Memoria*.

34. Symptomatic is the slogan 'class against class'.

35. Our argument here is that Gramsci's notes on economism and the full discussion of the war of position not only are objectively in disaccord with the Comintern policy of the third period but that they also imply a criticism of the limitations of the theoretical under-pinnings of the previous period.

36. See Buci-Glucksmann, *Gramsci and the State*, p. 19.

13. Passive Revolution: a Strategy for the Bourgeoisie in the War of Position

1. See *SPN*, footnote 11, p. 59, which says in part, 'In [Cuoco's] "Historical Essay on the Neapolitan Republic of 1799", he described the episode as a passive revolution because it was the work of an "enlightened" bourgeois class, imitating French models and involved no mass participation. In the years which followed he came, paradoxically, to argue precisely in favour of such "passive revolutions", in that his main thesis was the need to put through reforms in order to prevent revolution on the *French* model.' Cuoco had read Edmund Burke and admired him and we find a parallel with Edmund Burke's argument that the aim of reform should be to restore aspects of the social order. I have expanded the discussion in this chapter in an article on the passive revolution in *A Gramsci Reader*.

2. *SPN*, p. 59f.

3. *SPN*, p. 114.

4. *SPN*, p. 90.

5. See *SPN*, pp. 104-6.

6. See *SPN*, p. 116. See also *Q*, p. 149.

7. See *SPN*, p. 58f, p. 97 and *Q*, pp. 962-4.

8. See *Q*, p. 1325.

9. See *Q*, pp. 1636-8. For the organic crisis or the crisis of hegemony see *Q*, pp. 1602-4 and *SPN*, pp. 60-1.

10. *Q*, pp. 1638-9.

11. See Gramsci's discussion of the modes of the reorganisation of capitalism and the relation of new economic and political forms in his notes on 'Americanism and Fordism'. *SPN*, pp. 279-318. Gramsci is concerned in these notes to consider the effects of changes in the area of the economy for the relationship between economics and politics and between the mass of the population in the State, continuing themes from his earlier works. See Franco De Felice's introduction and notes to Antonio Gramsci, *Quaderno 22, Americanismo e Fordismo* (Einaudi, Turin, 1978).

12. Fascism also claimed explicitly to overcome the split between civil society and political society. Gentile provided an articulation of this. See *Q*, pp. 691-2.

13. See also *SPN*, p. 114, p. 177. The passage in Marx was one of the bases of a mechanistic interpretation of Marx in the Second International. See Badaloni, 'Libertà e uomo collettivo in Gramsci', in *Politica e storia in Gramsci*, pp. 22ff.

14. See *Q*, p. 1638.

15. This, of course, does not mean that there is no conflict but that the bourgeoisie avoids a head-on clash with the feudal classes doing without the equivalent of a Terror.

16. See *SPN*, pp. 117-18, and 80. He makes the point that the fear of the 'spectre of communism' which was promoted by Metternich was in fact a fear of

agrarian reform since presumably the participation of the masses in a period when a proletariat was extremely small could only have been based on changes in the social relations in the countryside. See *Q*, p. 131 and p. 1834.

17. *Q*, p. 1815.

18. See *SPN*, p. 109 and *Q*, p. 1782.

19. See *SPN*, p. 74.

20. See for example, *SPN*, pp. 117-18, pp. 109-10, p. 100; *Q*, p. 1782, p. 1930.

21. See *SPN*, pp. 101-2.

22. Gramsci refers to Marx's argument against Proudhon in *The Poverty of Philosophy*, *SPN*, p. 109, *Q*, pp. 1220-1, and to Croce, *Q*, pp. 1326-7.

23. *Q*, p. 1328. Gramsci is specifically discussing Croce here, but it is clear that he considers Croce's work as part of the revision of Marxism in the tradition of the Second International. See *Q*, p. 1325.

24. This was part of Bernstein's rejection of the dialectic as he understood it.

25. There is a parallel in this argument with Lenin's *Two Tactics of Social Democracy* where he argues the case for the proletariat in Russia to lead the bourgeois democratic revolution. See Franco Calamandrei, 'L'iniziativa politica del partito rivoluzionario da Lenin a Gramsci', *Critica Marxista*, vol. 5, nos. 4-5 (July-Oct. 1967), pp. 67-8.

26. See *Q*, pp. 1221, 1325-7, and 1327-8.

27. *SPN*, p. 114.

28. In Gramsci's view, therefore, politics does not disappear but is rather transformed. He thus goes a good deal of the way to answering those critics of Marxism who maintain that the negation of politics altogether is impossible. It should be noted that Anderson's discussion of Gramsci's ideas on the State 'The Antinomies of Antonio Gramsci', ignores the concept of passive revolution completely.

29. See *SPN*, pp. 107, 114, and footnote 101, p. 107. One of the implications of Gramsci's argument is that the very attempt by the bourgeoisie to carry out a passive revolution is a result of the ability of the working class to organise itself which represents a threat which the bourgeoisie wants to overcome. Thus the activities of the adversary must always be considered in part a result of the activities of the progressive forces, successful or not. Ragionieri makes a similar point. with regards to caesarism as a mode of unifying the bourgeois forces, a mode which has a direct and inverse relationship to the existence of a revolutionary working-class party. 'Gramsci e il dibattito teorico', p. 141.

30. See *SPN*, p. 114.

31. Gramsci distinguishes between an *élite* which as an organic relationship to a mass movement and a voluntarist leadership is cut off from such a movement. See *Q*, p. 1623.

32. See *SPN*, pp. 219-20. In the same note Gramsci explains that it is the organisation of masses of people in the modern period which characterises Caesarism and differentiates it as a political phenomenon from the *coups d'états* and military interventions of traditional Bonapartism.

33. See *SPN*, pp. 119-20.

34. This is Christine Buci-Glucksmann's phrase. See 'On the Political Problems of the Transition, the Working Class and the Passive Revolution', in Mouffe, *Gramsci and Marxist Theory*.

35. An example would be the vastly improved productivity through technical change which at the moment is producing pools of the permanently unemployed instead of resulting in a dramatic decrease in the working week which is a prerequisite for an expansion of democratic control and for overcoming the present sexual division of labour.

36. See for example *SPN*, pp. 221-2.

37. See *SPN*, p. 116.

14. The Party as the Decisive Element

1. This is the sense of Gramsci's emphasis on subjective conditions. See *Q*, p. 1781. See also Massimo Salvadori's discussion of subjectivity in Gramsci's work in *Gramsci e il problema storico della democrazia*, particularly p. 126.

2. See *SPN*, p. 185.

3. Gramsci describes this disjuncture and indicates the importance of the potential of objective developments in an important passage, 'mass ideological factors always lag behind mass economic phenomenon . . . hence . . . there must be a conscious, planned struggle to ensure that the exigencies of the economic position of the masses . . . are understood. An appropriate political initiative is always necessary to liberate the economic thrust from the dead weight of traditional policies.' *SPN*, p. 168.

4. Gramsci's argument is not a defence of the Jacobins' political wisdom *in toto* but merely a description of the way in which they brought the bourgeois revolution to fruition. If they went beyond what the historical premises would allow and politically there had to be a turn backward, this in no way harms his argument that the Jacobins, unlike the makers of passive revolutions, did at least push political development as far as was possible.

5. Gramsci emphasises, in counterposition to his earlier interpretation of the Jacobins in articles immediately after the Russian Revolution (see our discussion above), that 'It is necessary to insist . . . that the Jacobins were realists of the Machiavelli stamp and not abstract dreamers'. *SPN*, p. 78.

6. *Q*, p. 1361.

7. Gramsci's criticism of lack of realism in the various approaches to the problem of the unification of Italy is a central element in his notes on the Risorgimento. See *SPN*, pp. 55-120. It is important to note that his argument is *not* that a completely different outcome was possible, but that this outcome might have been more advanced had the policies of the progressive forces been based on a more realistic analysis of the concrete situation. I take this up in 'Hegemony and Political Intervention' in Sally Hibbin (ed.), *Politics, Ideology and the State* (Lawrence and Wishart, London, 1978). Most of the discussion about Gramsci's interpretation of the Risorgimento has missed this point.

8. Note the way he contrasts the postulation of the permanent revolution by Trotsky in 1905 with the way Lenin posed the question of an alliance with the poor peasants. *SPN*, pp. 84-5, footnote.

9. In this case a correct approach to the agrarian question. See *SPN*, p. 102.

15. Conclusion: The Party, the State, and Democracy

1. Probably the best known of his arguments in this regard is found in *Left-wing Communism, An Infantile Disorder*. It was also one of the main themes of his interventions at the III Congress of the International against a number of Western European communist parties, the Italian included.

2. See Cerroni, 'Gramsci e il superamento della separazione tra società e Stato', in Garin *et al.*; Bobbio, 'Gramsci and the Concept of Civil Society', in Mouffe, *Gramsci and Marxist Theory*; Buci-Glucksmann, *Gramsci and the State*, pp. 282-90. Portelli, *Gramsci e il blocco storico*, pp. 36-41; Nardone, *Il pensiero di Gramsci*, pp. 163-4. One of the themes in Badaloni's book, *Il marxismo di Gramsci*, is what he calls the 'socialization of politics'.

3. See Badaloni, *Il marxismo di Gramsci*, p. 182.

4. See *SPN*, p. 133. See Luciano Gruppi's criticism 'Machiavelli e Gramsci', p. 90.

5. See *SPN*, pp. 148, 54.

6. See Umberto Cerroni. 'Esiste una scienza politica marxista? Discutendo con Norberto Bobbio', in *Rinascita* (21 Nov. 1975), no. 46, pp. 21-3 for some indications

which can be drawn from Gramsci along these lines.

7. See *SPN*, p. 152.

8. The chief examples are Bobbio's articles, 'Esiste una dottrina marxista dello Stato?' and 'Quale alternativa alla democrazia rappresentativa', and Salvadori's article, 'Gramsci and the PCI: Two Conceptions of Hegemony'.

9. I have developed these themes further in 'Gramsci: A New Concept of Politics and the Expansion of Democracy', in Alan Hunt (ed.), *Marxism and Democracy* (Lawrence and Wishart, London, 1980).

10. *SPN*, p. 268.

11. For a discussion of this theme see Nicola Badaloni *Per il communismo* (Einaudi, Turin, 1972), in particular pp. 171-205.

12. See, *Q*, pp. 236-7 where Gramsci criticises Michel's notion of an 'iron law of oligarchy'.

13. *SPN*, p. 190, Gramsci is referring to a passage in Marx's *Eighteenth Brumaire of Louis Bonaparte.*

14. The reference to Mussolini is quite transparent in certain passages. See *SPN*, p. 150 and *Q*, p. 772.

15. See *Q*, pp. 749-51 and 1706-7 and *SPN*, p. 187, footnote 83.

16. See *Q*, p. 1056.

17. See, for example Peter Bachrach, *The Theory of Democratic Elitism* (University of London Press, London, 1969) and C.B. Macpherson, *The Life and Times of Liberal Democracy* (Oxford University Press, 1977).

BIBLIOGRAPHY

Primary Works

References to Gramsci's writings which are inserted in the text use abbreviations which are found in parentheses.

Caprioglio, Sergio (ed.), *Antonio Gramsci, Scritti 1915-1921, Nuovi Contributi* (I Quaderni de 'Il Corpo', 1969)

Gramsci, Antonio. *La costruzione del partito communista 1923-1926* (Einaudi, Turin, 1971) (*CPC*)

———. *Lettere dal carcere* (Einaudi, Turin, 1965) (*Lettere*)

———. *L'Ordine Nuovo 1919-1920* (Einaudi, Turin, 1955) (*ON*)

———. *Political Writings, 1910-1920* (Lawrence and Wishart, London, 1977) (*PWI*)

———. *Political Writings, 1921-1926* (Lawrence and Wishart, London, 1978) (*PWII*)

———. *Quaderni del carcere*, vols 1-4 (Einaudi, Turin, 1975) (*Q*)

———. *Scritti giovanili, 1914-1918* (Einaudi, Turin, 1958) (*SG*)

———. *Selections from the Prison Notebooks* (Lawrence and Wishart, London, 1971) (*SPN*)

———. *Socialismo e fascismo. L'Ordine Nuovo 1921-1922* (Einaudi, Turin, 1966) (*SF*)

Martinelli, Renzo (ed.), *Per la verità, Scritti 1913-1926* (Editori Riuniti, Rome, 1974)

Togliatti, Palmiro. *La formazione del gruppo dirigente del PCI nel 1923-24* (Editori Riuniti, Rome, 1974) (*La form.*)

Secondary Works

Alcara, Rosa. *La formazione e i primi anni del Partito comunista nella storiografia marxista* (Jaca Books, Milan, 1970)

Althusser, Louis. *For Marx* (Vintage Books, New York, 1970)

———. 'Ideology and Ideological State Apparatuses', in *Lenin and Philosophy and Other Essays* (New Left Books, London, 1971)

———. *Lire le capital* (Maspero, Paris, 1968)

Anderson, Perry. 'The Antinomies of Antonio Gramsci', *New Left Review*, no. 100 (Nov. 1976-Jan. 1977)

Andreucci, Franco and Sylvers, Malcolm. 'The Italian Communists Write Their History', *Science and Society*, vol. 40, no. 1 (Spring 1976)

Auciello, Nicola. *Socialismo ed egemonia in Gramsci e Togliatti* (De Donato, Bari, 1974)

Bachrach, Peter. *The Theory of Democratic Elitism* (University of London Press, 1969)

Badaloni, Nicola. '"Direzione consapevole" e "spontaneità"', in Nicola Badaloni, *et al. Ideologia e azione politica* (Editori Riuniti, Rome, 1972)

———. *Il marxismo di Gramsci* (Einaudi, Turin, 1975)

———. *Per il comunismo* (Einaudi, Turin, 1972)

Bates, T.R. 'Antonio Gramsci and the Soviet Experiment in Italy', *Societas*, vol. 4, no. 1 (Winter 1974)

———. 'Gramsci and the Theory of Hegemony', *Journal of the History of Ideas*, vol. 36, no. 2 (April-June 1975)

Berti, Giuseppe. Introduction, *I primi anni del PCI* (Feltrinelli, Milan, 1967)

Bobbio, Norberto. 'Esiste una dottrina marxista dello Stato?' *Mondoperaio*, no. 8-9 (Aug.-Sept. 1975)

———. 'Gramsci and the Conception of Civil Society', in Chantal Mouffe (ed.), *Gramsci and Marxist Theory* (Routledge and Kegan Paul, London, 1979)

———. 'Nota sulla dialettica in Gramsci', in Garin *et al.*, *Studi gramsciani*.

———. *Politica e cultura* (Einaudi, Turin, 1955)

———. 'Quale alternativa alla democrazia rappresentativa', *Mondoperaio*, no. 10 (Oct. 1975)

Buci-Glucksmann, Christine. *Gramsci and the State* (Lawrence and Wishart, London, 1980)

Calamandrei, Franco. 'L'iniziativa politica del partito rivoluzionario da Lenin a Gramsci e Togliatti', *Critica marxista*, vol. 5, no. 4-5 (July-Oct. 1967)

Cammett, John M. *Antonio Gramsci and the Origins of Italian Communism* (Stanford University Press, Stanford, California, 1967)

———. 'Two Recent Polemics on the Character of the Italian Risorgimento' *Science and Society*, vol. 27, no. 4 (Fall 1963)

Caracciolo, Alberto. 'A proposito di Gramsci, la Russia e il movimento bolscevico', in Garin *et al., Studi gramsciani*.

——— (ed.). 'Il movimento torinese dei consigli di fabbrica', in *Mondo operaio*, vol. 40, no. 2 (Feb. 1958)

——— and Scalia, Gianni (eds). *La città futura: Saggi sulla figura e il pensiero di Antonio Gramsci* (Feltrinelli, Milan, 1959)

Cerreti, Giulio. *Con Togliatti e Thorez, Quarant'anni di lotte politiche* (Feltrinelli, Milan, 1973)

Cerroni, Umberto. 'Gramsci e il superamento della separazione tra società e stato', in Garin *et al. Studi gramsciani.*

———. *Teoria politica e socialismo* (Editori Riuniti, Rome, 1973)

Cicerchia, Carlo. 'Rapporto col leninismo e il problema della rivoluzione italiana', in Caracciolo and Scalia, *La città futura*

Cirese, Alberto M. 'Conception of the World, Spontaneous Philosophy, Folklore', in Anne Showstack Sassoon (ed.), *A Gramsci Reader* (Writers and Readers Publishing Co-operative, London, 1981)

Clark, Martin. *Antonio Gramsci and the Revolution that Failed* (Yale University Press, London, 1977)

———. 'Factory Councils and the Italian Labour Movement 1916-1921' (unpublished Ph.D. thesis, University of London, 1966)

Cohen, Stephen F. *Bukharin and the Bolshevik Revolution, A Political Biography, 1888-1938* (Vintage Books, New York, 1975)

Cortesi, Luigi. 'Alcuni problemi della storia del PCI', *Rivista storica del socialismo*, vol. 8, no. 24 (Jan.-April 1965)

Davidson, Alistair. *Antonio Gramsci: Towards an Intellectual Biography* (Merlin Press, London, 1977)

———. 'Gramsci and Lenin, 1917-1922', in *Socialist Register* (1974)

———. 'Gramsci and Reading Machiavelli', *Science and Society*, vol. 37, no. 1 (Spring 1973)

De Clementi, Andreina. *Amadeo Bordiga* (Einaudi, Turin, 1971)

———. 'La politica del PCI nel 1921-22 e il rapporto Bordiga-Gramsci', *Rivista storica del socialismo*, vol. 9, no. 28 (May-Aug.) and no. 29 (Sept.-Dec. 1966)

De Felice, Franco. *Serrati, Bordiga, Gramsci e il problema della rivoluzione in Italia, 1919-1920* (De Donato, Bari, 1971)

———. 'Una chiave di lettura in "Americanismo e Fordismo"', *Rinascita* (22 Oct. 1972)

De Felice, Franco and Valentino Parlato. Introduction, *La questione meridionale* (Editori Riuniti, Rome, 1970)

De Giovanni, Biagio. *La teoria politica delle classi nel 'Capitale'* (De Donato, Bari, 1976)

——— *et al. Egemonia Stato partito in Gramsci* (Editori Riuniti, Rome, 1977)

De Leon, Daniel. *Socialist Reconstruction of Society* (no place of publication, 1905)

Femia, J. 'Hegemony and Consciousness in the Thought of Antonio Gramsci', *Political Studies*, vol. 23, no. 1 (March 1975)

Ferri, Franco. 'Consigli di fabbrica e partito nel pensiero di Antonio Gramsci', *Rinascita*, vol. 14, no. 9 (1957)

────── . 'La situazione interna della sezione socialista torinese nell'estate del 1920', *Rinascita*, no. 4 (April 1958)

────── (ed.). *Politica e storia in Gramsci* (Editori Riuniti, Rome, 1977)

Fiori, Giuseppe. *Antonio Gramsci* (New Left Books, London, 1970)

Galasso, Giuseppe. 'Gramsci e i problemi della storia italiana', in Garin *et al., Gramsci e la cultura contemporanea*

Garaudy, Roger. 'Révolution et bloc historique', *L'homme et la société*, no. 21 (July-Aug. 1971)

Garin, Eugenio. 'Politica e cultura in Gramsci (il problema degli intellettuali)' in Garin *et al., Gramsci e la cultura contemporanea.*

────── *et al. Gramsci e la cultura contemporanea* (Editori Riuniti, Rome, 1969)

────── *et al. Studi gramsciani. Atti del convegno* (Editori Riuniti, Rome, 1958)

Gerratana, Valentino. 'La ricerca e il metodo', *Rinascita*, no. 30 (25 July 1975)

Gerschenkron, Rosario. 'Rosario Romeo e l'accumulazione primitiva del capitale', *Rivista storica italiana*, vol. 71, no. 4 (1960)

Gobetti, Piero. *La rivoluzione liberale* (Einaudi, Turin, 1948)

Gruppi, Luciano. *Il concetto di egemonia in Gramsci* (Editori Riuniti, Rome, 1972)

────── . 'Machiavelli e Gramsci', *Critica marxista*, vol. 7, no. 3 (May-June, 1969)

Hoare, Quintin. Introduction, *Selections from the Prison Notebooks* (Lawrence and Wishart, London, 1971)

Hughes, H. Stuart. *Consciousness and Society* (Alfred A. Knopf, New York, 1958)

Jocteau, Gian Carlo. *Leggere Gramsci. Una guida alle interpretazioni* (Feltrinelli, Milan, 1975)

Kosík, Karel. 'Gramsci e la folosofia della praxis', in Garin *et al. Gramsci e la cultura contemporanea*

Lenin, V.I. 'Left-wing Communism. An Infantile Disorder', in *Selected Works* (Foreign Languages Publishing House, Moscow, 1946)

────── . 'Two Tactics of Social Democracy', in *Selected Works* (Foreign Languages Publishing House, Moscow, 1946)

────── . 'What Is To Be Done?' in *Selected Works* (Foreign Languages Publishing House, Moscow, 1946)

Lepre, Aurelio. 'Bordiga e Gramsci di fronte alla guerra e alla Rivoluzione d'ottobre', *Critica marxista*, vol. 5 (July-Oct. 1967)

Lisa, Athos. *Memoria. In carcere con Gramsci* (Feltrinelli, Milan, 1973)

Lombardi, Satriani, Luigi M. 'Gramsci e il folclore: dal pittoresco alla contestazione', in Garin *et al. Gramsci e la cultura contemporanea*

Lopuchov, Boris. 'Gramsci e l'elemento storico-nazionale nella lotta politica', in Garin *et al. Studi gramsciani*

Luporini, Cesare. 'Autonomia del pensiero di Gramsci e di Togliatti', *Rinascita*, no. 9 (1 March 1975)

———. 'Il rapporto con Sorel', *Rinascita*, no. 9 (1 March 1975)

———. 'La metodologia filosofica del marxismo nel pensiero di Gramsci', in Garin *et al. Studi gramsciani*

Macciocchi, Maria Antonietta. *Per Gramsci* (Il Mulino, Bologna, 1974)

Macpherson, C.B. *The Life and Times of Liberal Democracy* (Oxford University Press, 1977)

Magri, Lucio. 'Problems of the Marxist Theory of the Revolutionary Party', *New Left Review*, no. 60 (March-April 1970)

Marek, Franz. 'Gramsci e la concezione marxista della storia', in Garin *et al. Gramsci e la cultura contemporanea*

Marx, Karl. Preface, *A Contribution to the Critique of Political Economy* (Progress Publishers, Moscow, 1970)

Matteucci, Nicola. *Antonio Gramsci e la filosofia della prassi* (Giuffre, Milan, 1951)

Merrington, John. 'Theory and Practice in Gramsci's Marxism', *Socialist Register* (1968)

Miliband, Ralph. *The State in Capitalist Society* (Weidenfeld and Nicolson, London, 1969)

Mouffe, Chantal (ed.). *Gramsci and Marxist Theory* (Routledge and Kegan Paul, London, 1979)

Mouffe, Chantal and Showstack Sassoon, Anne. 'Gramsci in France and Italy—a Review of the Literature', *Economy and Society*, vol. 6, no. 1 (Feb. 1977)

Napolitano, Giorgio. 'Roger Garaudy e il nuovo blocco storico', *Rinascita* (20 March 1970)

Nardone, Giorgio. *Il pensiero di Gramsci* (De Donato, Bari, 1971)

Natta, Alessandro. 'Il partito politica nei Quaderni del carcere', *Prassi rivoluzionaria e storicismo in Gramsci, Critica marxista*, Quaderno no. 3 (1967)

Nenni, Pietro. *Storia di quattro anni* (Einaudi, Rome, 1946)

Paggi, Leonardo. *Antonio Gramsci il moderno principe* (Editori Riuniti, Rome, 1970)

———. 'Gramsci's General Theory of Marxism' in Mouffe, *Gramsci and Marxist Theory*

Paris, Robert. 'Gramsci e la crisi teorica del 1923', in Garin *et al. Gramsci e la cultura contemporanea*

Piotte, Jean-Marc. *La pensée politique de Gramsci* (Editions Anthropos, Paris, 1970)

Pizzorno, Alessandro. 'Sul metodo di Gramsci: dalla storiografia alla scienza politica', in Garin *et al. Gramsci e la cultura contemporanea*

Portelli, Hughes. *Gramsci e il blocco storico* (Laterza, Bari, 1973)

———. *Gramsci et la question religeuse* (Editions Anthropos, Paris, 1974)

———. 'Jacobinisme et anti-jacobinisme de Gramsci', *Dialectiques*, no. 4-5 (March 1974)

Poulantzas, Nicos. *Political Power and Social Classes* (New Left Books, 1973)

Pozzolini, A. *Antonio Gramsci, An Introduction to His Thought* (Pluto Press, London, 1970)

Quercioli, Mimma Paulesu. *Gramsci vivo nelle testimonianze dei suoi contemporanei* (Feltrinelli, Milan, 1977)

Ragionieri, Ernesto. 'Gramsci e il dibattito teorico nel movimento operaio internazionale', in Garin *et al. Gramsci e la cultura contemporanea*

Romeo, Rosario. *Risorgimento e capitalismo* (Laterza, Bari, 1959)

Rossi, Paolo. 'Antonio Gramsci sulla scienza moderna', *Critica marxista*, vol. 14, no. 2 (March-April 1976)

Sabetti, Alfredo. 'Il rapporto uomo-natura nel pensiero del Gramsci e la fondazione della scienza', in Garin *et al. Studi gramsciani*

Salvadori, Massimo L. 'Gramsci and the PCI: Two Conceptions of Hegemony' in Mouffe, *Gramsci and Marxist Theory*

———. *Gramsci e il problema storico della democrazia* (Einaudi, Turin, 1970)

Santarelli, Enzo. *La revisione del marxismo in Italia* (Feltrinelli, Milan, 1964)

Sassoon, Donald. 'An Introduction to Luporini', *Economy and Society*, vol. 4, no. 2 (May 1975)

Scalia, Gianni. 'Il giovane Gramsci', *Passato e presente*, no. 9 (1959)

Sereni, Emilio. 'Blocco storico e iniziativa politica nell "elaborazione gramsciana e nella politica del PCI"', *Critica marxista*, Quaderno 5 (1971)

Showstack Sassoon, Anne. 'Gramsci: A New Concept of Politics and the Expansion of Democracy' in Alan Hunt (ed.) *Marxism and Democracy* (Lawrence and Wishart, London, 1980)

———. 'Hegemony and Political Intervention' in Sally Hibbin (ed.). *Politics, Ideology and the State* (Lawrence and Wishart, London, 1978)

Soave, Emilio. 'Appunti sulle origini teoriche e pratiche dei Consigli di fabbrica a Torino', *Rivista storica del socialismo*, vol. 7 (Jan-April 1964)

Spriano, Paolo. 'Gramsci dirigente politico', *Studi storici*, vol. 8, no. 2 (April-June 1967)

———. *Gramsci e l'Ordine Nuovo* (Editori Riuniti, Rome, 1966)

———. *Antonio Gramsci and the Party: the Prison Years* (Lawrence and Wishart, London, 1979)

———. 'Il dibattito tra il "Soviet" e "l'Ordine Nuovo"', *Rinascita*, no. 1 (Jan 1961)

———. *Storia del partito comunista italiano. Da Bordiga a Gramsci*, vol. 1 (Einaudi, Turin, 1967)

———. *Torino operaia nella grande guerra* (Einaudi, Turin, 1960)

Tasca, Angelo. *I primi dieci anni del PCI* (Laterza, Bari, 1971)

Texier, Jacques. 'Gramsci, nécessité et créativité historique', *La nouvelle critique*, vol. 69 (1973)

———. 'Gramsci, Theorist of the Superstructure' in Mouffe, *A Gramsci Reader*

Togliatti, Palmiro. 'Gramsci e il leninismo', in Garin *et al. Studi gramsciani*, now in Togliatti, *Gramsci and Other Essays* (Lawrence and Wishart, London, 1979)

———. 'Il leninismo nel pensiero e nell' azione di Gramsci' in Garin *et al. Studi gramsciana.* (Now in *Gramsci and Other Essays.*)

———. *La formazione del gruppo dirigente del PCI nel 1923-24* (Editori Riuniti, Rome, 1974). (See *Gramsci and Other Essays.*)

———. *Lectures on Fascism* (Lawrence and Wishart, London, 1976)

Tronti, Mario. 'Alcuni questioni interno al marxismo di Gramsci', in Garin *et al., Studi gramsciani*

Vacca, Giuseppe. 'Discorrendo di socialismo e di democrazia II', *Mondoperaio*, vol. 19, no. 2 (Feb. 1976)

———. 'L'occasione "Politecnico" (Note su alcuni elementi della politica culturale di Togliatti)', *Lavoro critico*, vol. 5 (Jan-March 1976)

Vaccaro, Nicola. 'La dialettica quantità-qualità', in Garin *et al. Studi gramsciani*

Williams, Gwyn A. 'The Concept of "egemonia" in the Thought of Antonio Gramsci', *Journal of the History of Ideas*, vol. 21, no. 4 (Oct.-Dec. 1960)

———. *Proletarian Order* (Pluto Press, London, 1975)

Zanardo, Aldo. 'Il "manuale" di Bukharin visto, dai comunisti tedeschi e da Gramsci', in Garin *et al. Studi gramsciani*

Zangheri, Renato. 'La mancata rivoluzione agraria nel Risorgimento e i problemi economici dell'unità', in Garin *et al. Studi gramsciani*

INDEX

Alcara, Rosa 18, 57
Americanism and Fordism 116, 216, 244
Anderson, Perry 19, 60, 106-7, 232-3, 235, 242-3
Andreucci, Franco 18
Auciello, Nicola 232, 234, 242-3
Avanti! 22, 100

Bachrach, Peter 247
Badaloni, Nicola 60, 234-6, 244, 246-7
Bates, Thomas R. 232, 241
Benda, Julien 236
Bernstein, Eduard 188, 213, 245
Bobbio, Norberto 18, 233, 246-7
Bolsheviks 28-30, 44, 59, 64-5, 69, 80, 93, 97, 126, 130, 198, 202, 222
Bonaparte, Napoleon I 219
Bordiga, Amadeo 13, 15-17, 22, 35, 57, 61, 63-72, 77, 79-80, 82-4, 86-9, 94-8, 101-2, 105-7, 148, 161-5, 168, 170-2, 175, 188, 201, 219, 230, 241, 243
Buci-Glucksmann, Christine 61, 232, 234-5, 239-40, 242, 244-5
Bukharin, Nikolai 19, 120, 232
Burke, Edmund 244

Calamandrei, Franco 241-2, 245
Cammett, John M. 18, 60, 235
Caracciolo, Alberto 59
Cavour, Camillo Benso Conte di 207, 211-12
centralism 66-7, 69, 71-2, 85-6, 162
 bureaucratic/organic 163, 164, 167, 176, 231, 239
 democratic 162-5, 162, 227-8, 239
Cerroni, Umberto 234, 238, 246
CGdL *see* General Confederation of Labour
civil society 65, 111-14, 117, 122, 130-1, 135-6, 147-8, 150, 194, 196, 198-203, 210, 222-7, 233, 240, 243-4
Clark, Martin 60

coercion 109-10, 113, 131, 135, 215, 222-3, 226, 232, 242
Cohen, Stephen F. 19
collective will 100, 150-3, 155, 168, 170, 178-9, 185, 221, 229, 231
Comintern *see* Third International
common sense 117
Communist International *see* Third International
Communist Party of the Soviet Union (CPSU) 79, 92, 106-7
compromises 116, 191-2, 229
consent 112, 122, 130, 187, 197, 208, 214, 221, 223
Conservative Party 61
corporativism 61, 74, 107, 197, 220, *see also* economic-corporative
Cortesi, Luigi 57
Croce, Benedetto 13, 24, 26, 120, 135, 142, 144-5, 217, 236, 245
Cuoco, Vincenzo 204, 244
Cromwell, Oliver 219
culture 22, 25-6, 58

Davidson, Alistair 18, 57, 59, 237
De Clementi, Andreina 57, 107
De Felice, Franco 58, 60-1, 105, 108, 234, 241, 244
De Giovanni, Biagio 18
De Leon, Daniel 31, 59
Della Volpe, Gaetano 240
democracy 60, 87, 153, 222-3, 226-8, 246
 bourgeois 50-1, 72, 82
 direct 50
 extended/expanded 84, 226, 228-31, 239
 internal to party *see* political party
 liberal 49-51, 231
 new concept of 155
domination/dominance 111, 113, 127

economic base *see* structure
economic-corporative 84, 92, 116-17, 119, 123, 126, 133, 138, 148-9,

United Front 63-4, 66, 73, 105

Vacca, Giuseppe 19, 233, 236-7

war of movement 193-203, 241,
  243

war of position 193-204, 210, 213-14,
  221-2, 241-2, 244
Weber, Max 18
Williams, Gwyn 60, 232

☆ p 24. Grace eventually saw how fundamentally he differed from Croce — ... or unity of ... / practica of of 1233 ~ until he fully developed this he remained greatly influenced by Croce!